Le Corbusier in Detail

For Alice, Otilia and Emilia

Le Corbusier in Detail

Flora Samuel

AMSTERDAM • BOSTON • HEIDELBERG • LONDON • NEW YORK • OXFORD
PARIS • SAN DIEGO • SAN FRANCISCO • SINGAPORE • SYDNEY • TOKYO

Architectural
Press

Architectural Press is an imprint of Elsevier Ltd
Linacre House, Jordan Hill, Oxford OX2 8DP
30 Corporate Road, Burlington, MA 01803

First edition 2007

British Library Cataloguing in Publication Data
A catalogue record for this book is available from the British Library

Library of Congress Cataloging in Publication Data
A catalog record for this book is available from the Library of Congress

ISBN 978-0-75-066354-0

For information on all Architectural Press publications
visit our website at www.books.elsevier.com

Typeset by Integra Software
Printed and bound in The Netherlands

07 08 09 10   10 9 8 7 6 5 4 3 2 1

Working together to grow
libraries in developing countries

www.elsevier.com | www.bookaid.org | www.sabre.org

ELSEVIER   BOOK AID
             International   Sabre Foundation

Contents

List of Figures   vii
Figure Credits   xv
Acknowledgments   xvii

Introduction   **1**

1   Standardization and unity   **15**

1.1   Standardization   15
1.2   Standard materials   18
1.3   Standard structures   20
    1.3.1   Concrete frames   20
    1.3.2   Steel structures   24
    1.3.3   Vaulted roofs   28
1.4   Conclusion   33

2   Somatic detail   **39**

2.1   Anthropomorphism   41
2.2   Touch   44
    2.2.1   Walls and pilotis   45
    2.2.2   Door handles and handrails   47
    2.2.3   Furniture   59
    2.2.4   Floors   61
2.3   Colour   64
2.4   Space   64
2.5   Sound   65
2.6   Conclusion   66

3   Light and dark   73

3.1   Meaning   73
3.2   Windows   75
       3.2.1   Horizontal windows   76
       3.2.2   Glass walls (pan de verre)   78
       3.2.3   Brise soleil   79
       3.2.4   Ondulatoires   82
3.3   Rooflights   84
3.4   Reflection   89
3.5   Artificial lighting   91
3.6   Conclusion   96

4   Framing   101

4.1   Views   101
4.2   Objects   107
4.3   Space   116
4.4   Conclusion   122

5   Elements of the architectural promenade   127

5.1   Doors   130
5.2   Stairs and ramps   149
5.3   Conclusion   165

6   Rituals   169

6.1   Altars   170
6.2   Fire – the hearth   175
6.3   Water   181
6.4   Conclusion   192

7   Clouds 1959   195

7.1   Brazil   198
7.2   Geography lesson   199
7.3   Perspective   203
7.4   Interior urbanism   206

Conclusion   215

Select bibliography   219
Index   227

List of Figures

Unless stated otherwise all the buildings, drawings and paintings cited are by Le Corbusier and are in France. Dates shown are completion dates for built projects.

0.1	Expansion joint in parapet on the roof of the Unité Marseilles (1952)	2
0.2	Le Corbusier by his bed in his apartment at 24 Rue Nungesset et Coli (1934) in front of a painting by André Bauchant	3
0.3	Sliding door on the balcony of the hotel of the Unité, Marseilles (1952)	5
0.4	Some of the many sketches of fixings for the Bat'a boutique (1935). FLC 17984 and 17953	6
0.5	Le Corbusier on the site of the Unité Marseilles	7
0.6	The team who built the Notre-Dame du Haut, Ronchamp (1955). Photo taken from Le Corbusier's book *The Chapel at Ronchamp*	8
0.7	Notre-Dame du Haut, Ronchamp (1955)	9
0.8	Drawing of a stone taken from Le Corbusier's *The Poem of the Right Angle* (1955)	10
1.1	Maison Domino (1914)	22
1.2	Structure of Pavillon Suisse (1933)	25
1.3	Drawing of 'a primitive temple' from *Towards a New Architecture* (1923), p. 67	26
1.4	Pavillon des Temps Nouveau (1937)	27

1.5   Philips Pavilion exterior, Brussels International
      Exhibition (1958)   27
1.6   Proposition for 'vitrines parasol', 1956, FLC 17826   28
1.7   Heidi Weber Haus, Zurich (1968)   29
1.8   Sign of the 24-hour day   29
1.9   Interior of Heidi Weber Haus, Zurich (1968)   29
1.10 The 'fundamental Roman forms' Drawing taken from *The
      Radiant City* (1935)   30
1.11 Maisons Monol (1919)   30
1.12 Petite Maison de Weekend showing gazebo (1935)   31
1.13 Jaoul Maison B (1955)   32
1.14 House from La cite permanente at La Sainte Baume
      (c. 1950)   33
2.1   Cleaning instructions, hall floor Jaoul Maison B   40
2.2   The 'skin' of Notre-Dame du Haut, Ronchamp (1955)   43
2.3   *Abstraction Ozon* (1946). Plan of Ronchamp   43
2.4   *Icône* (1955)   44
2.5   Altar rail at Notre-Dame du Haut, Ronchamp (1955), FLC
      07236   46
2.6   Sketches drawn for the balconies of the Unité at Meaux   46
2.7   Handle of main door of Cultural Centre, Firminy-Vert (1965)   47
2.8   Sketch of door handle for Bat'a (1935), FLC 17899   48
2.9   Maison Jaoul B (1955), box in entrance   49
2.10 Folding window of top storey apartment, Unité, Marseilles
      Michelet (1952)   50
2.11 The linear timber handles at the Maison du Brésel (1957).
      Taureau II (1953)   51
2.12 Handle of aerateur, Heidi Weber Haus, Zurich (1968)   52
2.13 Detail of dining room window shutter, Maison Jaoul B (1955)   52
2.14 Wooden latch of aerateur in cell, La Tourette (1959)   53
2.15 Details of exterior Maison Jaoul B (1955) and of La Tourette
      (1953–59)   53
2.16 Interior of the east side of Notre-Dame du Haut, Ronchamp
      (1955), showing east door at the zenith of the roof   54
2.17 Handle of east door. Working drawing   55
2.18 Handle of east door from exterior   56
2.19 Enamel door, Heidi Weber Haus, Zurich (1968)   57
2.20 Drawing of handle for ceremonial door of Mill Owners'
      Association Building, Ahmedabad (1954)   58
2.21 Furniture, Charlotte Perriand and Le Corbusier (1928)   60
2.22 Solarium of de Bestegui apartment (1930)   61
2.23 Floor beneath seating in Notre-Dame du Haut, Ronchamp
      (1955)   62
2.24 Floor of Church. La Tourette (1959)   63
3.1   Section across Le Corbusier's scheme for the Basilica at
      La Sainte Baume (c. 1948)   75
3.2   Sliding wooden window, Villa Savoye (1930)   77

3.3	Brise soleil, Unité, Marseilles Michelet (1952)	79
3.4	Cell, La Tourette (1959)	81
3.5	Brise soleil, Carpenter Centre, Boston, USA (1963)	82
3.6	Ondulatoire, La Tourette (1959)	82
3.7	Aerateur, La Tourette (1959), FLC 1011	84
3.8	De Bestegui apartment, roof garden. Photo from *Oeuvre Complète*	85
3.9	'Mitraillette' rooflights over the sacristy La Tourette (1959)	86
3.10	Interior of pink/red tower over chapel at Notre-Dame du Haut, Ronchamp (1955)	87
3.11	Rooflights over the Chapel of the Holy Sacrament, La Tourette (1959)	88
3.12	Interior of Villa Church (1929)	89
3.13	Floor of Church at La Tourette (1959)	90
3.14	Lighting drawing for Pavillon des Temps Nouveau (1937), FLC 31185	91
3.15	Lights in hall at base of pilotis, Unité, Marseilles Michelet (1952)	92
3.16	Photo of model of Unité, Marseilles Michelet (1952) from Le Corbusier, Special Edition L'Homme et L'Architecture, 12–13 (1947), p. 5	93
3.17	Lamps, Unité, Marseilles Michelet (1952), FLC 29271	93
3.18	Lamps in the Cabanon (1950)	94
3.19	Ramp through gallery of Villa La Roche (1925)	95
3.20	Dining table, penthouse, 24 Rue Nungesser et Coli (1934)	96
4.1	Window of solarium Villa Savoye (1930)	102
4.2	Window of Le Corbusier's desk at the Cabanon (1950)	103
4.3	Le Corbusier's desk in penthouse, 24 Rue Nungesser et Coli (1934)	104
4.4	Shutters in Maison Jaoul B (1955)	105
4.5	Concrete bead at ankle height on roof of Unité, Marseilles Michelet (1952)	106
4.6	Stairwell Villa Savoye (1930). Photo from Le Corbusier's *Oeuvre Complète*	107
4.7	Shelf library, Villa La Roche (1925)	108
4.8	'Apartment for a young man' at the Brussels Exposition (1935)	109
4.9	Unité apartment slotting into its frame	110
4.10	Embedded casier in side of brise soleil, as used today. Unité, Marseilles Michelet (1952)	111
4.11	Sketch of brise soleil, Unité, Marseilles Michelet (1952), showing inverted pyramids set into side wall, FLC 27213	112
4.12	'Le Modulor', Unité, Marseilles Michelet (1952), FLC 21044	113
4.13	'Le Modulor' at ground level, Unité, Marseilles Michelet (1952)	114
4.14	Casier in Pavillon d'Esprit Nouveau (1925)	114

4.15   Niche over fireplace penthouse, 24 Rue Nungesser et Coli (1934). Photo from Le Corbusier's *Oeuvre Complète*   115

4.16   'The audacity of square mouldings' from *Towards a New Architecture*   116

4.17   Chamfered windows south wall of Notre-Dame du Haut, Ronchamp (1955)   117

4.18   Chamfered windows of Pilgrims' house, Notre-Dame du Haut, Ronchamp (1955)   118

4.19   Le Corbusier, *Femme à la fenêtre de Georges*, 1943   119

4.20   Open air gathering of pilgrims at Notre-Dame du Haut, Ronchamp (1955). Photo from Le Corbusier's *Oeuvre Complète*   120

4.21   Section through niche Notre-Dame du Haut, Ronchamp (1955) indicating extent of shadow over figure of Virgin   121

4.22   Exterior of Villa Schwob (1917) Charles Edouard Jeanneret (Le Corbusier)   122

5.1   Entrance, Cité de Refuge (1933)   128

5.2   Section A5, *The Poem of the Right Angle* (1955)   130

5.3   'La main ouverte'. Section F3, *The Poem of the Right Angle* (1955)   131

5.4   Door between hall and living room, penthouse, 24 Rue Nungesser et Coli (1934)   133

5.5   Handles of the timber pivoting doors at the Heidi Weber Haus, Zurich (1968)   133

5.6   Cupboard door handles, studio of penthouse, 24 Rue Nungesser et Coli (1934)   133

5.7   Door from Cabanon into next door café, L'Etoile de Mer owned by the Rebutato family who were good friends of Le Corbusier (1950)   133

5.8   Door onto the roof of the Heidi Weber Haus, Zurich (1968)   134

5.9   Door into lift lobby of Unité, Marseilles Michelet (1952)   135

5.10   Drawing of door into life lobby of Unité, Marseilles Michelet (1952)   136

5.11   Detail of door into lift lobby of Unité, Marseilles Michelet (1952). Photo author   137

5.12   Bridged entrance to Mill Owners' Association Building, Ahmedabad (1954)   137

5.13   Door, Maison La Roche (1925)   138

5.14   Piero della Francesca, *Flagellation* (1455–60)   139

5.15   Door into Church, La Tourette (1959)   140

5.16   Door into Church at La Tourette (1959)   140

5.17   Handle of door into Church, La Tourette (1959)   141

5.18   View from bedroom side of door between bedroom and dining space, penthouse, 24 Rue Nungesser et Coli (1934)   142

5.19   Drawing of door between bedroom and dining space, penthouse, 24 Rue Nungesser et Coli (1934)   143

5.20   Detail of frame of door between hall and living room penthouse, 24 Rue Nungesser et Coli (1934)   143

5.21   Sketch showing one of the ways Le Corbusier thought of making a transition space between the bedroom (lower right-hand side) and the dining space penthouse, 24 Rue Nungesser et Coli (1934), FLC 15653   144

5.22   Door between the main hall and theatre of the Maison du Brésel (1957)   145

5.23   Door between the main hall and theatre of the Maison du Brésel (1957)   146

5.24   Ceremonial door at Notre-Dame du Haut, Ronchamp (1955). Photo author   146

5.25   Drawing from Le Corbusier, Section A5, Milieu, *The Poem of the Right Angle* (1955)   147

5.26   Working drawing of ceremonial door at Notre-Dame du Haut, Ronchamp (1955), FLC 07230 and photo of door open   147

5.27   Front door of Cabanon (1950)   148

5.28   Stair, penthouse 24 Nungesser et Coli. Stair Maison des Jeunes, Firminy. Fire stair Unité, Marseilles   150

5.29   Le Corbusier, *Nature morte géométrique et racine* (1930)   151

5.30   Exterior stair of Ozenfant Studio (1924), FLC 07823   151

5.31   An example of a cantilevered staircases – the Heidi Weber Haus (1968)   152

5.32   Stair up to pulpit, Notre-Dame du Haut, Ronchamp (1955)   153

5.33   Drawing of stair up to pulpit, Notre-Dame du Haut, Ronchamp (1955)   154

5.34   Stair up lift shaft on roof of Unité, Marseilles Michelet (1952)   154

5.35   Stair up lift shaft on roof of Unité, Marseilles Michelet (1952)   155

5.36   Bridge over to entrance of La Tourette (1959)   156

5.37   Bridge into Pilgrims house at Notre-Dame du Haut, Ronchamp (1955)   157

5.38   Drawing of stair Jaoul Maison B (1955)   158

5.39   Stair within apartment Unité, Marseilles Michelet (1952)   159

5.40   Stair from hall of Jaoul Maison B (1955)   159

5.41   Stair Jaoul Maison B (1955)   160

5.42   Rear terrace. Villa Stein-de-Monzie, Garches (1928). Photo from Le Corbusier's *Oeuvre Complète*   160

5.43   Ramp. Carpenter Centre, Boston, (1963)   161

5.44   Ground floor stair. Pavillon Suisse (1933)   162

5.45   Ramp in nursery school, Unité, Marseilles Michelet (1952)   163

5.46   Iconostasis, *The Poem of the Right Angle* (1955)   164

6.1   Le Corbusier's sketch of the altar at Notre-Dame du Haut, Ronchamp (1955)   171

6.2   Table in roof garden of Villa Savoye (1930)   172

6.3   Photomural in Pavillon Suisse (1933). Photo from
       Le Corbusier's *Oeuvre complète*   173
6.4   Original photomural Pavillon Suisse (1933)   174
6.5   Mural in Pavillon Suisse (1933), FLC 15653   174
6.6   Hatch from dining space to kitchen, Maison Jaoul B (1955)   176
6.7   Fireplace seen from dining space, Maison Jaoul B (1955)   176
6.8   Drawing for fireplaces in Villa Savoye (1930), FLC 19454   177
6.9   Sketches for fireplace Villa aux Mathes (1935), FLC 8399   177
6.10   Fireplace, Petite Maison de Weekend (1935)   178
6.11   Chimney, Maison Jaoul B (1955)   178
6.12   Fireplace, de Bestegui apartment (1930). Photo from Le
       Corbusier's *Oeuvre Complète*   179
6.13   'Perspective of Fire', La Sainte Baume, FLC 17730   180
6.14   Exterior altar at Ronchamp from Le Corbusier's *Le Livre de
       Ronchamp*   180
6.15   Gargoyle detail, La Tourette (1959)   181
6.16   Gargoyles La Tourette (1959)   182
6.17   Drawing of gargoyle, Notre-Dame du Haut, Ronchamp
       (1955), FLC 7201   182
6.18   Gargoyle, west façade of Notre-Dame du Haut, Ronchamp
       (1955)   183
6.19   Detail of gutter, St- Pierre, Firminy-Vert (started 1960, com-
       pleted 2006)   184
6.20   St-Pierre, Firminy-Vert (construction started 1960,
       completed 2006)   184
6.21   Entrance to director's apartment at the Maison du Brésel
       (1957)   185
6.22   Sink at entrance to Villa Savoye. Photo from Le Corbusier's
       Oeuvre Complète   186
6.23   'Weewee and Co.' from Le Corbusier's *The Nursery Schools*   187
6.24   Paddling pool on roof of Unité, Marseilles Michelet (1952)   189
6.25   *Se Laver'*, FLC 27064   189
6.26   Sink in Le Corbusier's bedroom penthouse, 24 Rue
       Nungesser et Coli (1934)   190
6.27   Shower pod, penthouse, 24 Rue Nungesser et Coli
       (1934)   191
6.28   Sketch of shower unit for Ceramic Pozzi   191
6.29   Kitchen, Villa Sayoye (1930) from Le Corbusier's *Oeuvre
       Complète*   192
7.1   Lobby, Maison du Brésel. Photo from *Oeuvre Complète*   196
7.2   Red cloud, lobby, Maison du Brésel (1957)   196
7.3   Lobby, Maison du Brésel (1957)   197
7.4   Le Corbusier's scheme for a stand at the Ideal Home
       Exhibition in London (1938–39)   198
7.5   Sketch of the Palais du Ministère de l'Éducation Nationale
       (1936)   200

7.6   'Minister Capanema's office'. Sketch of the Palais du
        Ministère de l'Éducation Nationale (1936)   201
7.7   'Artificial mountains' on roof of Unité, Marseilles Michelet
        (1952)   201
7.8   Framing of a view. Series of sketches from Le Corbusier,
        Oeuvre Complète, Volume 4   202
7.9   Le Corbusier, *Deux bouteilles (1926)*   204
7.10   Plan of Lobby Maison du Brésel (1957)   205
7.11   Cover of Le Corbusier's *Precisions*, based on his journey
        round South America   207
7.12   White leather banquettes. Maison du Brésel (1957)   207
7.13   Detail, Section A1, *The Poem of the Right Angle* (1955)   208
7.14   'Les îles sont des corps de femmes', FLC 4231 (1945)   208
7.15   Banquette. Pavillon Suisse (1957–59)   209
7.16   Pigeonhole block, Maison du Brésel (1957)   210
7.17   Detail, pigeonhole block, Maison du Brésel   211

Figure Credits

Acknowledgments

This book has been very much a cumulative effort. Juliet Odgers, Allison Dutoit, my parents, Stella and Edward Samuel, and my daughter Alice Ojeda helped with the survey and gave thoughtful commentaries. Sam Austin went beyond the call of duty in drawing up my surveys for publication. Sarah Menin read the draft and made comments. Tim Benton, William Curtis, Caroline Maniaque José Oubrerie and Robert Rebutato provided me with invaluable thoughts on my surmises. Jodie Cusack and Laura Sacha at the Architectural Press backed the idea. Peter Carolin, Adrian Forty, Jonathan Hale, Vaughan Hart, Simon Unwin and Russell Walden generously gave support to my work at vital junctures. At the Fondation Le Corbusier Arnaud Decelles, Delphine Studer and Paula De Sa Couto helped with a number of practical issues.

Thanks, in no particular order, are due to Jennifer Caras Vial, Denise Leitao of the Brazil Pavilion, Madame Gaelle Rio and Pilar, fortunate inhabitants of the Maisons Jaoul, M. Mathey at Ronchamp, Laurent Duport, José Oubrerie, Russell Walden, Patrick Lynch, Tim Offer, Kwan Phil Cho, Chris Richards, Lorna Davies, Mary McLeod, Gerard Monnier, Djamel Derdiche, Elodie Mazzola at the Cabanon and Inge Linder-Gaillard. Marie Gastinel-Jones helped me with French translation. Clarice Bleil da Souza helped with Portuguese and things Brazilian.

The members of the Architectural History and Theory Group of the Welsh School of Architecture, particularly Adam Sharr and Richard Weston, were continuously supportive and enthusiastic. Sylvia Harris, Paul Duerden and Lynn Phillips in the Architecture Library, Cardiff University supplied me with books. Todd Wilmert, Jorge Nudelman and the many other Le Corbusier scholars I have been fortunate to encounter continually provide me with food for thought. Jane McAllister and Ben Stringer gave me pictures of the Ahmedabad buildings. Paola Sassi, Jakob Hotz, Chris Loyn, Fiona Henderson and Ian Jones helped greatly with my knowledge of construction as did Nic and Richard Morgan, Pat, Dave, Dai, Elvis, John, Terry and Andrew – builders – whose thoughts and actions during the process of building my house and during the writing of this book have been more than instructive.

Like any of my efforts, this book could not have been written without the ceaseless support of my family, in particular Alex.

This book also could not have been written without the support of an Arts and Humanities Research Council grant for travel, a Leverhulme Fellowship for time out from teaching and British Academy funding for the use of copyright.

Bath 2007

Introduction

I would like to present architecture's true image. It is determined by spiritual values derived from a particular state of consciousness, and by technical factors that assure the practical strength of an idea.[1] It is further determined by the strength of the work, its effectiveness and permanence. Consciousness equals life-purpose equals man.[2]

The issue here is the meaning of detail and the way in which Le Corbusier used it as a means to convey aspects of his wider architectural philosophy.[3] While being loaded with meaning, Le Corbusier's details are astonishingly raw and risky (Figure 0.1). Although in many ways flawed, as Edward Ford states of Le Corbusier, 'there is a great deal to be learned by examining his buildings on their own terms'.[4] He praises Le Corbusier for his ability to 'develop detailing systems that reproduced, on a small scale, the organizational ideas of the buildings themselves'.[5] Not only do they express the organizational ideas, they also express Le Corbusier's philosophies which encompassed not just buildings, but his view of the entirety of existence. In *Towards New Architecture* Le Corbusier posed the question 'from what is emotion born?': 'From a certain harmony with the things that make up the site. From a plastic system that spreads its effects over every part of the composition. From a unity of idea that reaches from the unity of the materials used to the unity of the general contour'.[6] This 'unity of idea' is absolutely central to Le Corbusier's work – a desperate attempt to create order in what he perceived to be a fragmented and chaotic world. Nowhere is this quest better expressed than in the realm of detail, where philosophy and reality meet head on.

Le Corbusier stated that 'In Nature, the smallest cell determines the validity, the health of the whole'.[7] Such ideas emerge very directly from the

Figure 0.1
Expansion joint in parapet
on the roof of the Unité
Marseilles (1952)

lessons of his youth, when, in his original incarnation – Charles Édouard Jeanneret[8] – he learnt of the importance of close observation and drawing as a means to access the lessons of nature. The implication was that the cellular structures of nature were repeated throughout the universe both at small and large scale.[9] In his words 'Everything is arranged according to principles consistent with the whole', further 'every organism is a kind of link in the chain of variants around the axis between two poles'.[10] It follows that each architectural detail should contribute to the meaning of the whole, and represent a microcosm of the larger entity, *pars pro toto*. Indeed, Le Corbusier's one-time assistant, Jerzy Soltan, recalled that mantra 'from general to particular and from particular to general' was often to be heard during the period that he worked in Le Corbusier's Rue du Sèvres atelier.[11] Such ideas were entirely in keeping with his highly structured view of the world.

Le Corbusier's architecture was built around a philosophy of Orphism, based on the ancient mystery religion of that name.[12] Orpheus – linked to the figures of Dionysus and Apollo – is himself of course known for having charmed the gods with the beauty of his music. Put very crudely, Orphism was the belief, derived from the ideas of Pythagoras and Plato that the cosmos was held together by numbers and that geometry and proportion could be used to achieve harmony with nature – a process assisted by a balance of masculine and feminine.[13] His fascinations with ancient Greek philosophy, the kabbala, versions of Gnosticism, Catharism,[14] troubadours, masonry, alchemy, Neo-Platonism, Rabelais, Cervantes, Apollinaire and the Platonic androgyne are all, in essence, Orphic – his architecture providing a route of initiation into this belief in this Bacchic figure (Figure 0.2).

Figure 0.2 Le Corbusier by his bed in his apartment at 24 Rue Nungesset et Coli (1934) in front of a painting by André Bauchant

Le Corbusier's interest in Orphism gives rise to a series of key themes that are prevalent in his words, his paintings and his architecture. They are: asceticism and unity; the evocation of the body; light, dark and other oppositions such as sun and water; geometry; the route of initiation and ritual. The structure of this book – the chapter headings – emerge from these themes, yet Le Corbusier's details do not fall into easy typological categories, their multifarious nature being one of the real strengths of his work. A Corbusian window could, for example, simultaneously be categorized as furniture, a wall or a door (Figure 0.3). Soltan reminisced that: 'The holy Corbusierian principles of modern architecture would be kept: free plan, independent construction, free ground floor, free elevations and open roof. But then these principles *in turn expressed a variety of others*'.[15]

A limited repertoire of detail types, many derived from his study of nautical architecture, would appear repeatedly in Le Corbusier's buildings, as within his paintings, subject to minor variations across his career.[16] While it is important to make a distinction between Le Corbusier's early Purist (pre-1930) and late (1930 and onwards) more brutal work, his architectural philosophies remained roughly similar throughout, though they were expressed with an increasing level of subtlety and sensitivity to the vagaries of human existence.[17]

Prowess

Ford writes that 'Few major architects of the twentieth century have received as much criticism for the technical shortcomings of their buildings as Le Corbusier, and in truth, much of it is deserved'.[18] In William Curtis's belief, Le Corbusier was 'negligent over finishes and materials' citing the example of some of the early houses, problems with the concrete of the Millowner's Building and the roof of the Unité as cases in point.[19] However, others are more forgiving. Kenneth Frampton states poignantly that 'in the history of twentieth century architecture perhaps nothing is more unacknowledged than the emergence of tectonic form in the work of Le Corbusier'.[20] Reyner Banham believed that 'Le Corbusier's position of unrivalled esteem among architects make him too convenient a target for criticism, too obvious a colossus on whom to find feet of clay'.[21] Sekler and Curtis write that Le Corbusier's 'inventions for building are all the more stunning through contrast with the odds and ends surrounding them in the notebooks'.[22] These authors' account of the design and building of the Carpenter Centre demonstrates Le Corbusier's full engagement with the subject of detail. 'Le Corbusier the technician emerges in these letters: a man with a lifetime's experience of locksmiths tucked away in odd arrondissements'.[23] In Tim Benton's opinion he was 'almost obsessively fascinated by detailing'. He adds that some of Le Corbusier's most 'impressive drawings are for window mechanisms, gate latches, skylights, lamps and fitments'.[24] For Benton 'the story of Le Corbusier's detailing is a poignant one. Most of the houses

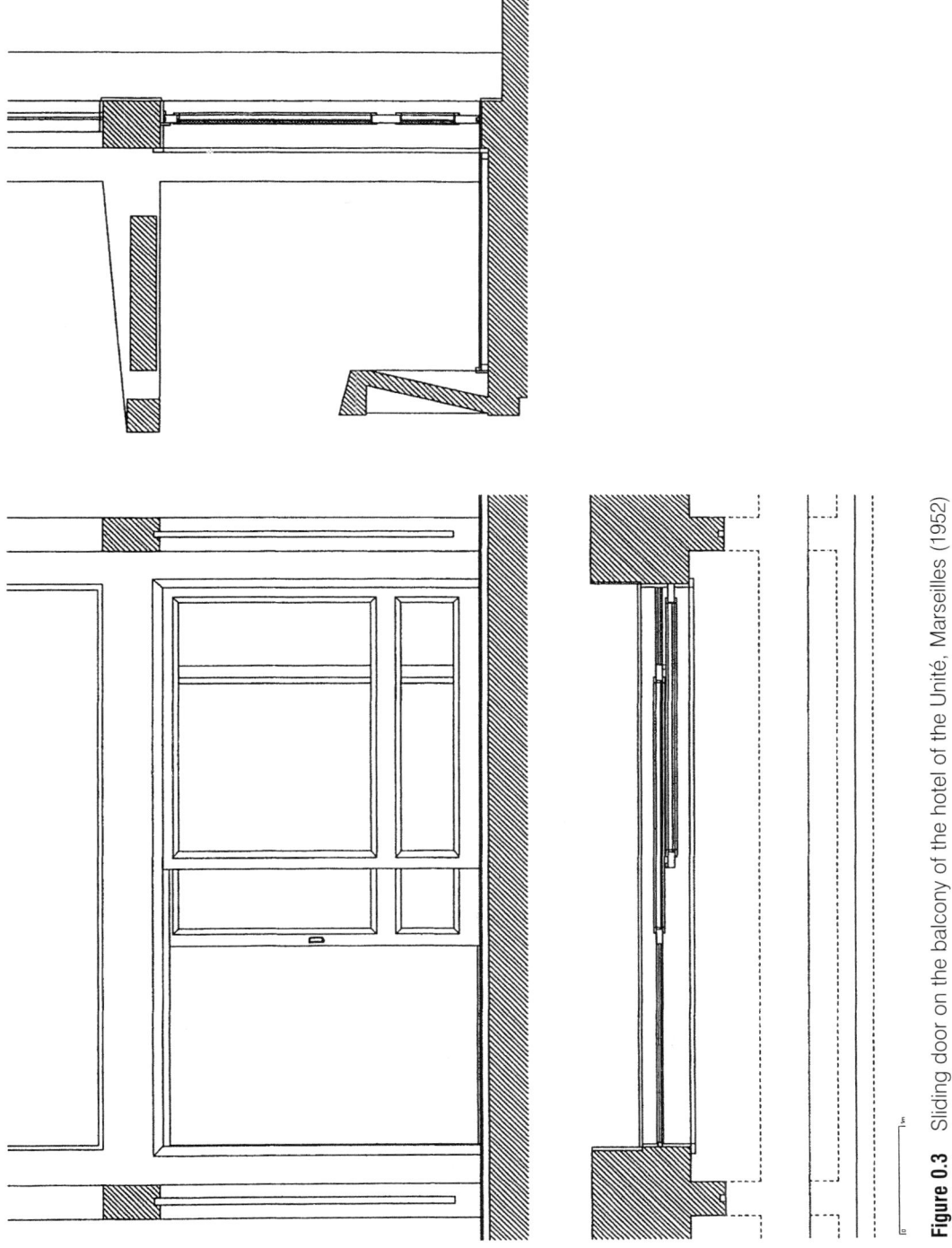

Figure 0.3   Sliding door on the balcony of the hotel of the Unité, Marseilles (1952)

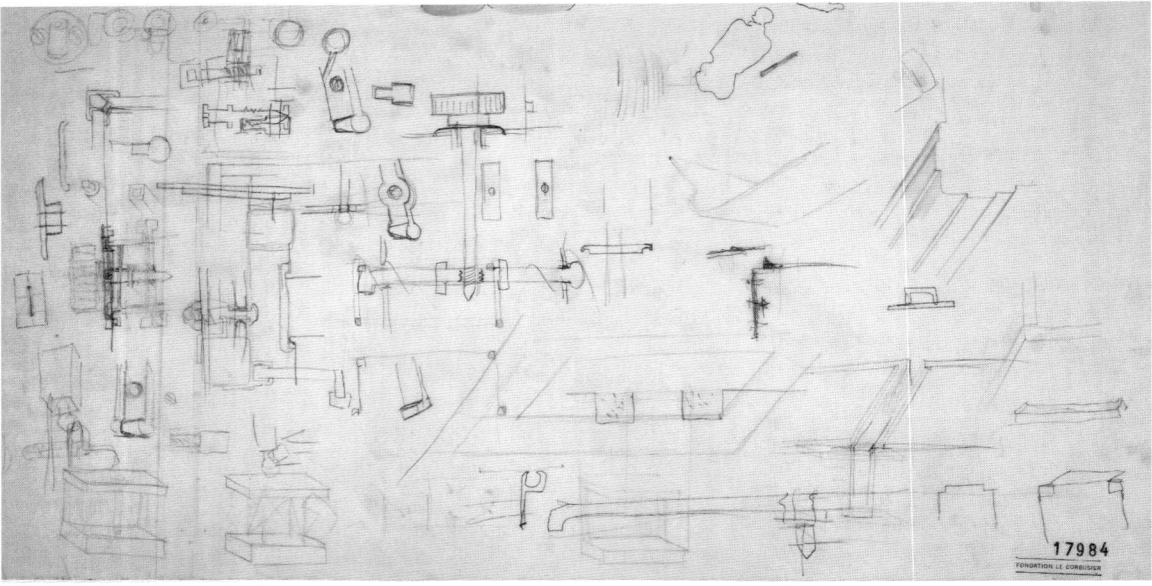

Figure 0.4   Some of the many sketches of fixings for the Bat'a boutique (1935). FLC 17984 and 17953

have a touchingly sincere craftsmanship about the details'. He refers to the little drainage channels to catch condensation beneath the windows, to the mechanisms of latches and door handles and the position of lights and skylights – 'these things provide real satisfaction to the visitor, and the correspondence is full of the record of struggle to make these details work' (Figure 0.4).[25]

So there is no overall consensus on the subject of Le Corbusier's ability in the area of detail. Many scholars make contradictory statements – vilifying his work one minute and applauding it the next. Rather than being a comment on the lack of rigour displayed by these writers, I believe that it reflects the all embracing nature of the subject in hand. If any assessment is to be made of the technical merits of Le Corbusier's work it is necessary to define the meaning of the word 'technology', in its earliest form – an amalgamation of *techne* and *logos*. Techne, as has frequently been reiterated, relates to art, craft and skill, but logos is something far more complex – in it its broadest possible sense it is about conveying meaning. If technology is about creating an artful combination of making and meaning – tectonics – then Le Corbusier can barely be faulted. If technology is, in its more recent sense to do with solving practical problems – construction – then his record is less than impeccable.

Ford, in his book *The Details of Modern Architecture*, examines Le Corbusier's early Purist villas and makes revealing comparisons between Le Corbusier's use of detail and that of his contemporaries. It is very difficult to make any definitive statements regarding the degree of originality attained by Le Corbusier in his approach to construction,[26] but it seems, as with most things to do with Le Corbusier, the more closely the cultural context of his endeavours is examined, the less radical they appear – the villa at Garches, for example, being built, in James Stirling's view, with 'quite conventional methods for its time'.[27]

Process

André Wogenscky, Le Corbusier's long-term assistant,[28] recalled that Le Corbusier had always been convinced of the need for the architect to be able to collaborate with all the technicians, starting with the elaboration of the very first drafts.[29] In post-Second World War France engineers were only involved in the later stages of the design process, so Le Corbusier set up ATBAT – The Atelier des Bâtisseurs – to work on the Unité Marseilles, with the precise aim of countering this trend.[30] The same assiduousness cannot be said of his attitude to the 'mechanicals' which, according to Curtis, he rarely considered until late in the design process 'when he would pack them in as best he could'.[31]

It is one thing to design a ground-breaking work of architecture. It is another to find somebody to build it. Certainly Le Corbusier was fortunate in his ability to find intrepid builders who were prepared to take the risk of working with his novel methods of construction. Indeed, it seems that many of the details of his buildings evolved on-site in discussion with the contractor and his team.[32] In spite of a number of legendary photo shoots on site (Figure 0.5) Le Corbusier was not diligent about visiting his work

Figure 0.5
Le Corbusier on the site
of the Unité Marseilles

under construction.[33] This was not a priority, given the variety of other claims on his time. Now most architects know that the minute that their back is turned something goes wrong on site and that a daily visit is often necessary to keep the project on track. For this reason, very often the task of site supervision frequently fell to one of Le Corbusier's representatives on site. In the case of the Millowner's Building at Ahmedabad, as Rémi Papillault has illustrated, the most basic plans were available to Balkrishna Doshi who was primarily charged with the task of getting it built.[34] This is an extreme case, given the geographic distance from Paris,[35] but similar cases of neglect are recorded elsewhere, for example at the Villa Savoye. It is for this reason that Benton gives credit to the team of builders and craftsmen who worked on the early villas,[36] suggesting that they played an important role in making Le Corbusier's details 'cumulative and coherent'. He stresses, for example, the importance of the input of the mason Aimonetti on the details of the Villa de Mandrot, a radical departure in terms of construction from Le Corbusier's early villas.[37] Later in his career Le Corbusier himself wrote of the way that he designed certain parts of the Unité to be modelled with a trowel by a particularly talented Sardinian concretor.[38] Indeed, a whole section of Le Corbusier's book on Ronchamp is devoted to the team of workmen that played such an active role in its creation (Figure 0.6).

Le Corbusier was usually involved in all aspects of design work, with his assistants working up his sketches into drawings that received his final stamp of approval, or were covered with a cross or scrawled with the word 'annulé'.[39] Benton records that Le Corbusier was impatient with construction, but was an assiduous critic of details drawn by others.[40]

Figure 0.6 The team who built the Notre-Dame du Haut, Ronchamp (1955). Photo taken from Le Corbusier's book *The Chapel at Ronchamp*

The true extent of Le Corbusier's input into his buildings is a subject for further research. However, Wogenscky stated categorically that: 'I can attest that he and he alone was the author of all of his projects. Even for small details, he drew up his own sketches and directions'.[41] This is one of the premises upon which the argument in this book is built.

Speaking detail

Le Corbusier never lost an opportunity to stress the amount of attention that he lavished on each of his works. At the Pavillon Suisse, for example, the 'Greatest care was taken over the smallest detail, visible as well as hidden'.[42] In terms of meaning, the Chapel at Ronchamp (Figure 0.7) was, similarly, the result of 'meticulous research', involving the continual adjustment of a 'thousand factors which in a true work, are all gathered and collected into a closely knit pattern – and even in the simple crossing of right angles, sign and symbol of an existence – these thousand factors about which no-one ought or would wish to speak of'.[43] Such an environment would be legible to those with eyes to see, as opposed to the 'eyes which do not see' berated by the architect through the polemic pages of his book *Towards a New Architecture* (1982).

Even the most laconic settings would convey meaning to their inhabitants:

> Let me recall to your mind that man of ours seated at his table: he has just got up and walked through his rooms. He listens to the language spoken by

Figure 0.7 Notre-Dame du Haut, Ronchamp (1955)

Figure 0.8 Drawing of a stone taken from Le Corbusier's *The Poem of the Right Angle* (1955)

the objects around him, his companions, the witnesses to his aspirations. Arranged in his home like a beautiful thought, they speak to him as he moves about. The furniture, the walls, the openings to the outside, this cozy den of his where minutes, hours, days and years of a lifetime unfold, all speak to him.[44]

Le Corbusier stressed that 'the furniture, the walls, the openings to the outside' all 'speak' to the inhabitant of the space. It is this idea, the idea of the 'speaking' detail, that is the central focus of this book.[45] Within the pages of *The Poem of the Right Angle* (1990), the book of lithographs and text that reflects most closely Le Corbusier's inner world, found objects – stones and bones – develop faces. They cease to be inanimate objects. They begin to communicate (Figure 0.8). In Le Corbusier's terms they are radiant.

Structure and fabric

The raw material for the writing of this book has, by and large, been the buildings themselves. Unless stated otherwise, the drawings are based on measurements made on site. I have not yet been able to visit Chandigarh and Ahmedabad in the course of my research. This has prevented me from discussing in any depth perhaps the most flawed of Le Corbusier's architecture, a fact that should be borne in mind. My attention is given more to the appearance and meaning of details than to their precise construction, as innovations in technology, ecological imperatives and, certainly in Britain, building regulations, mean that they cannot and should not be replicated in their entirety.

The seven volumes of Le Corbusier's *Oeuvre Complète*, written originally as a resource for students, have of course provided much material, but several commentators have noted that the drawings of buildings included in its 'mythopoetic pages'[46] do not represent the building as built, but usually an interim version uncompromised by the demands of reality.[47] The *Oeuvre Complète* contains a fairly limited amount of technical information. In the early volumes each section tends to begin with a description of the more technical aspects of the building,[48] revealing something about the nature of Le Corbusier's priorities or rather the way he wanted his priorities to be seen at that time. He took great care with the content of these volumes, a close inspection of which can reveal much to an inquisitive reader.

The 32 volumes of the Garland Series containing virtually all Le Corbusier's 'architectural' drawings, in the Fondation Le Corbusier, have provided an absolutely invaluable resource.[49] I have included original drawings wherever possible, often in preference to more standard views of particular building elements. Where I have not been able to include illustrations, reference can also be made to the new digital archive of Le Corbusier's working drawings.[50]

Undoubtedly the most useful texts for the writing of this book have been Benton's *The Villas of Le Corbusier* (1987), Caroline Maniaque's *Le Corbusier et les Maisons Jaoul* (2005) and Sekler and Curtis's *Le Corbusier at Work* (1978). All three books dwell on the intricacies of building in an exemplary manner. The latter gives comprehensive coverage of the processes involved in building the Carpenter Centre for the Visual Arts at Harvard University. The genesis of this building is important for two reasons: first, because the Carpenter Centre was the last building that Le Corbusier completed before his death and, second, because of his 'avowed intention to make it a special demonstration of his principles'.[51]

My book does undoubtedly require some foreknowledge of Le Corbusier's work on the part of the reader. This can be easily obtained from one of the many survey books on the subject which will introduce entire buildings rather than minute fragments. Le Corbusier's overall approach to structure, production and materials are, however, swiftly summarized in Chapter 1 of this book. I then illustrate the ways that Le Corbusier used detail to express aspects of his philosophical preoccupation with Orphism: body, light and dark, framing and geometry, promenade and ritual. The final chapter, 'Clouds 1959', is a more holistic exploration. It begins its evolution in a contemplation of one detail in the lobby of the Maison du Brésel, but extends out into the space beyond, making links to the landscape of details in the surroundings. Here a chain of possibility is presented by one eloquent tectonic gesture.

Notes

1 Le Corbusier, *Talks with Students* (New York, Princeton: 2003), p. 37. Originally published 1943.

2 Ibid.

3 It is important to note that Le Corbusier received much assistance and support from his cousin and sometime partner, Pierre Jeanneret particularly during the period 1922–40.

4 E.R. Ford, *The Details of Modern Architecture* (Cambridge, MA: MIT, 1990), p. 233.

5 Ford, *The Details of Modern Architecture*, p. 241. Similarly William Curtis writes of the Carpenter Centre that 'detailing and finish are integral with the overall forms and guiding ideas of the design'. E. Sekler and W. Curtis, *Le Corbusier at Work: The Genesis of the Carpenter Centre for the Visual Arts* (Cambridge, MA: MIT, 1978), p. 21.

6 Le Corbusier, *Towards a New Architecture* (London: Architectural Press, 1982), p.189. Originally published as *Vers une Architecture* (Paris: Crès, 1923).

7 Le Corbusier, *The Marseilles Block*, London: Harville, 1953), p. 17.

8 He was to change his name to Le Corbusier when working on *Esprit Nouveau* with Amédée Ozenfant in the early 1920s.

9 See S. Menin and F. Samuel, *Aalto and Le Corbusier: Nature and Space* (London: Routledge, 2003) for an expansion of this discussion.

10 Le Corbusier, *The Decorative Art of Today* (London: Architectural Press, 1987), p. 175.

11 J. Soltan, 'Working with Le Corbusier' in H. Allen Brooks (ed.), *The Le Corbusier Archive, Volume XVII* (New York: Garland, 1983), pp. ix–xxiv (xvii). Hereafter referred to as Allen Brooks, *Archive*.

12 Orphism was also an art movement started by Guillaume Apollinaire, who Le Corbusier held in high esteem.

13 F. Samuel, 'Orphism in the work of Le Corbusier with particular reference to his unbuilt scheme for La Sainte Baume', unpublished PhD thesis, Cardiff, 2000.

14 It is impossible to overstate the seriousness with which Le Corbusier treated his supposed ancestral connection with the Albigensian Cathars, a Manichaean heretical sect prevalent in the Languedoc area of France during the twelfth and thirteenth centuries. Le Corbusier, *Sketchbooks Volume 3 1954–1957* (Cambridge, MA: MIT, 1981), p. 26.

15 Soltan, 'Working with Le Corbusier', p. xvi.

16 Sekler and Curtis, *Le Corbusier at Work*, p. 241.

17 I. Zaknic, *The Final Testament of Père Corbu: a Translation and Interpretation of Mise au Point* (New Haven, CT: Yale University Press, 1997), p. 100.

18 Ford, *The Details of Modern Architecture*, p. 233.

19 W. Curtis, *Le Corbusier: Ideas and Forms* (Oxford: Phaidon, 1986), p. 224.

20 K. Frampton, *Studies in Tectonic Culture: The Poetics of Construction in Nineteenth and Twentieth Century Architecture* (Cambridge, MA: MIT, 1996), p. 343.

21 R. Banham, *The Architecture of the Well-tempered Environment* (London: Architectural Press, 1969), p. 143.

22 Sekler and Curtis, *Le Corbusier at Work*, p. 52.

23 Ibid., p. 175.

24 T. Benton, *The Villas of Le Corbusier 1920–1930* (London: Yale, 1987), p. 12.

25 Ibid.

26 Each month during the 1940s and 1950s a 'review of building techniques and industrial design' appeared at the end of the *Architectural Review*. These provide a useful source of comparison.

27 See F. Choay, *La Règle et le Modèle* (Paris: Seuil, 1996, 2nd edn), p. 317. Evenson, N. 'Yesterday's city of tomorrow today' in Allen Brooks, *Archive*, vol. 15, p. xiv.

28 He began working with Le Corbusier in 1936 and continued in his atelier for some twenty years.

29 Ibid, p. x.

30 A. Wogenscky, 'The Unité d'Habitation at Marseille' in Allen Brooks, *Archive, Volume XVI*, p. ix.

31 Sekler and Curtis, *Le Corbusier at Work*, p. 136.

[32] Judi Loach has interviewed many members of Le Corbusier's atelier. See for example J. Loach, 'Le Corbusier at Firminy-Vert' in T. Benton (ed.), *Le Corbusier Architect of the Century* (London: Arts Council, 1987), pp. 338–43 for a brief discussion of office processes.

[33] This fact emerged in a discussion at the conference 'Le Corbusier Moments biographiques' held at the Fondation Le Corbusier, 8–9 December 2006.

[34] Rémi Papillault, 'Sur le chantier d'Ahmedabad', paper at Le Corbusier Moments biographiques held at the Fondation Le Corbusier, 8–9 December 2006. To be published shortly by Editions de la Villette.

[35] Caroline Maniaque gives a highly detailed account of Le Corbusier's part in the building of the Maisons Jaoul. C. Maniaque, *Le Corbusier et les Maisons Jaoul* (Paris: Picard, 2005), p. 58.

[36] These were 'the mason, Summer; the carpenter and joiner, Louis; the painter and glazier, Celio; the plumber, Pasquier and the electrician, Barth'. Benton, *The Villas of Le Corbusier*, p. 12.

[37] T. Benton, 'Villa Savoye and the Architect's Practice' in Allen Brooks, *Archive, Volume VII*, p. x.

[38] Le Corbusier, *Oeuvre Complète Volume 5, 1946–1952* (Zurich: Les Editions d'Architecture, 1995), p. 191. Originally published in 1953.

[39] Soltan, 'Working with Le Corbusier', p. xii.

[40] Tim Benton in conversation with the author, December 2006.

[41] Wogenscky, 'The Unité d'Habitation at Marseille', p. x.

[42] Le Corbusier and Pierre Jeanneret, *Oeuvre Complète Volume 2, 1929–34* (Zurich: Les Editions d'Architecture, 1995), p. 16. Originally published in 1935.

[43] Le Corbusier, *The Chapel at Ronchamp* (London: Architectural Press, 1957), p. 6.

[44] Le Corbusier, *Talks with Students*, p. 54.

[45] As Colin Rowe suggests in his discussion of La Tourette, those 'sceptical of the degree of contrivance' and 'temperamentally predisposed to consider the game of hunt-the-symbol as an overindulgence in literature' really need to look at the architecture once more. C. Rowe, *The Mathematics of the Ideal Villa and Other Essays* (Cambridge, MA: MIT, 1976), p. 189.

[46] Sekler and Curtis, *Le Corbusier at Work*, p. 2.

[47] Ibid.

[48] See, for example, the Cité de Refuge, 1932. Le Corbusier and Jeanneret, *Oeuvre Complète Volume 2, 1929–34* p. 98.

[49] Allen Brooks, *Archive*, vols 1–32.

[50] Le Corbusier Plans, Echelle 1, Fondation Le Corbusier DVD, 2006.

[51] Sekler and Curtis, *Le Corbusier at Work*, p. 2.

Standardization and unity

1

'I am obsessed by this law of economy to which I give a meaning going beyond that of the wallet . . .'[1] Le Corbusier's espousal of rational structures, simple materials and standardization had profound roots in the ascetic and harmonious doctrines of Orphism. Le Corbusier emulated the life of a monk, spending long hours in retreat.[2] His vision of the simple contemplative life, discovered most famously on his visit to the monastery at Ema, was one that he wished to share 'to discover, to create a different, other architecture, unique and original in its essential nudity'.[3] One of Le Corbusier's prime objectives was to assist people in the process of 'savoir habiter': knowing how to live.[4] Put simply, this meant understanding and fully appreciating the important things in life, sun, sea, space, greenery and love. He wrote in *When the Cathedrals were White*: 'Knowing how to live is the fundamental question before modern society, everywhere, in the whole world. An ingenuous question and one that could be considered childish. How to live? Do you know reader? Do you know how to live soundly, strongly, gaily, free of the hundred stupidities established by habit, custom and urban disorganization?'[5]

Le Corbusier's quest for clarity would take many forms. Here I focus on his attitude to standardization, materials and structure, in doing so providing the framework, both philosophically and physically, for the rest of his tectonic decisions.

1.1 Standardization

Le Corbusier's ideas on standardization and rationalism in the domestic sphere were clearly informed by ideas about the order of nature – his enthusiasm for the homes of ants and honey bees and his continued references to the biology of the city. There seem to be three motives behind his obsession with this subject: first, of course, to provide cheap high-quality homes; second, to make life more simple, and third, and less easy to grasp, to connect people together through their shared use of standard elements.

His ideas on standardization received their most famous airing within the pages of *Towards a New Architecture* in the chapter entitled 'Mass-production housing' where he focuses on the 'spirit' of 'constructing', 'living in' and 'conceiving' mass-production houses.[6] It is my suggestion that for Le Corbusier mass production was in fact a highly spiritual matter.[7] It was as much, if not more, about creating commonality between people and things as it was about economics. Central to Le Corbusier's idea of community was the concept of the Radiant City which received its full expression in the book of the same name published in 1933.[8] 'Therefore, radiant, therefore ineffable, this total potential with banal materials to make our cities, our homes, our houses and our countrysides, the modern world "radiant".'[9] A radiant building, object or work of art would influence everything around it, like the Parthenon, which Le Corbusier described as generating 'lines spurting, radiating out as if produced by an explosion' linking it to its environment and beyond.[10] Radiant architecture would impose its influence upon the surroundings. It would be connected with other edifices, both old and new, built in the same spirit and with the same sensitivity to geometry. Furthermore, architecture could be 'made radiant' through the use of the Modulor,[11] Le Corbusier's own system of proportion, evolved from his researches into ancient architecture, art, history, religion, science, technology and the natural world.[12]

Le Corbusier emphasized the importance of relationship and communication in bringing about the higher form of civilization that he sought. Such ideas would be inculcated, for example, in the children at the 'radiant school' on the top of the Unité.[13] Le Corbusier wrote that 'when nature integrates' itself in architecture it is then that one approaches unity and then affirmed 'I believe that unity is that stage to which the unceasing and penetrating work of the mind leads'.[14] Clearly standardization would play a key role in such a process. 'For the mass-production house will impose unity in the various elements, windows, doors, methods of construction, materials. Unity in detail and general lines – this was the demand, in Louis XVI's reign, in the muddled, congested and inextricable and uninhabitable Paris of that time, of a very intelligent *abbé*, Laugier, who busied himself with town planning: Uniformity in detail and variety in the general effect . . .'[15]

In *Towards a New Architecture* Le Corbusier called for 'a minute study of every detail connected with the house, and a close search for a standard, that is for a type'.[16] This pursuit would continue to the very end of his career. A variety of schemes for mass-produced houses or 'House–Tool'[17] are described in the pages of the *Oeuvre Complète*, perhaps the best known example being the Citrohan house, 1921 – citrohan, of course, being a pun on citroen – in other words a house like a car.[18]

'One thing leads to another, and as so many cannons, airplanes, lorries and wagons had been made in factories, someone asked the question: "why not make houses?"'[19] It quickly became apparent to Le Corbusier that this was the best place to produce high-quality standard construction components. Elements would be constructed in metal-fabricators' work-shops and transported by trucks straight to the site, where they could be assembled in a matter of days.[20]

His 'Houses in dry construction' 1939/40 were to be built of standard-ized elements: 'metal stanchions, metal beams, sheet metal ceiling unit, cladding units'. The stairs were to be standard, as were the windows, doors, kitchens, and sanitary fittings.[21] Factory production, especially Taylorism,[22] appealed to Le Corbusier's spirit of orderliness,[23] an infi-nite improvement on contractor's yards which he described as 'sporadic dumps in which everything breathes confusion', a description which will be familiar to many.[24]

Clearly the celebration of factory production would have implications for the vexed issue of craftsmanship. Although he never received any formal instruction in architectural design, Le Corbusier was raised up and trained within the craft tradition of Swiss watch making.[25] Le Corbusier's first building, the Villa Fallet, is full of intricate, nature-based timber dec-oration reflecting his interest in the arts and crafts at that time. When asked whether there will be 'a more intimate collaboration between the architect and other technicians' in the future, Le Corbusier responded 'That is a question! That is a question! It is a crucial problem of archi-tectural education' and then went on to describe his own apprenticeship into the subject as being very much on site.[26] However, he eventually rejected the word craftsman in favour of the clinical and pristine 'techni-cian'.[27] Indeed he suggested that 'the French send their craftsmen to visit American engineers' in order to be thus transformed.[28] These desires underpin such ambiguous statements as 'let the craft be present at all times, from the first day, the true facts about technological methods, the real qualities of the materials, the reality of the workyard', their confusion reflecting real turmoil in Le Corbusier's mind.[29]

'Unity in detail, tumult in the ensemble'[30] was Le Corbusier's stated objective in his early work. Le Corbusier was largely able to maintain a uni-formity in detail of his buildings partly because of the skill and dedication of his employees, 'the date palms',[31] partly because of the degree of his involvement in all aspects of design (in spite of long periods of absence), partly through the use of a limited family of forms often derived from his paintings, partly through the – more orthodox, but limited – use of sched-ules of standard details,[32] and partly because of the *Oeuvre Complète*. Jerzy Soltan recalled that Le Corbusier frequently told his employees to "Go and check this in the Girsberger" in this way 'assuring his work's continuity, saving time and money'.[33] The role of the Modulor in all of this is, of course, significant. Wogenscky observed that:

In reality, the Modulor is a tool that helps one to 'tune' dimensions to each other just as one tunes the strings of a piano. It does not help one to determine sizes, but rather to arrange them, to prevent them from being in arbitrary relation to one another, to make them adjust precisely to one another, to bring them together in one single family. It is this 'single family' that gives a strange unity to any composition made with the Modulor . . . The apartments of the Marseilles Unité were designed with just fifteen different dimensions, and these can be found repeated and harmonized with one another everywhere, as in a living being created by nature.[34]

However, he was not always rigid in the use of his system of proportion. Soltan recalled that when Le Corbusier discovered a less than satisfactory design on the drawing board of one of his assistants he would ask "How did you get to this proposal?", "The Modulor suggested it," ran the answer,[35] to which Le Corbusier would reply, 'To hell with the Modulor! When it doesn't work, you shouldn't use it'.[36]

1.2   Standard materials

So zestful was Le Corbusier about standardization that he sought a standard palette of materials with which to create his new architecture stating in *Towards a New Architecture* that 'natural materials, which are infinitely variable in composition, must be replaced by fixed ones'.[37] By 'fixed' he meant that their character was predictable and unvarying, the product of a production line – such as steel, reinforced concrete and glass[38] or the Solomite compressed straw panels used, for example, in the Esprit Nouveau Pavilion.[39] In addition, aluminium was applauded for being lightweight – it also contributed to the sense of luxury in houses such as Villa Church[40] – while Pierre Chareau's Maison de Verre[41] had impressed upon Le Corbusier the poetic possibilities of glass block.[42] He also took a liking to factory produced timber board, as he particularly hated to see 'artistic veins' in wood, an abhorrence that he would retain to the end of his career, presumably because these blemishes interfered with the planar quality of his work.[43]

Materials, in Le Corbusier's mind sat within two discrete categories, natural and artificial.[44] In his early work he treated concrete as a 'fixed' material, as opposed to a natural material, as he was at that time interested in creating a pristine finish, or at least the illusion of a pristine finish. However, in his later work all this would change. Concrete became for him a 'material of the same rank as stone, wood or baked earth'. He added that the 'experience is of importance. It seems to be really possible to consider concrete as a reconstructed stone'.[45] Beton brut came into being apparently by accident, as the contractor was under the impression that the concrete would be plastered over. Le Corbusier recalled:

Beton brut was born at the Unité d'Habitation at Marseilles where there were 80 contractors and such a massacre of concrete that one simply could not dream of making useful transitions by means of grouting. I decided: let us leave all that brute. I called it 'beton brute' [bare concrete]. The English immediately jumped on the piece and treated me (Ronchamp and Monastery of La Tourette) as 'Brutal' – beton brutal – all things considered, the brute is Corbu. They called that 'the new brutality'. My friends and admirers take me for the brute of the brutal concrete![46]

Whether Le Corbusier would have chosen such a finish for his building is not clear, certainly the concrete in such late buildings as the Carpenter Centre is beautifully smooth.

There is a growing tension in Le Corbusier's work between his desire for a pristine factory finish, with guaranteed structural capabilities and the need to work with the materials and skills found on site, as he was to do at the Maison Errazuriz. It is expressed clearly in such statements as the following, made in *Talks with Students* originally published in 1943:

materials used should be safe, tested, subjected to strict control, synthetic wherever possible, and governed by constant coefficients of resistance. Such modern materials as Portland cement and various kinds of steel are good examples. In the process of construction, one can see that the building does not draw exclusively on any rigid procedure; instead, the erection of the walls, floors, arches, materials used locally in timber-work, joinery, stone and brickmasonry, etc. These materials may be natural substances like stone or slate, or fabricated products traditional in certain regions such as tile or brick.[47]

Clearly an enthusiasm for standardization was at odds with an enthusiasm for regionalism, yet this did not stop Le Corbusier from becoming increasingly interested in 'the possible splendours of an architecture adapted to the surroundings and local materials'.[48] 'Part of the daily environment, their familiar traits unite the present with the past. Custom, for some of them a thousand years old, has made of them the companions of our lives. This friendly pact with one's environment is something to consider. From it, we can get a feeling of security, or belonging, and in just this we have the secret, the precious source from which all architecture springs'.[49]

In the opinion of Benton the vernacular could only become a source of inspiration if 'stripped of its nationalist and traditionalist associations and rediscovered as a fragment of "nature" – in other words a form of objets trouvés'.[50] While, at times, Le Corbusier would be sensitive in the extreme to regionalist issues of material, for example at La Sainte Baume,[51] at others his insensitivity was on a grand scale. David Leatherbarrow writes, for example, of the decision to build in concrete at Chandigarh when it was 'obvious that there was not an already existing local capacity to build in this material.'[52] Photographs of the hordes of women and men carrying and constructing on the building site for Mill-owners' Building at Ahmedabad indicate the sheer human effort of constructing a concrete building in such an environment. Le Corbusier was, however, keen to emphasize the universal and unifying qualities of his structural solutions: 'In our own day, the technology of steel and reinforced concrete has a similarly universal character. Everyone has access to these materials. No patch of sky or piece of earth can claim sole ownership'.[53] He clearly had a love affair with the monumental possibilities of concrete construction and had difficulties in conceiving a public architecture in any other material.

Although Le Corbusier is perhaps best known for his use of concrete and steel, brick, earth, 'moellon' rubble blocks (ubiquitous in Paris)[54] and, even, rough hewn logs[55] were to become important elements in his constructional repertoire. Le Corbusier described the materials of the Petite Maison de Weekend (1935) as 'very traditional' with the masonry left visible and the chimney made of ordinary bricks.[56] This would be true if reinforced concrete, steel-framed plate glass, glass lenses and plywood panelling fell within the category of 'traditional'. Both modern and archaic in its construction, Le Corbusier emphasized the latter to acknowledge his loss of faith in technological progress. Indeed Frampton writes that this building 'evokes a kind of eternal return in which neither the archaic nor the modern predominate'.[57]

1.3   Standard structures

Fundamental to the pursuit of standardized housing was the pursuit of a standardized structure to support it. Le Corbusier would reuse structures again and again, his aim being to find the ideal structural solution for the particular material in hand, almost as though it had been refined through the processes of natural selection. The dormitory block of Maison du Brésel is, for example, supported by beams that appeared much earlier in the nearby scheme for the Pavillon Suisse.[58] Le Corbusier learnt the potential of concrete and steel from Auguste Perret and Tony Garnier on his early forays to Paris. From that point onwards his buildings became highly experimental both philosophically and physically, 'laboratories' in every sense of the word – his most notorious experiment, executed with the aid of a most indulgent client, M. Fruges, an altruistic industrialist from Bordeaux who apparently said to Le Corbusier "I would like you to apply your theories" to his scheme for worker's housing at Pessac.[59]

1.3.1   Concrete frames

Fully aware that it might be one of his last built works, it was Le Corbusier's intention that the Carpenter Centre would provide 'the key to the solution of reinforced concrete'[60] – indeed he believed that there were certain ideal – in the Platonic sense – forms to which a particular material might aspire. A brief scan of the chapter 'Mass-production houses' in *Towards a New Architecture* reveals that, even at that early stage in his career, he had already experimented with various different structural forms for concrete, but the one that was to have the greatest longevity in his work was based on the domino frame which first entered his work in 1914 (Figure 1.1).[61] Here a floor slab, a first floor slab and a roof garden slab are linked by a simple dogleg stair and supported on slim columns to which the façade and the walls have relinquished their former structural role, giving them the freedom to be positioned at the will of the architect. The lowest slab was raised from the ground on blocks, a suitably indeterminate and universal foundation condition. Revealing the political implications of something as seemingly innocuous as a structural frame, Colin Rowe wrote of the Maison Domino and its off-spring, the Villa Savoye, as being 'symbols of emancipation' which carry implications of 'social liberty'.[62] Its development was paralleled by Le Corbusier's statement on the 'five points of a new architecture' – pilotis, horizontal windows, free façade, free plan and roof garden, the various aspects of which will be touched upon in the course of this argument.

Le Corbusier's famous 1914 image of the domino frame, what Curtis calls 'an industrialised equivalent of Laugier's Primitive Hut',[63] is actu-ally deceptive – the idealized smooth slabs and pilotis never built.[64] The slabs of Le Corbusier's concrete buildings were not in fact of a uniform flush thickness.[65] The majority were built with the Hennibique system, a ribbed slab produced by placing hollow clay tiles on a flat wooden scaffolding with spaces between, the result being a lighter, stronger and cheaper structure. When the formwork is removed the tiles remain in place leaving a flush surface on the soffit. Smooth slabs do not reflect the structural tensions that reside within them and do not make the best use of the material which should decrease in depth as the forces within the slab decrease. Le Corbusier had observed that: 'There is much to be learned from the study of material phenomena: unity of structure, purity of outline. A gradual but total distribution of all sec-ondary elements; an infinite gearing down of the system to its furthest extremities. The result, an entity'.[66] His work was not, however, always so rational.[67]

Of the pilotis that supported the slabs, Le Corbusier wrote: 'Please admit in passing that "naked man", what I call pure man, has used this resource in all times and places'.[68] One such column could take on several forms and meanings. Curtis writes that:

> It might serve to lift the body of the building into space, to define a route, to introduce a cadence into the interior; it might be round or oval in plan, parallel-sided or tapering in elevation, smooth or rough in finish. And, depending upon the weights to be borne and complex of intentions sur-rounding its use, the piloti might evoke different references. In the entrance hall of the Villa Stein de Monzie the four oval pilotis suggest simultaneously the idea of a classical vestibule (Palladio's four-column idea) and the notion of aviomorphic struts.[69]

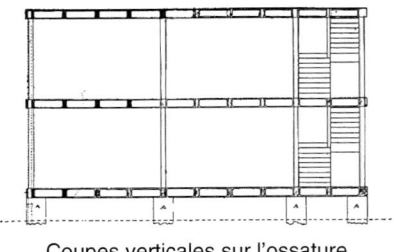
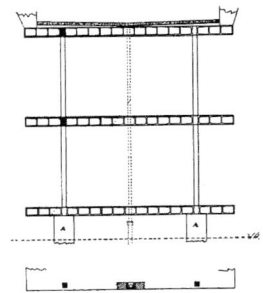

Coupes verticales sur l'ossature

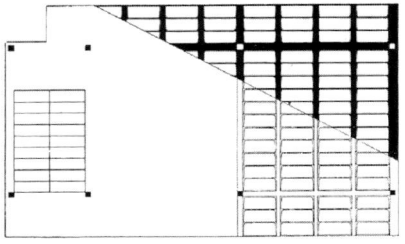

Coupe sur le plafond

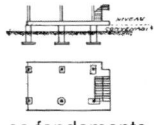

Les fondements

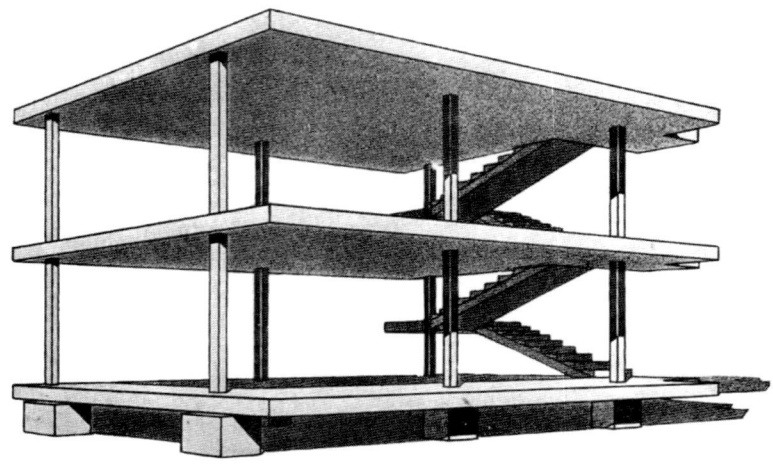

Figure 1.1
Maison Domino (1914)

L'ossature standard «Dom-ino», pour exécution en grande série

Columns, circular in plan, were favoured by Le Corbusier, perhaps because they alluded to the Doric order that he so admired.[70] For Rowe the circular section 'tended to push partitions away from the column', which meant that it did not aid the delineation of structural cells. It 'offered a minimum of obstruction to the horizontal movement of space' and 'tended to cause space to gyrate around it'.[71] By far the majority of Le Corbusier's pilotis have neither base nor capital.[72] Describing them as 'atectonic' Frampton calls such columns 'abstractions of the idea of support' owing to the fact that beams are not expressed in the flush plane of the ceiling.[73] With regard to structure Le Corbusier himself asked:

> How should it be built? By 'suppressing I do not mean repressing or condemning. By 'expressing the structure' I mean: affirming its structural components, making them visible and making of this tendency the central postulate in our architecture. Whether we express a column or not (beyond its task of helping support the building) is just a question of one's aesthetic, and we need not quibble over it. We can go from one extreme to the other, which will only indicate the range of the infinitely varied modalities for possible solutions. If you relish such things, you can easily begin petty bickering.[74]

When, for example, it was found that extra reinforcement was needed at the head of each piloti, just beneath the slab of the Carpenter Centre, Le Corbusier toyed with the idea of creating a mushroom capital as was used on a massive scale on the Parliament Building at Chandigarh.[75] However, the illusion that the slabs were hovering would be spoilt by drawing attention to the way in which they were being supported. Fortunately for him the requirement for an 'air floor' made the formation of smooth slabs possible as the capitals of the columns could be recessed within the depth of this void. At the same time the extra reinforcement that was needed at the cantilevered edges could be similarly masked, once again creating the flush plane so necessary to Le Corbusier's aesthetics.

Soltan often had his architectural sensibilities offended when working with Le Corbusier – 'sometimes, he did not exclude the possibility of raping (a little) the virtue of architectural chastity' – presumably rational structure and a pragmatic use of materials.[76] Emil Hervol, the engineer for the Carpenter Centre, also experienced numerous instances in which Le Corbusier's philosophies took priority over pragmatism as Curtis has recorded:

> For example, he suggested an optimal slab thickness in the overhanging areas which [the job architect] Sert disallowed 'Because of Corbu's blue system or something' . . . [77] And when everyone was confronted with the problem of the auditorium span, Hervol suggested that the span be reduced by the placement of hidden columns in the auditorium's side walls – a suggestion that was greeted with horror by the Cambridge architects who felt it was dishonest and anyway broke the grid. But when Hervol left out the redundant column next to the weight bearing stair wall to save cost, he was chided: evidently the architects preferred structural dishonesty to breaking the grid.[78]

Indeed 'Emergency measures' had to be used to support the cantilevered curved studios, including a brise soleil which extended down to ground level to become a pier.

A further instance of structural 'dishonesty' is cited by Curtis. The pilotis of the Carpenter Centre vary in girth, supposedly in recognition of the amount of weight that they carry. Taken to its logical extreme this idea would have resulted in pilotis of innumerable different diameters spread around the building. Instead, however, the columns were sized according to the load that they seemed to be carrying:

> the column becoming an increment thicker for each additional floor supported. In some cases this system resulted in slender columns rising unbraced through clear space for two stories. These had to be so packed with steel reinforcing that concrete could not be poured but had to be crammed manually. The diminishing column sizes were not equal to standard formwork dimensions, and standardized reinforcing solutions were found to be impossible too. The reason for this, of course, was that the weights above were actually varying, even when the column size did not acknowledge it. Columns of the same size would often require totally different reinforcing solutions from the engineer despite the assertion of the architect that they were 'bearing the same weight'.[79]

In spite of this Curtis refers to the structural skeleton as 'extremely elegant'[80] with 'parallels' in the 'classical orders used in combination, or even (since the architect himself spoke of a "forest of firs") the diminution towards the tops of trees'.[81] Certainly Le Corbusier seemed to have been more interested in issues of composition and geometrical harmony than he was in any sense of structural honesty. As he wrote in *Towards a New Architecture*, with regard to the 'delicate distortions' employed by Phidias and his workers on the Parthenon, 'the engineer is effaced and the sculptor comes to life – contours go beyond the scope of the practical man, the daring man, the ingenious man; they call for the plastic artist'.[82]

1.3.2 Steel structures

While Le Corbusier is known for his love affair with concrete, close inspection of the *Oeuvre Complète* reveals an equivalent passion for steel. So admiring was he of the towers of the George Washington bridge over the Hudson that he wrote effusively that 'here, finally, steel architecture seems to laugh'.[83] Further, he referred to the details of the PFSF bank in Philadelphia as 'gods . . . a perfection which reaches the highest nobility'. So seductive did he find the building that he was to describe it as 'coquetry in choice steels'.[84] Steel performed a primary role in his vision of dry construction, as used, for example, in the upper stone clad reaches of the Pavillon Suisse (1933) 'a spider's web of metal' where, as he wrote excitedly (Figure 1.2):[85]

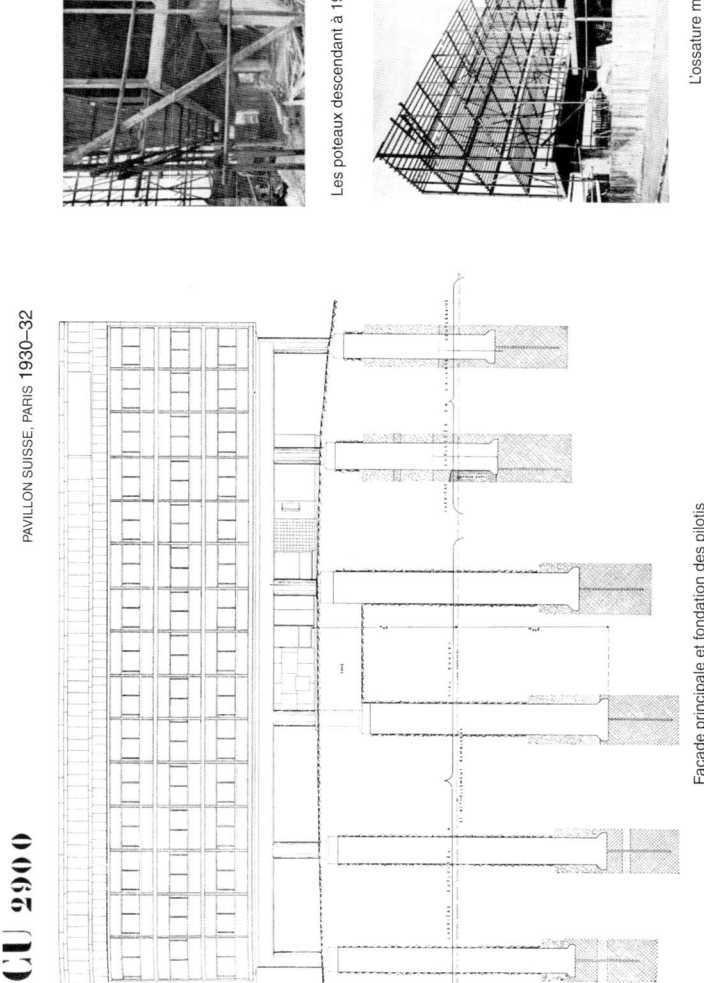

PAVILLON SUISSE. PARIS 1930–32

CU 2900

Les poteaux descendant à 19,50 mètres dans le sol

L'ossature métallique

Façade principale et fondation des pilotis

Figure 1.2   Structure of Pavillon Suisse (1933)

By means of brackets we are going to hang vertical steel sections, well adjusted, really vertical, 25cm in front of these ribbons of concrete. Then, across them, inside or outside, horizontal steel sections at distances determined by the glass or plate glass sizes available on the market . . . I shall build window walls, stone cladding (veneer, brick, artificial panels of cement or other materials), and mixed walls small windows or glass panes scattered like portholes in the stone cladding.[86]

He also took a particular interest in the tensile qualities of steel. When offered the opportunity to make a temporary exhibition pavilion he invariably returned to the archetype of the tent, intrigued as he was by nomadic lifestyles.[87] His interest in the tent as a primary form was evoked as early as 1923 in the pages of *Towards a New Architecture* where he included an illustration showing a reconstruction of 'a primitive temple' (Figure 1.3), one that withstands comparison with the Pavillon des Temps Nouveaux (Figure 1.4) where guy ropes extend at right angles to the tent itself.[88] Le Corbusier did not re-create the pitched roof of the temple tent, preferring instead to keep the interior free of structure – the roof hangs in an inversion of the vaulted form of which he was to become so fond.

The Philips Pavilion for the Brussels World Fair clearly represents the climax of Le Corbusier's experimentation with tents (Figure 1.5). Here, as Frampton observes, he was to 'reconcile both tent and vault into one complex hyperbolic, cable-stayed volume'.[89] But, as Marc Treib records, Le Corbusier's office was only really responsible for the design – its

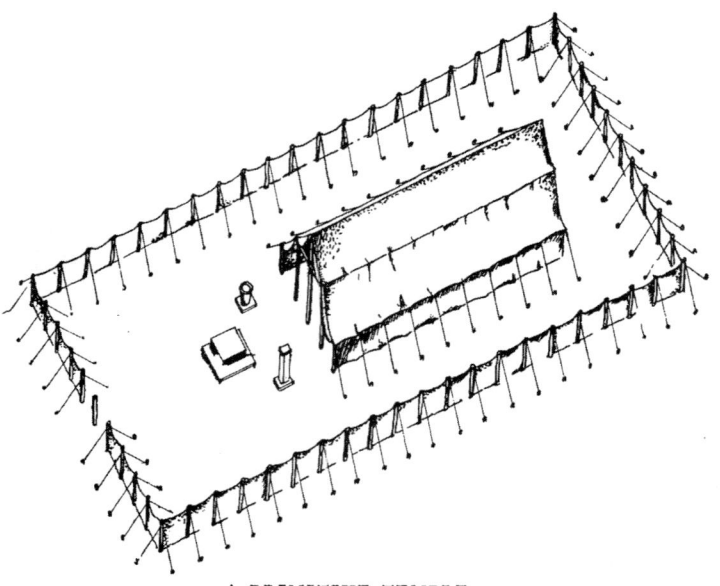

REGULATING LINES

A PRIMITIVE TEMPLE

Figure 1.3 Drawing of 'a primitive temple' from *Towards a New Architecture* (1923), p. 67

Figure 1.4   Pavillon des Temps Nouveau (1937)

Figure 1.5
Philips Pavilion exterior,
Brussels International
Exhibition (1958)

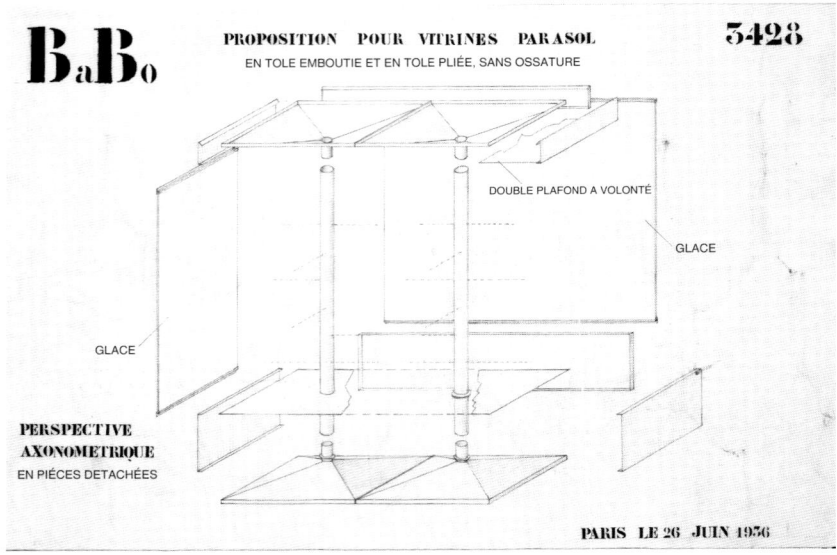

Figure 1.6 Proposition for 'vitrines parasol', 1956, FLC 17826

cable-driven form, its ingenious construction of precast panels was in fact the conception of the contractor.[90]

Late in Le Corbusier's career a further roof type would enter his repertoire, the parasol roof, a protective overhanging structure supported either on arches, piers or pilotis (Figure 1.6).[91] It sheltered buildings from the sun while allowing them to benefit from cool breezes and it would become a unifying feature in the design of Chandigarh, a clear example being the convex curved roof of the Parliament building.[92] This line of enquiry would culminate in a steel building, simultaneously exhibition pavilion and house, the Heidi Weber Haus in Zurich (Figure 1.7), itself derived from an idea developed in the 1930s.[93] In 1965, Le Corbusier asked Weber whether she would mind if the structure was built in steel, a suggestion that 'thrilled' his client who proudly proclaims that 22,000 screws were used in its production. In its form the parasol roof of flat steel plates forms a flattened wave clearly evoking Le Corbusier's sign of the 24-hour day (Figure 1.8). In some parts of the building there appears to be an excessive amount of structure. It almost seems as though Le Corbusier was trying to re-create the feeling of the 'forest of firs' that he alluded to at the Carpenter Centre, perhaps in the manner of his friend Aalto (Figure 1.9).[94]

1.3.3   Vaulted roofs

Another friend, the artist Constantino Nivola, wrote that Le Corbusier never 'lost sight of the intimate continuity that ties the past to the present, the recurring forms that are visible only to those who know how to see them and

Figure 1.7
Heidi Weber Haus, Zurich
(1968)

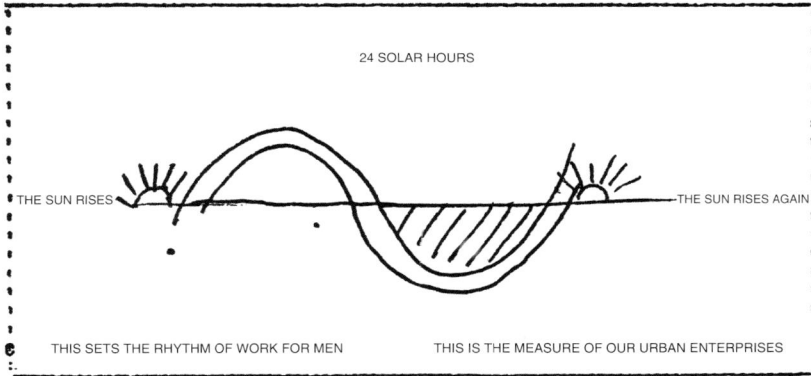

Figure 1.8
Sign of the 24-hour day

Figure 1.9
Interior of Heidi Weber
Haus, Zurich (1968)

order them into a universal language'.[95] In *The Radiant City* Le Corbusier drew a sketch of what he called the 'fundamental Roman forms'. These consisted of arches, apses and barrel vaults. He wrote that they were 'so intimately the outcome of a dominating, organising type of thought that they will always continue to haunt all human creations' (Figure 1.10).[96]

The Monol House of 1919 (Figure 1.11) is the first of a lineage of vaulted schemes which would include the Petite Maison de Weekend at La Celle St Cloud of 1935, the Permanent City at La Sainte Baume, the Maisons Jaoul of 1955, as well as the Villa Shodhan of 1956, but unlike these other dwellings (to be built of materials raw in the extreme), it was to be prefabricated in the factory with ceilings and floors of arched corrugated asbestos sheets, which would act as permanent shuttering for 'a coating of concrete an inch or so thick'.

The beauty of the vaulted roof was that a house could be made up of repetitive modules or cells. Le Corbusier wrote 'The designing of such a house demanded extreme care since the elements of construction were the only architectonic means'.[97] Le Corbusier celebrated this fact at the Petite Maison de Weekend (Figure 1.12) where 'a typical bay'[98] broke off from the house and became a gazebo in the garden, what Frampton

Here are the fundamental Roman forms:

They are so intimately the outcome of a dominating, organizing type of thought that they will always continue to haunt all human creations.

Figure 1.10 The 'fundamental Roman forms' Drawing taken from *The Radiant City* (1935)

Maisons «Monal» (deux étages)

Figure 1.11 Maisons Monol (1919)

Situation de la maison dans le terrain

Figure 1.12 Petite Maison de Weekend showing gazebo (1935)

calls 'an al fresco primitive hut', its thin concrete piers replaced by heavy masonry cross walls in the house itself.[99]

Colin Rowe wrote of Le Corbusier's passion for walls, one that seems to belie the opportunities afforded by the domino system.[100] However the adoption of a vaulted structural system would allow Le Corbusier's innate love of walls to come back into play as it did at the 'Residence inside an agricultural estate near Cherchell, North Africa' of 1942. Here 'Three types of wall would support the vaulting in regular spans – the square pier, the half bay wall, the full bay wall' in what Le Corbusier called a 'play of combinations'.[101] Generally the walls carry the load from the vaults but, for example, in the case of the catalan vaults of the Maisons Jaoul (Figure 1.13), there are massive concrete lintels at the bottom of each arch which distribute the load of the vaults across the varied openings beneath.[102] Le Corbusier stated that: 'The composition consists of opening holes in these parallel walls and playing the solid/open game, but playing intensely the architectural game'.[103]

The walls of the vaulted houses generally were to be built of brick or rammed earth – pisé construction (as at La Sainte Baume). The brick used for the Jaoul houses was, according to Laurens Duport (responsible for their recent renovation), 'irregular and very common' coming 'by the heap load' from demolition sites.[104] Le Corbusier had very definite ideas of the type of brick and joints to be used and was adamant that the same should be used both internally and externally, presumably to blur the boundaries between inside and outside space.[105] 'We are not bourgeois, we appreciate the roughness of raw brick'.[106]

The idea of using pisé had come to Le Corbusier when working on his scheme for refugee housing, the Maisons Murondins in 1940.[107] These houses, designed in anticipation of a postwar housing shortage, were to be constructed simply and inexpensively out of pisé blocks which

Figure 1.13 Jaoul Maison B (1955)

were to be cast on site.[108] For Le Corbusier pisé, connected with the earth, was a material charged with enormous symbolic potential. 'Life within this pisé has perhaps a total dignity and gives back to men of the machine civilisation the sense of fundamental resources, human and natural'.[109] His enthusiasm for vaults seems to have been fuelled by an interest in living beneath the earth, in catacombs and in caves – indeed he invariably chose to cover his vaulted roofs in grass, ostensibly because of the cooling benefits achieved in this way, but also for more mnemonic purposes. Le Corbusier hoped that the materials and forms of his buildings would act upon their inhabitants in a subliminal way, encouraging and reinforcing particular modes of existence. The scheme for the housing at La Sainte Baume provides a case in point. The interior finishes of each earth built house were to be simple in the extreme – timber and quarry tiles contributing to the primitive feeling of the whole – the roof covered in grass. In his own copy of Ernest Renan's *La Vie de Jesus* Le Corbusier underlined the words, 'the founders of the kingdom of God are the humble'.[110] It seems that by creating such elemental homes Le Corbusier hoped to instil in those that lived within them an appreciation of a simple and ascetic existence. Indeed, he wrote of the interior of La Tourette 'the interior displays a total poverty'.[111] The earthern architecture of the La Sainte Baume houses would evoke simultaneously the cave of Mary Madgalene, the spiritual heart of the scheme, and the tomb, the catacombs of ancient Rome acting as a precedent for the complex as a whole.[112] In an 'aspect géométral de la cité, faisant face à

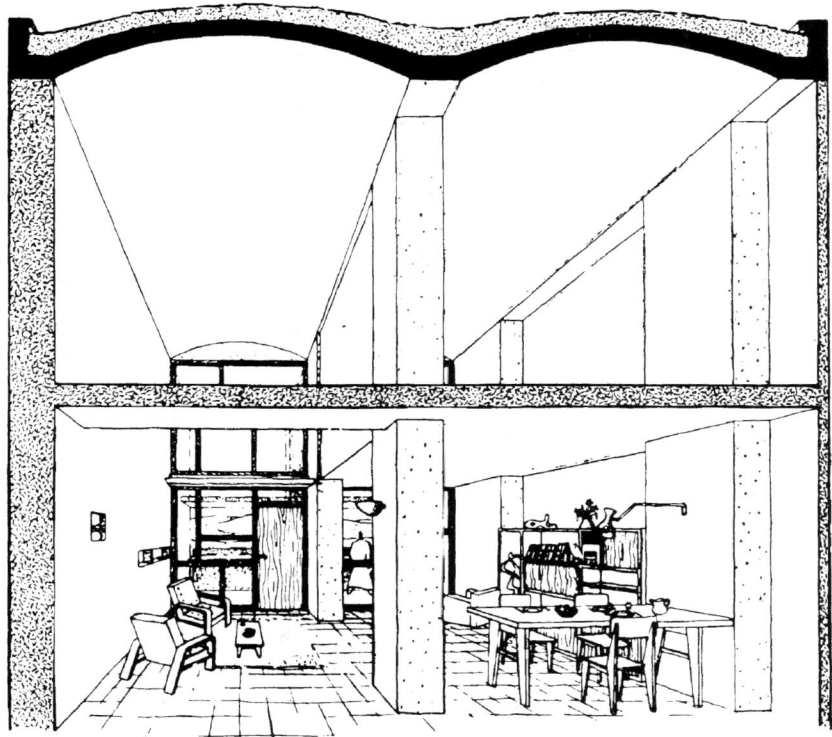

Figure 1.14 House from La cite permanente at La Sainte Baume (c. 1950)

la chaine des rochers', a drawing in the *Oeuvre Complète*, the Permanent City appears like a wall of tombs, each house occupying two arched bays (Figure 1.14). Embodying a return to 'terre mere', the materials of the building suggest a narrative of birth and death entirely in keeping with the scheme as a whole. To live within what Stirling called the 'consistently subdued light'[113] of a vaulted home was to live within the earth, to be reminded of death, the architect's intention being to focus the attention of the inhabitant upon 'the transience of our lives and the irreparable loss of time'.[114]

1.4   Conclusion

Although conceived to save time and money, making standardized buildings was not the simple process that Le Corbusier originally professed it to be. A great many errors were made along the way. These are illustrated in great detail in Benton's piece 'Pessac and Lège revisited: standards, dimensions and failures'. Here Le Corbusier used:

standard prefabricated metal windows, standard roller blinds, standard door, standard staircases inside and out, standard fittings (window and door handles, locks, etc.) an innovatory chemical septic tank (the 'Perfection', manufactured by Stupfel), Odelin-Nettey-Bourdon's range of Robur combined kitchen stove and hot air hearing system and, notionally at least, a standard plan and the use of the famous cement cannon manufactured by Ingersoll-Rand.[115]

The account Benton gives is a chapter of accidents – of vacillation over standards, of the concrete frame not conforming to the dimensions of the standard windows, of vast unnecessary expenses and wasted materials. This might be understandable in such an early experimental building – an inevitable step along the way to future more successful schemes – however, the vision of standardization to which Le Corbusier aspired was never really to be achieved. Like most buildings, his were a combination of the standard and the site specific, his ideals deeply compromised by reality and in conflict with his vision of a poetic architecture individually tuned to each client.

Undoubtedly Le Corbusier was hampered in his pursuit of unification by a construction industry that was not yet ready for his ideas. Although – because of his disillusionment with both industry and government – he seemed to lose faith in the application of industrial methods to architecture, he remained very interested in the issue of standardization throughout his career.[116] Indeed, he returned to this issue for his last, most modular scheme of all, the Venice hospital. However, in the intervening years other factors seem to have come to the fore, both pragmatic – relating to the availability of materials and skills in the lean war years – and poetic – relating to the body, its size and its experiences. Standardization could not provide a formula for architecture. Neither a 'pleasing detail' nor a rational structure was as important as creating an overall feeling of order, leading, by implication, to a well-ordered existence.[117]

Notes

[1] Le Corbusier, *Precisions on the Present State of Architecture and City Planning* (Cambridge, MA: MIT, 1991), p. 54.

[2] 'My life is more or less exactly that of a Trappist or any other kind of monk of your choosing (except for the vow of chastity).' Letter Le Corbusier to Sigismond Marcel, 28 January 1925, FLC (Fondation Le Corbusier, hereafter referred to as FLC), Dossier La Roche, doc.131. Quoted and translated by T. Benton 'The Sacred and the Search for Myths' in T. Benton (ed.), *Le Corbusier Architect of the Century* (London: Arts Council, 1987), p. 243.

[3] Xenakis, I., 'The Monastery of La Tourette' in H. Allen Brooks (ed.), *The Le Corbusier Archive, Volume 28* (New York: Garland, 1983), p. ix. Hereafter referred to as Allen Brooks, *Archive*.

[4] Le Corbusier, *The Marseilles Block* (London: Harvill, 1953), p. 34. Originally published as *L'Unité d'habitation de Marseille* (Mulhouse: Editions Le Point, 1950). See also 'Eyes that do not see' in Le Corbusier, *Towards a New Architecture* (London: Architectural Press, 1982), p. 9. Originally published as *Vers une Architecture* (Paris: Crès, 1923).

[5] Le Corbusier, *When the Cathedrals were White: A Journey to the Country of the Timid People* (New York: Reynal and Hitchcock, 1947). Originally published as Quand les cathédrales étaient blanches (Paris: Plon, 1937), p. xvii.

[6] Le Corbusier, *Towards a New Architecture*, p. 210.

[7] Ibid.

[8] Le Corbusier, *The Radiant City* (London: Faber, 1967), p. i. Originally published as Le Corbusier, *La Ville Radieuse* (Paris: Éditions de l'Architecture d'Aujourd'hui, 1935).

[9] Le Corbusier, 'Où est-on 26 ans après la Charte d'Athènes,' May–June 1962, 18 pp. Typed MS (unpublished, intended for M.P. Delouvrier's book *Le District de Paris*), p. 14, FLC A3 01 365.

[10] Le Corbusier, *Modulor 2* (London: Faber, 1955), p. 26. Originally published as *Le Modulor II* (Paris: Editions d'Architecture d'Aujourd'hui, 1955).

[11] Ibid., p. 306.

[12] J. Soltan, 'Working with Le Corbusier' in H. Allen Brooks (ed.), *The Le Corbusier Archive, Volumes XVII* (New York: Garland, 1983), pp. ix–xxiv (p. xviii). Hereafter referred to as Allen Brooks, *Archive*.

[13] Le Corbusier, *The Nursery Schools* (New York: Orion, 1968), p. 63.

[14] Le Corbusier, *Precisions*, p. 245.

[15] Le Corbusier, *Towards a New Architecture*, p. 247.

[16] Ibid., p. 246.

[17] Ibid., p. 245.

[18] Framework of concrete, girders made on the site and raised by a hand-winch. Hollow walls of 1 1/8′ concrete and expanded metal with a $7\frac{1}{2}′$ cavity; all floor slabs on the same unit of measurement; the factory window frames, with adaptable ventilating on the same unit. The arrangements in conformity with the running of the household. Ibid., p. 223.

[19] Ibid., p. 216.

[20] Le Corbusier and P. Jeanneret, *Oeuvre Complète Volume 1, 1910–1929*, (Zurich: Les Editions d'Architecture, 1995), p. 199, Originally published in 1937.

[21] Le Corbusier, *Oeuvre Complète, Volume 4*, (Zurich: Les Editions d'Architecture, 1995), p. 38. Originally published in 1946.

[22] Frederick Taylor wrote *The Principles of Scientific Management* in 1911. Urging that standardized tools should be used for standardized tasks and bemoaning the waste caused through inefficiency, it is no surprise that Taylor's ideas received such a warm welcome from the architect. See also M.F. Guillén, *The Taylorized Beauty of the Mechanical. Scientific Management and the Rise of Modernist Architecture* (Princeton, NJ: Princeton University Press, 2006).

[23] Le Corbusier and Jeanneret *Oeuvre Complète Volume 1*, p. 78.

[24] Le Corbusier, *Towards a New Architecture*, p. 217.

[25] See J. K. Birksted, ' "Beyond the clichés of the hand-books": Le Corbusier's architectural promenade', *The Journal of Architecture*, 11:1 (2006), pp. 55–132 for a discussion of Le Corbusier's milieu at that time.

[26] Le Corbusier, *When the Cathedrals were White*, p. 208.

[27] For a discussion of the mythologizing of craft roots read B. Colomina, 'Mies Not' in Detlef Mertens (ed.), *The Presence of Mies* (New York: Princeton Architectural Press, 1994), p. 202.

[28] Le Corbusier, *When the Cathedrals were White*, p. 64.

[29] Ibid., p. 120.

[30] Le Corbusier and P. Jeanneret *Oeuvre Complète, Volume 1, 1910–1929* (Zurich: Les Editions d'Architecture, 1995), p. 132. Originally published in 1937.

[31] During the rather depressed period towards the end of Le Corbusier's life he referred to his employees, rather paternalistically, as date palms irrigated by the water of Le Corbusier's own artistic inspiration. Le Corbusier, 'Les dattiers royaux', Paris 11 July 1957, FLC S3.5.217.

[32] See for example FLC 17396 in Allen Brooks *Archive, Volume XXIX*, p. 392 or FLC 5461 in Allen Brooks *Archive, Volume XXV*, p. 405.

[33] Soltan, 'Working with Le Corbusier', p. xxiii.

[34] A. Wogenscky, 'The Unité d'Habitation at Marseille' in Allen Brooks *Archive, Volume XVI*, p. xvii.

[35] Soltan, 'Working with Le Corbusier', p. xxiii.

[36] Wogenscky, 'The Unité d'Habitation at Marseille', pp. xvii.

[37] Le Corbusier, *Towards a New Architecture*, p. 214.

[38] Ibid., p. 214.

[39] T. Benton, 'Pessac and Lège revisited: standards dimensions and failures', *Massilia*, 3 (2004), pp. 64–99.

[40] T. Benton, *The Villas of Le Corbusier* (London: Yale University Press, 1987), p. 112.

[41] W. Curtis, *Le Corbusier: Ideas and Forms* (Oxford: Phaidon, 1986), p. 111.

[42] See FLC 26783 for a construction section through a Nevada glass panel in the Unité. Allen Brooks *Archive, Volume XVII*, p. 223.

[43] E. Sekler and W. Curtis, *Le Corbusier at Work: The Genesis of the Carpenter Centre for the Visual Arts* (Cambridge, MA: MIT, 1978), p. 187.

[44] Le Corbusier and Jeanneret, *Oeuvre Complète Volume 2*, p. 16.

[45] Le Corbusier, *Oeuvre Complète, Volume 5, 1946–1952* (Zurich: Les Editions d'Architecture, 1995), p. 191. Originally published in 1953.

[46] Letter, Le Corbusier to Sert, 26 May 1962 reproduced in Sekler and Curtis, *Le Corbusier at Work*, p. 302. According to Banham 'Behind all aspects of New Brutalism, in Britain and elsewhere, lurks one undisputed architectural fact: the concrete-work of Le Corbusier's Unité d'Habitation at Marseilles'. R. Banham, *The New Brutalism, Ethic or Aesthetic* (London: Architectural Press, 1966), p. 16.

[47] Le Corbusier, *Talks with Students* (Princeton Architectural Press), 1999, p. 51.

[48] Le Corbusier, *Oeuvre Complète Volume 4*, p. 116.

[49] Le Corbusier, *Talks with Students*, 1999, p. 51.

[50] T. Benton, 'The petite maison de weekend and the Parisian suburbs', in M. Mostafavi (ed.), *Le Corbusier and the Architecture of Reinvention* (London, AA Publishing, 2003), pp. 118–39.

[51] Le Corbusier, *Talks with Students*, Princeton Architectural Press, 1999, p. 51.

[52] D. Leatherbarrow, *The Roots of Architectural Invention* (Cambridge: Cambridge University Press, 1993), p. 148.

[53] Le Corbusier, *Talks with Students*, p. 51.

[54] Benton, 'From Jeanneret to Le Corbusier', pp. 28–39.

[55] See the 1940 Murondin houses: 'The roofing materials; timber is cut and cleared, it is made into uniform logs. The branches are trimmed as laths. The twigs are made into faggots. Elsewhere, on the grassland, turf is removed by spades.' Le Corbusier, *Oeuvre Complète Volume 4*, p. 95.

[56] Le Corbusier and P. Jeanneret, *Oeuvre Complète Volume 3, 1934–38* (Zurich: Les Editions d'Architecture, 1995), p. 125. Originally published in 1938.

[57] K. Frampton, *Studies in Tectonic Culture: The Poetics of Construction in Nineteenth and Twentieth Century Architecture* (Cambridge, MA: MIT, 1996), p. 345.

[58] I. Zacnic, *Le Corbusier: Pavillon Suisse: The Biography of a Building* (Basel: Birkäuser, 2004), p. 133.

[59] Le Corbusier and Jeanneret *Oeuvre Complète Volume 1*, p. 80.

[60] Letter Le Corbusier to Sert, 28 February 1961 reprinted in Sekler and Curtis, *Le Corbusier at Work*, p. 294.

[61] For a discussion of the possible origins of the domino frame see Curtis, *Le Corbusier: Ideas and Forms*, p. 42.

[62] C. Rowe, *The Architecture of Good Intentions* (London: Academy Editions, 1994), p. 57. The same cannot be said of its usage in modern-day office plans.

[63] Curtis, *Le Corbusier: Ideas and Forms*, p. 43.

[64] G. Martin Moeller observes a 'moralizing' tendency in early twentieth-century concrete discourse – rigorous use of concrete being seen as symptomatic of other virtues. G. Martin Moeller, 'Reinforced concrete and the morality of form' in J.L. Cohen, and M.G. Mueller, *Liquid Stone: New Architecture in Concrete* (Basel: Birkäuser, 2006), pp. 156–8.

[65] FLC 15398 in Allen Brooks, *Archive, Volume VIII*, p. 201.

[66] Le Corbusier, *Oeuvre Complète Volume 4*, p. 62.

[67] 'Le Corbusier was building in *béton brut*, which with its messiness and considerable redundancy of material presented an aesthetic totally at variance with the refinement of shell structures'. A. Forty 'A material without a history' in Cohen and Mueller, *Liquid Stone* pp. 34–35.

[68] Le Corbusier, *Precisions*, p. 45.

[69] Curtis, *Le Corbusier: Ideas and Forms*, p. 226.

[70] Le Corbusier, *Towards a New Architecture*, pp. 187–93.

[71] C. Rowe, *The Mathematics of the Ideal Villa and Other Essays* (Cambridge, MA: MIT, 1976), p. 145.

[72] At the Villa Savoye they appear on a 5 metre by 5 metre grid.

[73] Frampton, *Studies in Tectonic Culture*, p. 177.

[74] Le Corbusier, *Talks with Students*, p. 56.

[75] Sekler and Curtis, *Le Corbusier at Work*, p. 146.

[76] Soltan, 'Working with Le Corbusier', p. xxiii.

[77] He refers to Le Corbusier's blue Modulor scale.

[78] Sekler and Curtis, *Le Corbusier at Work*, p. 207.

[79] Ibid., p. 164.

[80] Ibid.

[81] Ibid.

[82] Le Corbusier, *Towards a New Architecture*, p. 202.

[83] Le Corbusier, *When the Cathedrals were White*, p. 75.

[84] Ibid., p.64.

[85] Le Corbusier and Jeanneret, *Oeuvre Complète Volume 2*, p. 121.

[86] Le Corbusier, *Precisions*, p. 55.

[87] See also Pavillon Nestlé, 1928 in Allen Brooks, *Archive, Volume V*, pp. 13–22.

[88] Le Corbusier, *Towards a New Architecture*, p. 67.

[89] Frampton, *Studies in Tectonic Culture*, p. 346.

[90] M. Treib, *Space Calculated in Seconds* (Princeton, NJ: Princeton University Press, 1996), p. 51.

[91] See for example the Villa Chimnabhai project of 1953 in Allen Brooks, *Archive, Volume XXVI*, p. 3.

[92] Curtis, *Le Corbusier: Ideas and Forms*, p. 192.

[93] See Pavillon de la France à l'Exposition de l'Eau, Liège, 1937. Allen Brooks, *Archive, Volume XIV*, p. 3.

[94] S. Menin and F. Samuel, *Aalto and Le Corbusier: Nature and Space* (London: Routledge, 2002).

[95] C. Nivola, 'Le Corbusier in New York, in R. Ingersoll, *A Marriage of Contours* (Princeton, NJ: Princeton Architectural Press, 1990), p. 6.

[96] Le Corbusier, *The Radiant City*, p. 185.

[97] Le Corbusier and Jeanneret, *Oeuvre Complète Volume 3*, p. 125.

[98] Ibid.

[99] Frampton, *Studies in Tectonic Culture*, p. 345.

[100] Rowe, *The Mathematics of the Ideal Villa*, p. 196.

[101] Le Corbusier, *Oeuvre Complète, Volume 4*, p. 122.

[102] See for an account of the development of these vaults C. Maniaque, *Le Corbusier et les Maisons Jaoul* (Paris: Picard, 2005), pp. 84–7.

[103] Le Corbusier, *Oeuvre Complète Volume 5*, p. 173.

[104] L. Duport, *Le Corbusier: Les Maisons Jaoul* (Les Lieux Editions, 2004), n.p.

[105] Maniaque, *Le Corbusier et les Maisons Jaoul*, p. 74.

[106] Letter Le Corbusier to Professor Fueter, 17 March 1950, FLC I2 (7) 14. Published in Maniaque, *Le Corbusier et les Maisons Jaoul*, p. 127.

[107] FLC 28928 in Allen Brooks, *Archive, Volume XIV*, p. 709.

[108] K. Frampton, 'The other Le Corbusier: primitive form and the linear city 1929–52', in Benton (ed.), *Le Corbusier Architect of the Century*, p. 31.

[109] Ibid.

[110] 'Les fondateurs du royaume de Dieu seront les simples.' E. Renan, *La Vie de Jesus* (Paris: Calmann-Levy, 1906), p. 124 in FLC.

[111] Le Corbusier, *Oeuvre Complète Volume 7, 1957–1965* (Zurich: Les Editions d'Architecture, 1995)

[112] Compare the section through with La Sainte Baume with T. Rollet, *Les Catacombes de Rome: Histoire de l'art et des croyances religiuses pendant les premiers siècles du Christiarme, vol. 2* (Paris: Morel, 1881), illustrations not numbered.

[113] The 'dark clay tile' on the underside of the vaults did little for the quality of light in Stirling's opinion. James Stirling, 'From Garches to Jaoul' 1955. p. xi.

[114] Le Corbusier, *Precisions*, p. 5.

[115] T. Benton, 'Pessac and Lège revisited: standards dimensions and failures', *Massilia*, 3 (2004), p. 84.

[116] See for example FLC 21941 showing the prefabricated cladding panels posited for the Unité at Meaux in 1957.

[117] See A. Colquhoun, 'The significance of Le Corbusier' in Allen Brooks, *Archive, Volume I*, pp. xxxvi.

Somatic detail 2

Le Corbusier was very preoccupied with the manner in which the body would respond to art and to architecture. 'I have a body like everyone else, and what I'm interested in is contact with my body, with my eyes, my mind'.[1] In *The Decorative Art of Today* he wrote of the way in which the 'emotion leading to action' could be felt in 'our inner depths, before even the formulation of a theory'.[2] Further, in *Precisions* he observed that: 'Architecture is a series of successive events . . . events that the spirit tries to transmute by the creation of relations so precise and so overwhelming that deep physiological sensations result from them, that a real spiritual delectation is felt at reading the solution, that a perception of harmony comes to us from the clear-cut mathematical quality uniting each element of the work'.[3] 'But how do you receive an architectural sensation? By the effect of the relationships you perceive'.[4] Building on the ideas of Plato,[5] Le Corbusier believed that the primary means to influence thought was by influencing the body at a subconscious level,[6] the 'joys of the body' being 'interdependent to intellectual sensations'.[7] The body would in turn send signals to the brain which would eventually result in a change of consciousness. Nowhere in architecture is the potential of bodily contact felt more readily than in the realm of detail, designed specifically to be touched or seen at close quarters – here 'the architectural work enters the plane of sensitivity' and 'We are moved'.[8]

As Christopher Green has observed, Le Corbusier was 'always willing as figure painter to acknowledge and exploit his sexual responses', in other words to use the body as a means of accessing knowledge.[9] 'Art, product of the reason–passion equation' was for him 'the site of human happiness'.[10] It may be for this reason that 'The rebirth of the body' was one of the central tenets of his Radiant City plan. The occupants of a Radiant building, for example the Unité in Marseilles, would have access to sun, space and greenery, each promoting individual well-being. A shorter working day and decreased travel to and from work would also allow men and women to spend more time together, resulting in an improvement in their relationships. 'A woman, a man, and a few children, elements of the harmony of the hearth. But, today, the mother of the family is crushed by housework'[11] wrote Le Corbusier. 'A hard lot hers and such a common one that she deserves all our consideration.'[12] A point emerges whose great importance will only resonate with those people who are intimate with the subject of housework – as its seems was Le Corbusier. 'It is absolutely imperative that women are liberated from the domestic drama (which results in problems for men)'.[13] His Unité, conceived with great consideration for issues of cleaning,[14] would for this reason provide 'the solution to modern life'.[15] Le Corbusier's designs for streamlined homes, labour-saving kitchens[16] with washable seamless surfaces, free-form curves, largely free of cornices, skirtings, mouldings and other dust-collecting details were conceived with the feather duster and mop very much in mind – 'economy in your actions, your household management and in your thoughts'[17] – the ultimate aim being to relieve housewives from their exhausting burden, leaving them free to enjoy other more important concerns (Figure 2.1).[18] At the same time the inhabitants of the Radiant City would learn from their homes, their bodies responding

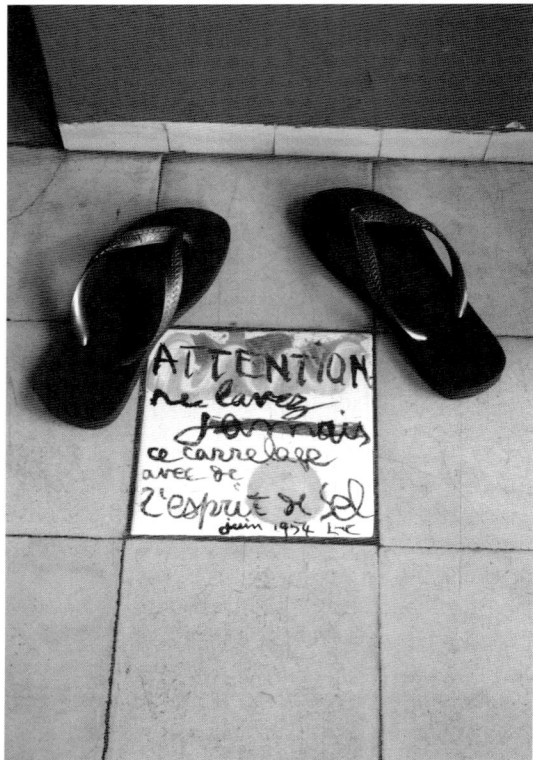

Figure 2.1
Cleaning instructions, hall floor Jaoul Maison B

at an innate level to the proportions of the space that they occupied. The Unité in Marseilles, for example, was detailed in a way that would make people 'think and reflect'.[19]

Le Corbusier's architecture would appeal to the senses in a variety of different ways. This chapter focuses on the issues of anthropomorphism, touch, colour, space and sound, all of which were manipulated by Le Corbusier with the specific intention of moving and arousing the body, awakening the inhabitants of his buildings to the possibilities of 'savoir habiter' – knowing how to live within 'Materials friendly to Man'.[20]

2.1   Anthropomorphism

Le Corbusier wrote of his plan for the Radiant City in terms of a balance between masculine and feminine elements. 'This prodigious spectacle has been produced by the interplay of two elements, one male, one female: sun and water. Two contradictory elements that both need the other to exist. . .'[21] Further, he defined 'Male' architecture as 'strong objectivity of forms, under the intense light of a Mediterranean sun', while 'female' architecture was described in terms of 'limitless subjectivity rising against a clouded sky',[22] in other words, more nebulous.[23] His architecture became a marriage of these two opposites types – opposite in both meaning and appearance – in alchemical terms, a highly charged and erotic interplay intended to awaken echoes deep within its inhabitants.[24]

Even in its earliest manifestations Le Corbusier's architecture was focused on the body. Kenneth Silver observes that the bottles and jars, subjects of Ozenfant and Le Corbusier's Purist paintings have 'an almost anthropomorphic quality' and even 'an emotive life'.[25] Their love affair with flesh is made clear in a passage within the pages of *After Cubism* (1918) in which they describe a scene, a possible subject for a painting:

The wallpaper is quite idiosyncratic and resembles some of Picasso's surfaces; the wood of the table has an interesting matte quality; the sheets of paper give off a rigorously modulated light; the knife gleams, the violin has gentle curves: a classic still life. The potted palm introduces vegetation into the room and the complexity of superior organisms. But the figure is enthroned as queen and reduces the still life to role of décor.

The flesh of the woman's face has a matte quality still more beautiful than that of the wood, the light on her forehead is more beautiful than that on the sheets of paper, the gleam in her eyes is more beautiful than that from the knife.

The human body is organized in accordance with the laws of symmetry as legible as those that determined the construction of the violin; the whole of the room is a lucky anecdote, a fortunate happenstance that would make for a good choice; but a single thing encompasses and exceeds the beauty of the others; the human figure; it is this that promises the highest plastic yield.[26]

In 1928 Le Corbusier 'threw open a window on the human figure'[27] expressing an uneasiness with abstraction – he felt a need 'to keep contact with living beings'.[28] Given that his paintings were, for Le Corbusier, a source of architectural form, it follows that his buildings too would retain echoes of the body from which they were conceived. Frampton writes of 'Le Corbusier's observation that the more intimate our relations are to an object, the more it will reflect our anthropomorphic figure; conversely, the more distant, the more it will tend to abstraction',[29] yet his work seems to me to reflect the body at every scale.

Le Corbusier was fond of making analogies between building and body – his new architecture would be 'naked in the sunlight – cleansed, muscled, supple' no longer 'painfully pierced with windows' with plenty of space for 'the organs of private life'.[30] Indeed, conduits and wires circumnavigate Le Corbusier's buildings like the veins and tubes of the anatomical drawings that he so admired. In the opinion of Rowe there is a 'far from casually composed piece of symbolism' that focuses on the telephone in the early work of Le Corbusier. The wires of the telephone, like the pipes for the water, are the 'entrails' of the building. 'We are making visible the ligaments (supposedly like those of the human body) which attach "modern man" to the "modern environment"'.[31] Further, 'We have insisted that the viscera should be on the inside, classified, tucked away, and that only a clear form should be apparent. Not as easy as it sounds!'.[32] Just as, in later life, he liked to colour-code his drawings in crayon, Le Corbusier also liked to colour-code his buildings in terms of their services. Throughout the Heidi Weber Haus, for example, sockets are housed in tiny yellow cubes standing proud of the floor in separation of its function. Red, on the low-level radiators and heating duct indicate the presence of heat. Colour, as in an anatomical diagram, is used to differentiate between the main and the secondary structures, the body and the building, similarly rational in conception.

Christopher Pearson makes the point that, within Le Corbusier's domestic architecture, a work of art was intended, amongst other things, to act as a 'carefully sited anthropomorphic presence within the building, which could dramatise . . . the visitor's relationship to and participation in the architectural space by the creation of a sympathetic bond between visitor and sculpture'.[33] Le Corbusier would similarly adopt anthropomorphic forms into his architecture in order to maximize its psychological impact on the visitor. 'I believe in the *skin* of things, as in that of women', wrote Le Corbusier in *When the Cathedrals were White*[34] – a quote that his friend the photographer Lucien Hervé reused, juxtaposed with an image of the gunnite curves of Ronchamp, looking remarkably like skin seen at very close quarters (Figure 2.2).[35] Le Corbusier was very clear that the form of Ronchamp was generated in order to stir 'the psychophysiology of the feelings' rather than to fulfil the requirements of religion.[36] In the opinion of Jaime Coll the plan of the chapel was derived from a sketch from Le Corbusier's Ubu series (Figure 2.3).[37] Certainly the similarities are striking. I would also suggest that the plan, and indeed the whole building, retains elements of the *Icône* series of paintings

Figure 2.2
The 'skin' of Notre-Dame
du Haut, Ronchamp
(1955)

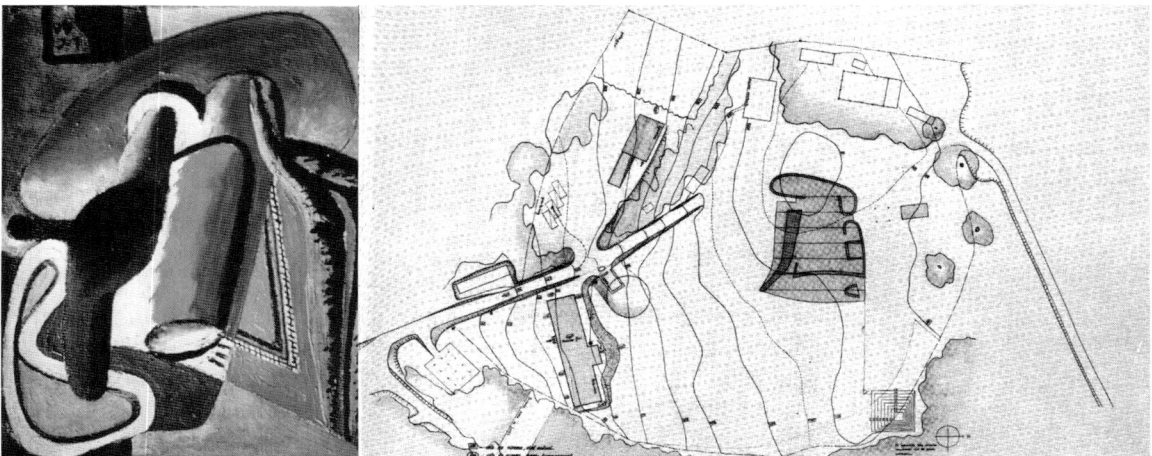

Figure 2.3   *Abstraction Ozon* (1946). Plan of Ronchamp

(Figure 2.4), a fact that seems to justify the suggestion that certain parts of the building might be compared with elements of a woman's body.[38] As Le Corbusier wrote of Ronchamp: 'I give you this chapel of dear, faithful concrete, shaped perhaps with temerity but certainly with courage in the hope that it will seek out in you (as in those who will climb the hill) an echo of what we have drawn into it.'[39] Further, 'The key is light and light illuminates the shapes and shapes have an emotional power'.[40]

Figure 2.4
Icône (1955)

2.2 Touch

> Hand kneading hand caressing
> Hand brushing. The hand and the seashell love each other[41]

The human hand attains the status of fetish in the work of Le Corbusier – his handprint is a mark of emphatic presence and knowledge, a knowledge gained through touch. Willing himself into a state of synaesthesia, Le Corbusier wrote that it was possible to 'hear' the 'music of visual proportion' of a building,[42] 'taste' a column with his 'eyes', and so on. His eyes awaken sensations in his mouth. His hands awaken his eyes. His paintings are populated with women who appear to see, like the goddess Baubo, through their extended nipple-like eyes, as he wrote in *The Poem of the Right Angle*:

> Life is tasted through
> the kneading of the hands
> eyesight resides in
> palpation[43]

Indeed, he believed that: 'Touch is a second kind of sight. Sculpture or architecture, when their forms are inherently successful, can be caressed; in fact, our hands are impelled towards them'.[44]

2.2.1   Walls and pilotis

Clearly Le Corbusier had an understanding with Hervé about the erotic nature of the textures in his buildings. On a further occasion he wrote him a note about the pilotis of the Carpenter Centre 'in beton brut, but smooth'.[45] Here 'Columns of reinforced concrete called "women's thighs" poured in half forms of *metal* (with crossed joints) the concrete is so smooth, so seductive that one puts one's hand there'.[46] Next to these words Le Corbusier drew a man with folded arms, presumably, as Curtis writes 'engaged in a battle of self restraint'.[47] 'Lisse' or smooth,[48] although they were built of concrete, Le Corbusier wrote of their 'softness' in terms of great affection.[49]

One of the more surprising aspects of Le Corbusier's architecture is that it is often very comfortable. The body finds itself supported, for example, on the sloped pilotis of the Maison des Jeunes at Firminy. The elbow finds it way onto the angled parapet of the Hotel in the Unité and it is positively pleasurable to lean on the altar rail of Ronchamp (Figure 2.5). At the Maison du Brésel the low walls at the back of the banquettes are formed of a very smooth concrete which dips slightly in the middle to accommodate and support the elbow while being flat enough to accommodate a drink. Sketches drawn for the balconies of the Unité at Meaux give some indication of the care that he took with such matters (Figure 2.6).[50]

Yet, by contrast, Le Corbusier also chose finishes precisely for their abrasive, unsympathetic and downright defensive qualities. At La Tourette the interior of the cells is finished in a render so outrageously rough that a smooth panel is provided next to the bed to avoid continual injury and snagging of blankets. For the interior of the cloister large stones were placed in the concrete mix close against the shuttering, leaving the surface of stones exposed when the boarding was removed.[51] Such materials, so painful to the touch, seem to express something of the hardships of the life of the monk or indeed the pilgrim.[52] A similarly repellant finish was achieved in the outbuildings of Ronchamp, except in reverse where imprints of stone can be seen in the surface of the concrete.

The experience of soft or abrasive materials would, of course, be heightened when they were placed in juxtaposition with one another. Particularly sensual is Le Corbusier's use of contrast, a key theme in his approach to design and indeed within his own personal view of the world; for example, he draw attention to the 'violent contrasts' of glass and beton brut at the principal entry to the Unité.[53] The use of contrast is one of the most common techniques used by architects and other designers to bring out the inherent beauty of differing textures and forms,[54] but in the work of Le Corbusier it is very often symbolic: 'A way

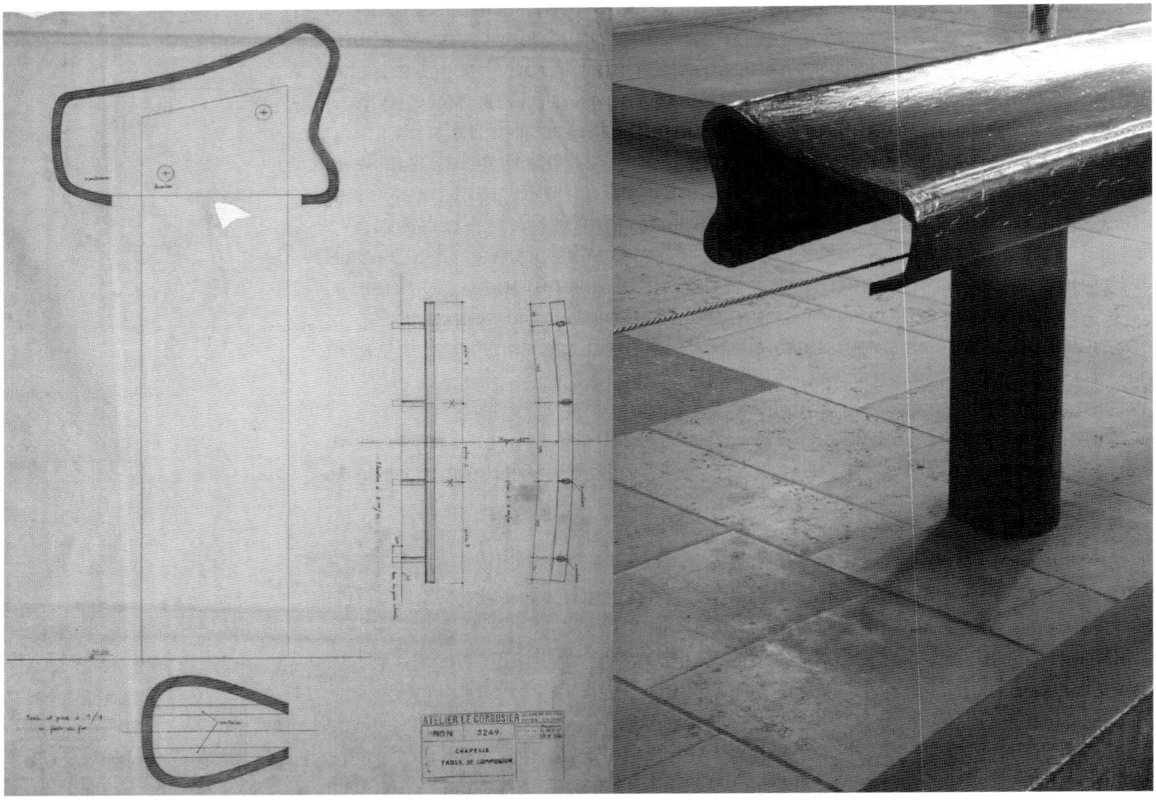

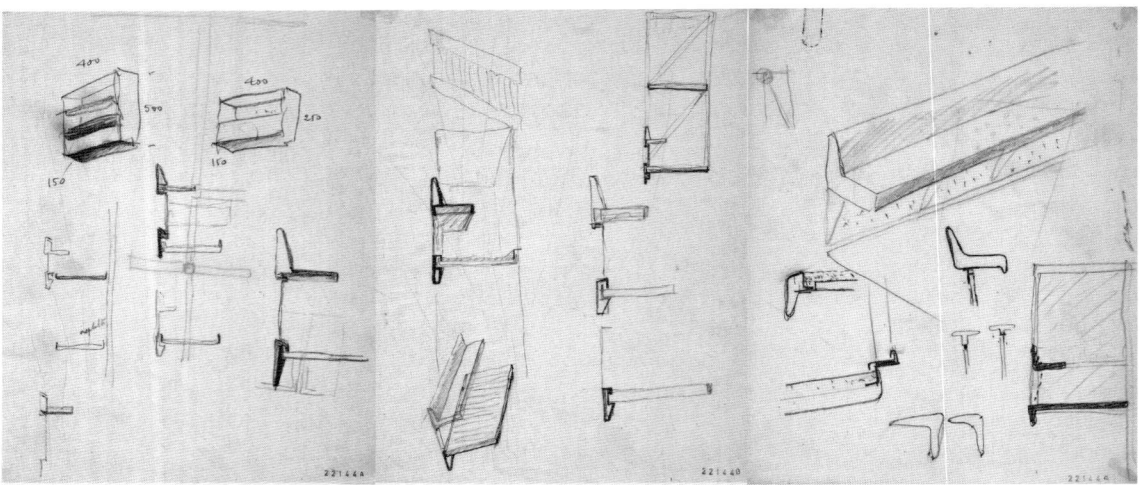

Figure 2.5   Altar rail at Notre-Dame du Haut, Ronchamp (1955), FLC 07236

Figure 2.6   Sketches drawn for the balconies of the Unité at Meaux

of dealing with the worst blemish of the Unite at Marseilles, which is the handrail of the ramp which runs up to the children's rest room on the roof, has occurred to me. I have decided to make beauty by contrast. I will find its complement and establish a play between crudity and finesse, between the dull and the intense, between precision and accident.'[55]

The details of the Unité speak of Le Corbusier's philosophy of opposition and harmony. 'Equilibrium is the sign of undying movement. Equilibrium is not sleep, ankylosis, lethargy or death. Equilibrium, it is the place of meeting of all forces. Unanimity.'[56]

2.2.2   Door handles and handrails

The meaning and significance of doors in the work of Le Corbusier is discussed in Chapter 5. What interests me here is the way that he designed door handles and handrails to invite touch and support the body. My hand is received by the handle; it is mirrored by its forms, like holding hands with another person. In order to open the door to the Maison des Jeunes at Firminy (Figure 2.7) I press my palm against the palm of the door in a gesture of greeting and I am mirrored by the

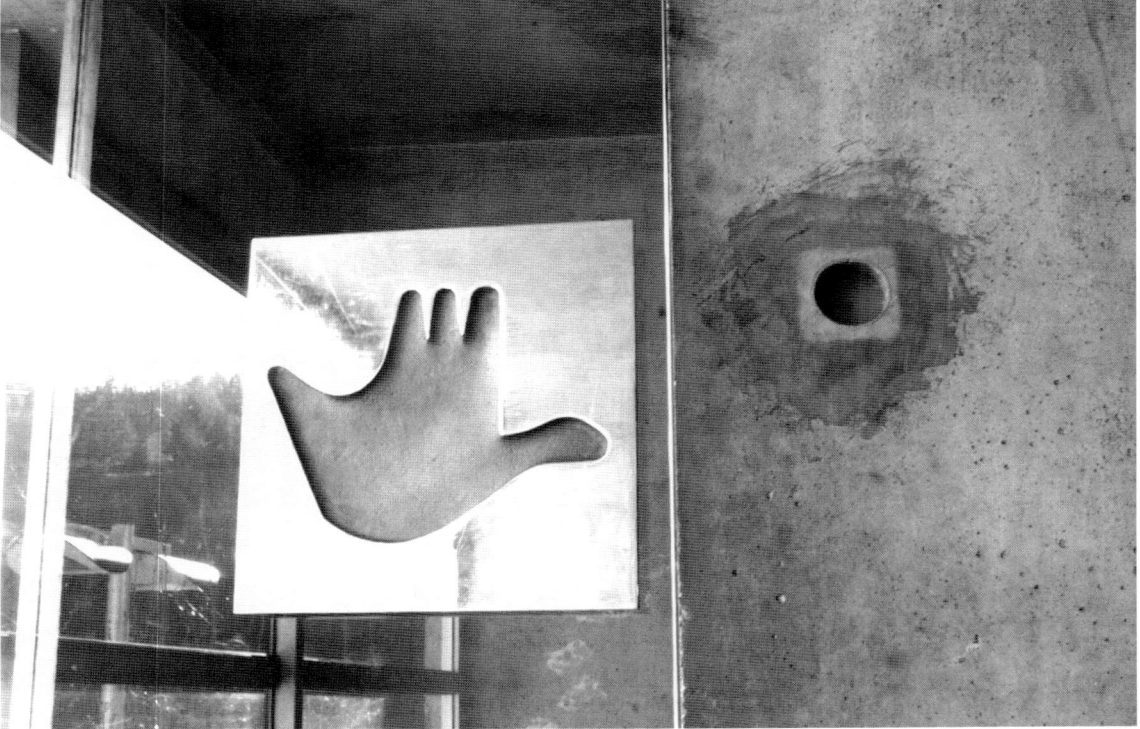

Figure 2.7   Handle of main door of Cultural Centre, Firminy-Vert (1965)

building.[57] Here a bright shiny square plate (320 mm by 320 mm), itself a mirror, set into the glass door has a cut-out in the shape of a hand. Beneath the cold metal at the place where my skin makes contact with the door there is a layer of the finest mortar, warm and smooth to the touch. In the highly abstracted façades of such early buildings as the Maisons La Roche Jeanneret the door handle gives scale and humanity to the whole.[58]

Le Corbusier was fully aware of the importance of choosing the correct ironmongery to fit his unified conception of architecture. Perhaps paradoxically it was often specially made, rather than bought off the peg.[59] James Stirling observed of the stairs on the north face of Ronchamp that, although the rails appeared to be mass produced, 'cut-offs from an extruded section of rolled steel joist are in fact specially cast and the top flange is set at an acute angle to the web'.[60] Certainly the archives contain many metal work drawings[61] which were developed with the help of particular 'serrurerie' with whom the atelier had a close relationship.

Although Le Corbusier's taste in handles and other small details changed across his career, they were always smooth and curved to the touch, with one notable exception, to be discussed later. In the early part of his career, long metal bars extending from floor to hand height formed the handles of Le Corbusier's glazed doors; for example, at the entrance to the Pavillon Suisse[62] or that proposed at one stage for the Bat'a boutique (1935) where a bar was to appear on the exterior of one of the double doors and another was to appear on the interior of the other double door, reflecting the act of entry or exit (Figure 2.8).[63]

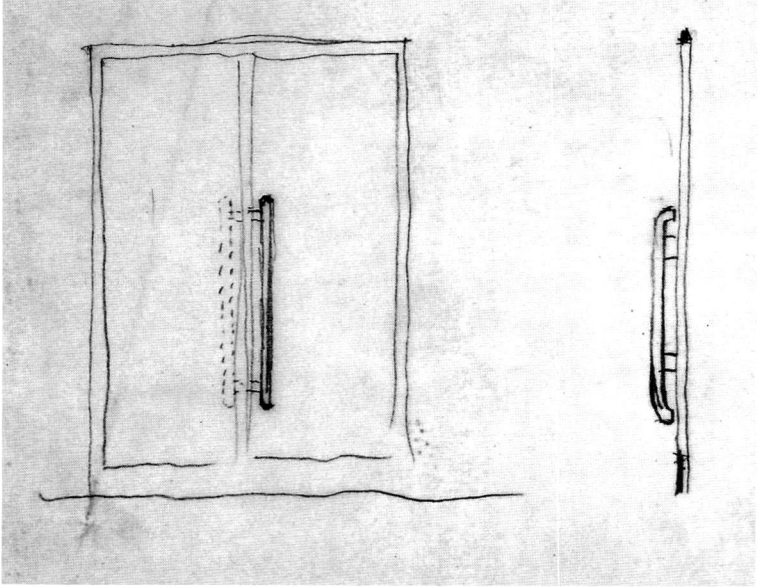

Figure 2.8   Sketch of door handle for Bat'a (1935), FLC 17899

Where a handle will be pushed rather than pulled, an acknowledgment is made in its form.

Le Corbusier clearly designed such hardware with the senses in mind. For the Bat'a boutique (1935) he devised door handles made of interlocking B's, their sleek curves appealing to touch. In plan or in elevation Le Corbusier's handles may look linear and sharp, but in section they are curved and enveloping, like the hands in his drawings. The concrete of the storage box at the base of the stairs in Jaoul Maison B (see Figure 5.4 in Chapter 5) is scooped out in a undulating curve to provide the necessary grip to lift its immensely heavy lid (Figure 2.9). The long timber linear handles of the furniture used repeatedly across Le Corbusier's work was sculpted sensuously for the hand in section, their smooth hooked form, drawn from the vocabulary of the 'Taureaux' paintings (see Figure 2.11).[64]

In Le Corbusier's post war work the frames are either strikingly absent or emphatically present. Where frames were inevitable, for example for the folding doors of the Unité apartment, large sections were used – smooth and almost malleable they attract our fingertips. A moulded timber rail straddles the window – again accommodating the elbow in a remarkable way (Figure 2.10). The most basic day to day actions are registered and catered for by Le Corbusier. They are made special. They are made easy.

Hidden within his later work are a number of references to the most ancient forms of timber construction and detail, detail that can be achieved with the most basic of tools. The handles of the aerateurs at

Figure 2.9   Maison Jaoul B (1955), box in entrance

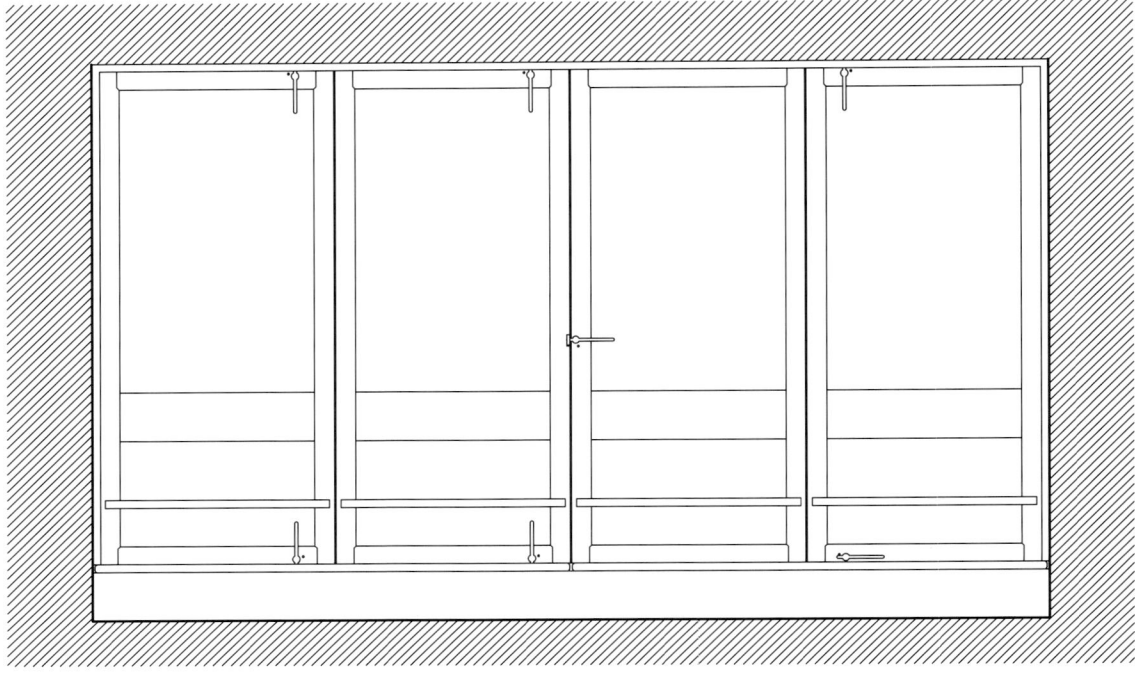

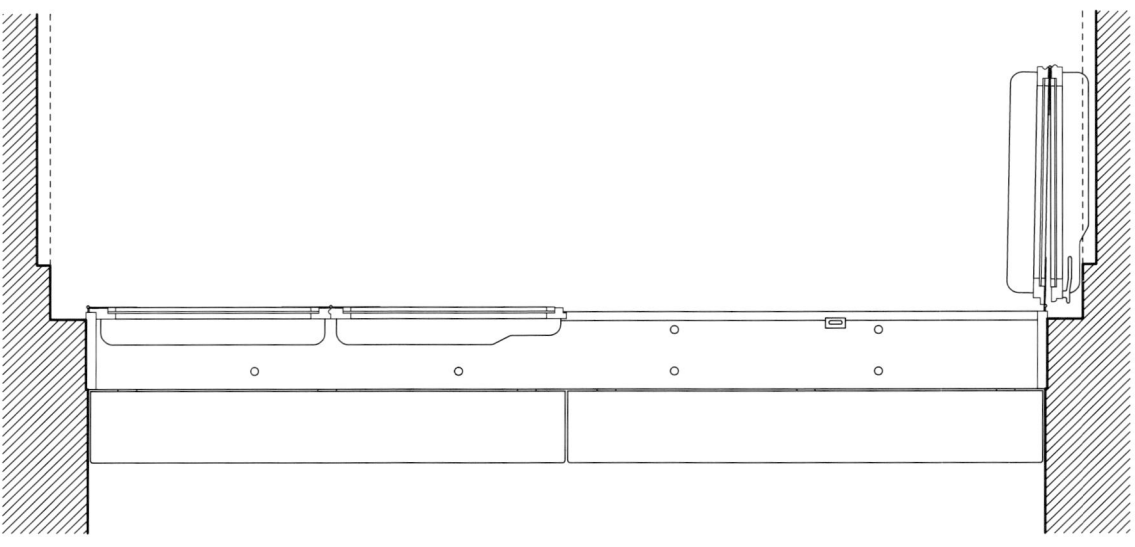

0   1m

Figure 2.10   Folding window of top storey apartment, Unité, Marseilles Michelet (1952)

Figure 2.11 The linear timber handles at the Maison du Brésel (1957). *Taureau II* (1953)

Zurich are formed of ostensibly simple metal bars that taper to fit into a hole (Figure 2.12) in a metal peg that brings down the metal latch, a version of the system used at the Unité Marseilles and Rezé les Nantes, La Tourette and elsewhere.[65] The pegged window of the Jaoul House B (Figure 2.13), the simple timber latches of the aerateurs in the cells of La Tourette (Figure 2.14),[66] the concrete logs that protrude from the side of Maison Jaoul B (Figure 2.15) and the sacristy at La Tourette all hark back to earlier forms of construction.[67] Robert Rebutato who was responsible for the prestressed concrete used at La Tourette told me that these logs were entirely decorative – there as a reminder of some more ancient architecture.[68] It is my suggestion that these almost archetypal – in the Jungian sense – details trigger a basic response from us. They seem supremely legible. We feel that we could perhaps make them ourselves without too great an effort. They evoke other details that we have engaged with in the past. Perhaps even as a child we played with such things. As such they feel satisfying and comfortable at the most fundamental level.

Occupying the position beneath the zenith of the great roof, the east door (1650 mm wide by 2220 mm high) at Ronchamp is at the climax of the Chapel (Figure 2.16). Formed in concrete, it evokes the stone rolled away from Christ's tomb, discovered by Mary Magdalene on his Resurrection. The handle of the door itself appears to take the abstract form of a woman's body (Figures 2.17 and 2.18) – its message similar to that of *The Poem of the Right Angle* is that it is necessary to engage with the body to be united with the spirit.[69] On the exterior it is juxtaposed

Figure 2.12
Handle of aerateur, Heidi
Weber Haus, Zurich (1968)

Figure 2.13   Detail of dining room window shutter, Maison Jaoul B (1955)

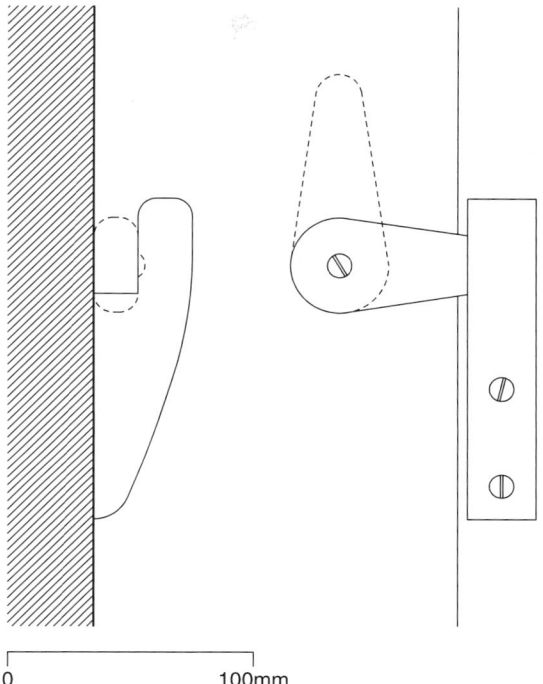

0   100mm

Figure 2.14
Wooden latch of aerateur
in cell, La Tourette (1959)

Figure 2.15   Details of exterior Maison Jaoul B (1955) and of La Tourette (1953–59)

Figure 2.16
Interior of the east side of
Notre-Dame du Haut,
Ronchamp (1955),
showing east door at the
zenith of the roof

with an imprint of a cockle shell (one of three on the door), linked with
woman – to Venus and to the Magdalene in the art of Le Corbusier –
as well as to the act of pilgrimage.[70] In *The Radiant City*, Le Corbusier
juxtaposed an image of a cockle shell with a pine cone next to the word
'harmonies'.[71] Here the pine cone, being a traditional symbol of masculine
creative force, combines with the cockle to create sexual balance. It also
appears in the pages of *The Poem* pointing directly towards the groin
of a naked woman on the opposing page, accompanied by the words
'to make architecture is to make a creature'.[72] In alchemical terms the
pine cone is the Roman symbol of Jupiter, associated with tin which
combines with copper (associated with Venus), to make the bronze of the
handle itself. Whether this was intentional or not one can only speculate,
although we do know that the architect was interested in the alchemical
metal symbolism and the possibility of bringing down beneficent forces
from the planets through their use.[73]

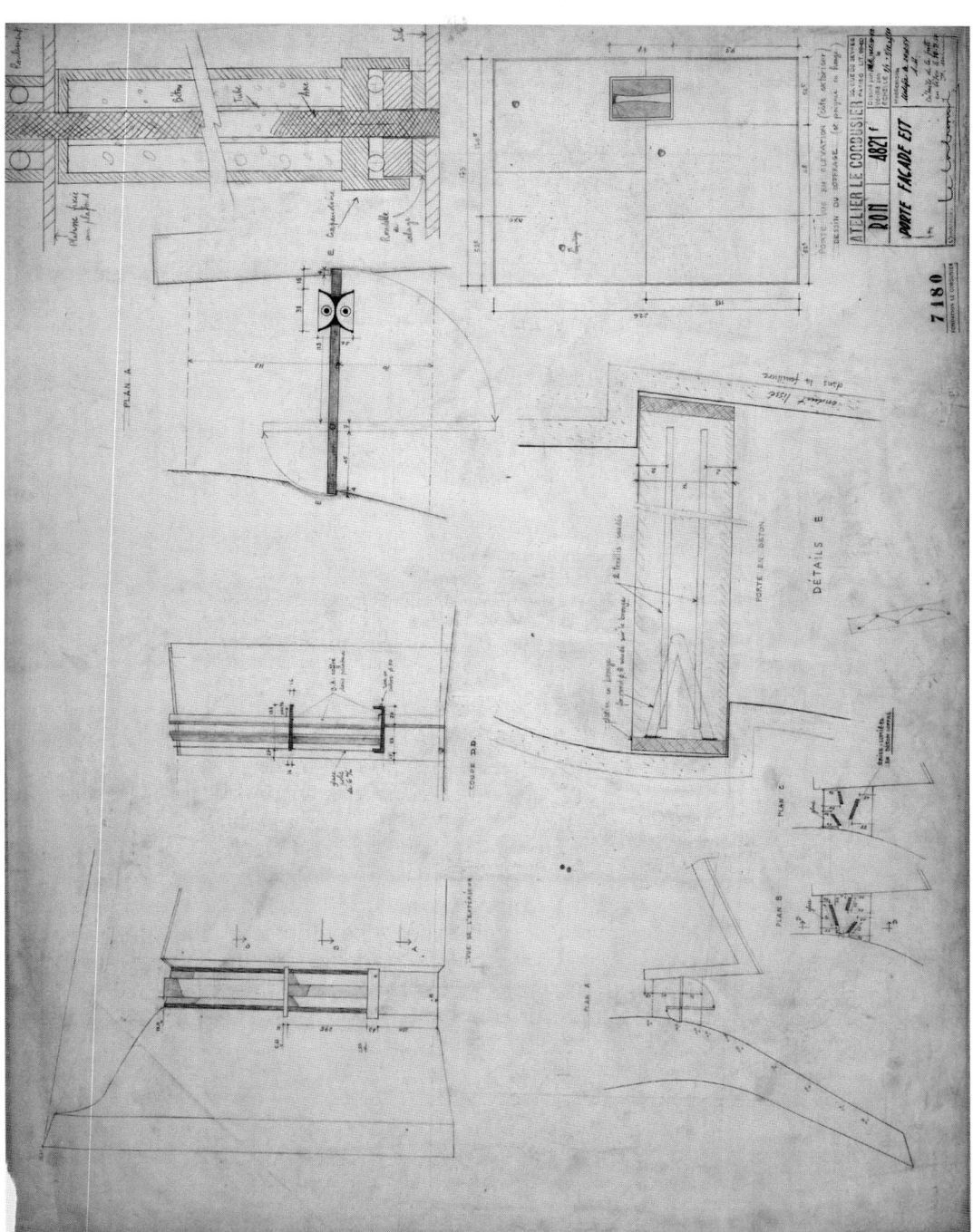

Figure 2.17   Handle of east door. Working drawing

Figure 2.18
Handle of east door from
exterior

Working drawings showing the door handle in plan reveal its uncanny likeness to a pair of breasts, a fact that could not have escaped Le Corbusier.[74] According to Krustrup, Le Corbusier associated his wife Yvonne with the figure of Venus,[75] who in turn has long been associated with that of Mary Magdalene, who, I would suggest, also has a place in the symbolism of this door.[76] She came to Christ's tomb on the third day, and was the first witness to his resurrection, carrying away with her his message to which she gave new life. Orientated to the rising of the sun, but startlingly cold to the hand, the door appears to symbolize the death and resurrection of Jesus. Simultaneously, in an alchemical sense, it alludes to the *petite morte* of sexual union, the relinquishing of the body and subsequent spiritual rebirth.

If the shell and the handle of the door represents the feminine, where is the masculine in this, Le Corbusier's, gender-balanced world? It is my suggestion that the male visitor to the building is himself written into its symbolism which is incomplete without his presence. Le Corbusier wrote of Ronchamp 'the drama is designed, installed. For you living men, to live the drama as well'.[77] Here the male visitor to the chapel is encouraged to engage with the building in a very physical way. What the female visitor should do remains unclear. It may be that Le Corbusier intended her to project herself into the Marian role, as generations of Catholic women have done before. Yet, rather than Mary the Virgin, it is Mary Magdalene who is offered up as an exemplar, admired by Le Corbusier, for her knowledge rather than her shame.

An identical handle appears set into yet another large door, this time that of the exterior wall of Heidi Weber's House in Zurich (Figure 2.19). Here the stark white enamel square bears an illustration of *Taureau*, the bull man, the Minotaure of Le Corbusier's paintings, locked in friendly embrace with a woman. Its message I would argue is the same as the door at Ronchamp although couched in rather different terms.

Yet another version of the handle was projected for a ceremonial door in the Mill Owners Association at Ahmedabad. Here the hand grasps what might be described as highly priapic, stubby metal cylindrical pole instead of the abstracted womanly form (it should be noted at this point that Le Corbusier was fully au fait with Freud and was never adverse to a ribald joke) at the groin height of Modulor man who looks on with interest (Figure 2.20).[78] The abstracted female handle is, however, used once more on the door of the Museum at Ahmedabad (1956) leading to a speculation as to whether Le Corbusier chose door handles based on the building type in question.[79]

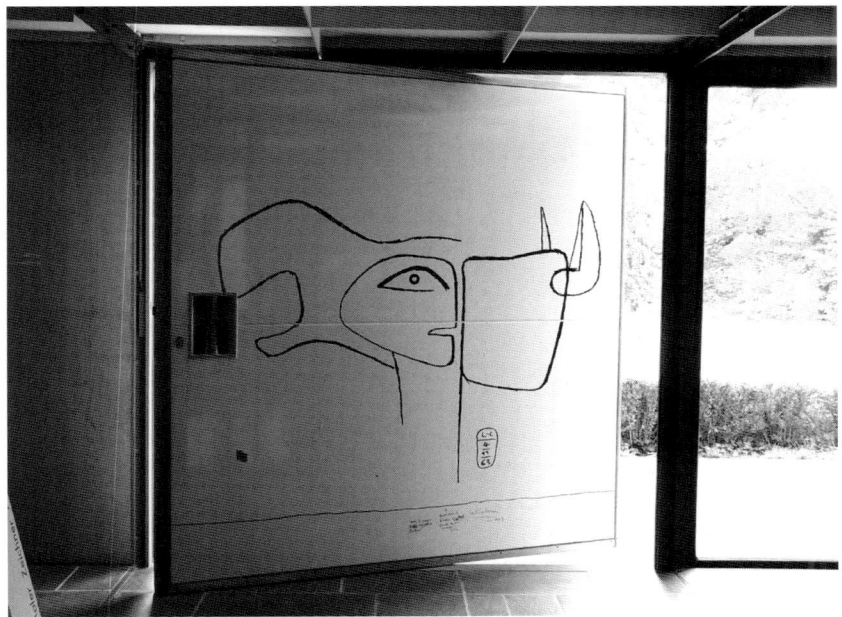

Figure 2.19   Enamel door, Heidi Weber Haus, Zurich (1968)

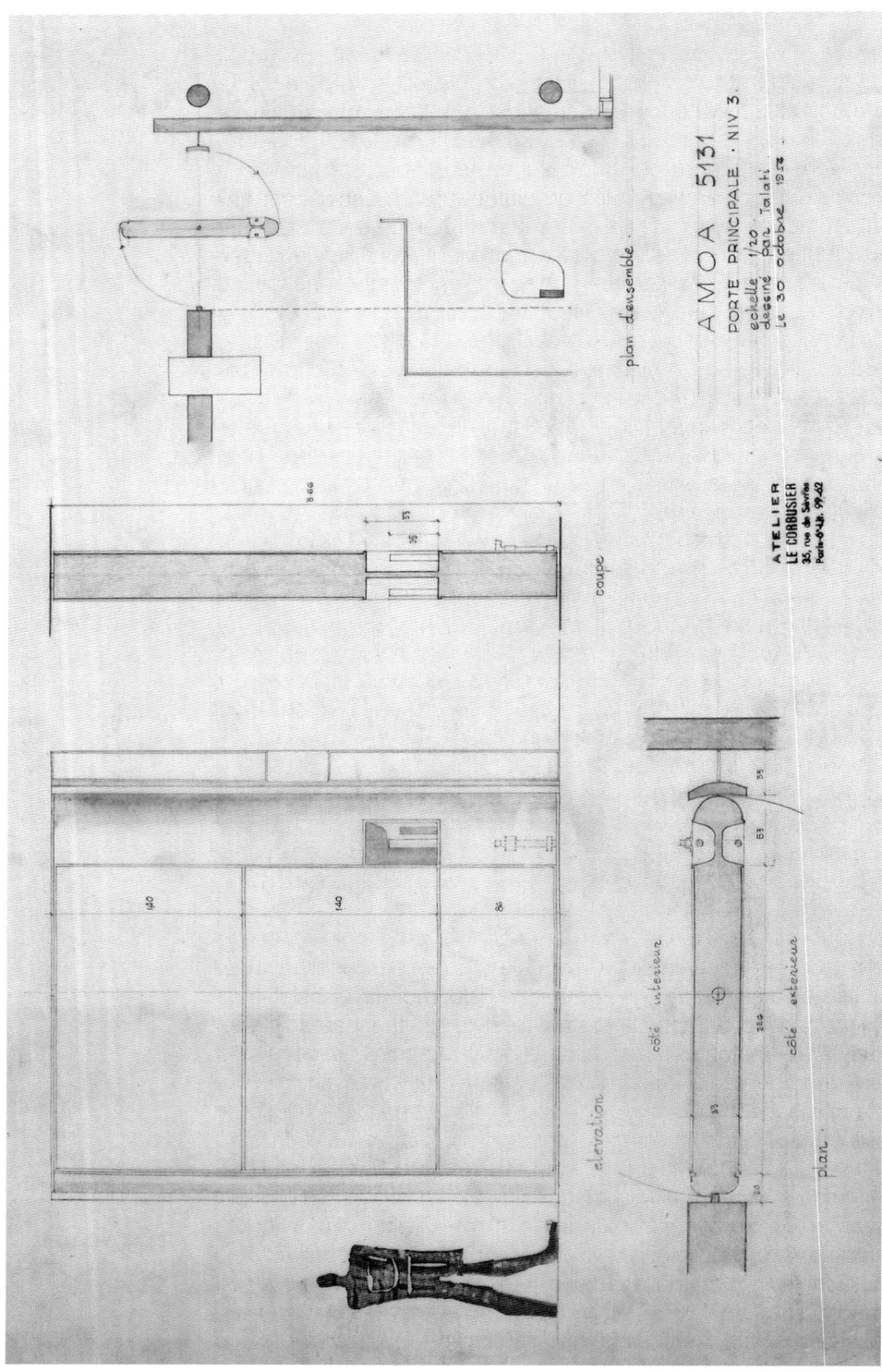

Figure 2.20 Drawing of handle for ceremonial door of Mill Owners' Association Building, Ahmedabad (1954)

2.2.3   Furniture

'A new term has replaced the old word furniture, which stood for fossilizing traditions and limited utilisation. That new term is equipment',[80] wrote Le Corbusier.[81] By dispensing with the word 'mobilier', his aim was to dispense with a particular way of life or 'usage' and to usher in 'a new era in domestic organisation'[82] an existence without clutter, leaving the inhabitants of his buildings better able to deal with the act of living well.

Le Corbusier divided his furniture into two distinct categories, movable furniture 'meubles') and storage – the latter discussed in more detail in Chapter 4. Much of his movable furniture was designed in conjunction with Charlotte Perriand, who gave him credit 'for setting the design parameters and for suggesting the basic form' according to McLeod.[83] Although a great deal has been written about their collaboration, it is worth mentioning their furniture once more as it brings to the fore those sensual and corporeal aspects that, I would argue, were so fundamental to Le Corbusier's architecture.

The furnishings of the home were for Le Corbusier 'human-limb objects', in other words an extension of the human body. In an article he wrote for *Harper's Bazaar*, accompanying a design for women's clothes, he blurred the boundaries between the padded clothing and furniture, both designed for comfort when sedentary.[84] 'The "human-limb object" is a docile servant. A good servant is discreet and self-effacing, in order to leave his master free'.[85] The idea of these 'auxiliary limbs' reinforces the message that furniture should be as efficient as any of the organisms of nature.[86] Thus 'these objects are in proportion to our limbs, are adapted to our gestures. They have a common scale, they fit into a module'.[87]

At the Pavillon Esprit Nouveau seating was organized according to function, not etiquette, a subject of which Le Corbusier was not overly fond.[88] A relinquishing of etiquette allowed for a relinquishing of complex dress codes, which limited people, particularly women, in their movements and their capabilities. He stressed that 'The evolution of the feminine toilette and the rules of decorum have authorised absolutely new attitudes'.[89] In this way the design of furniture held important social implications by promoting a more liberated lifestyle. In the past, different furniture had often been gendered but, as Mary McLeod has illustrated, the new metal and leather 'equipment' – created by Le Corbusier and Charlotte Perriand in tandem – was gender free. It is my suggestion that his interest in standardization sprang, partly, from concerns of gender, as well as social equality.[90] 'This new domestic equipment, which is no longer of wood but of metal, is made in the factories that used to manufacture office-furnishing'.[91] Le Corbusier himself wrote of the limitations of wood as a material for chairs, believing that metal construction lent itself to new ways of sitting.[92] Together with Perriand he conceived four different modes of emancipated sitting, each leading to a particular chair design.

The *siege à dossier basculant* (Figure 2.21) was a reworking of the standard colonial chair, its wooden legs replaced with steel. The seats and backs were of calfskin, wool or unbleached canvas, the armrests

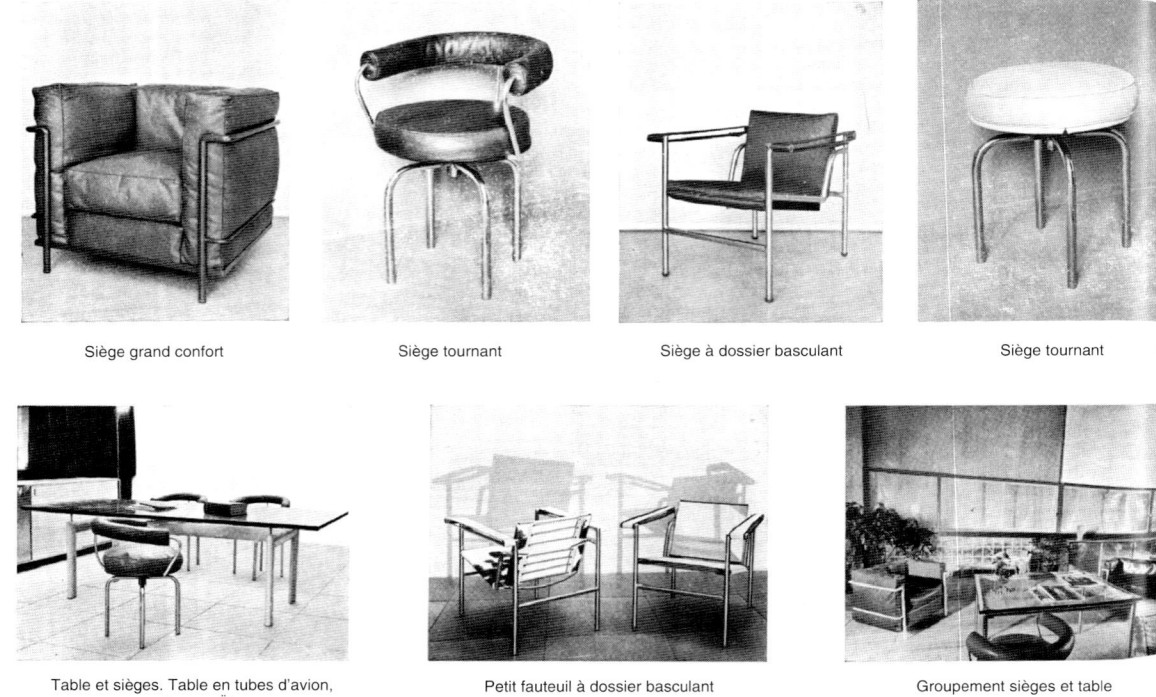

Siège grand confort   Siège tournant   Siège à dossier basculant   Siège tournant

Table et sièges. Table en tubes d'avion, section ovoîde   Petit fauteuil à dossier basculant   Groupement sièges et table

Figure 2.21 Furniture, Charlotte Perriand and Le Corbusier (1928)

leather straps.[93] As in all of Le Corbusier and Perriand's furniture, and indeed in Le Corbusier's architecture, the part that touches the body is expressed differently to the structure. McLeod suggests that the dimension of this chair 'suggest a female occupant or a slender man'.[94] She also reflects that it was 'not particularly innovative' unlike the *fauteuil grand confort* (1928).[95] A version of the traditional club armchair, this consisted of five overstuffed leather cushions squeezed into steel frame. It was made in two sizes reflecting, McLeod suggests, 'that both men and women could enjoy its enveloping pleasures'.[96] Further she writes of the 'serpentine' *chaise longue* that: 'Eighteenth century grace and eroticism have their twentieth century equivalent in this light, undulating structure poised on four points, so beautifully illustrated by the classic image of Perriand relaxing on its stretched canvas surface.'[97] She adds that 'the photo, like the chair, has a seductive charm'.[98] Even when empty, it evokes the body in its sensuous curves and sculptural form.

According to McLeod, Perriand and Le Corbusier 'regarded the chair's frames – which they designed as extensions of the human body – as universally applicable, and therefore capable of standardization, while materials, colours, and finishes could be tailored to individual preferences and particular settings'.[99] However, it does seem that the chairs were designed very much with contrast in mind, each material inviting touch and heightening the experience of the other through difference, as shown in the design for the Salon d'Automne 1929. There is nothing prim about fur, leather and steel, materials that lend themselves to touch, archetypal in their eroticism.

2.2.4 Floors

Not only are hands in contact with the fabric of a building – so are feet. A tacit hierarchy can be read, and indeed felt, through the finishes on the floor, intrinsic to the experience of the architectural promenade. In the Villa La Roche, as Tim Benton records, the majority of the floor surfaces are covered with small tiles coloured black in circulation areas and white in service spaces such as bathrooms. Brown linoleum covers the floors of the library and the bedrooms while the living room of the adjoining Jeanneret house is of parquet, the floor surfaces contributing to the sense of order within the building.[100] The grassed surfaces of the roof garden would then provide an appropriately tactile and scented denouement for the promenade architecturale;[101] Le Corbusier's own appreciation of the issue being brought into the relief by the famous image of the outdoor room on the roof of the Bestegui apartment where the grass appears as fitted carpet (Figure 2.22).

Floor surfaces were often used to acknowledge the presence of a special place in the architecture of Le Corbusier. The table at the centre of the gallery of Maison La Roche is set into black tile to give it extra emphasis. A square of parquet is, for example set into the tiled floor of Jaoul Maison B in order to delineate the dining space and, presumably,

Figure 2.22 Solarium of de Bestegui apartment (1930)

to contribute to the comfort of that area. Timber is similarly used in the floor beneath the seating at Ronchamp – a very simple mosaic of timber posts cut transversally it already, rather beautifully, shows signs of wear (Figure 2.23). At Ronchamp 'stone . . . paving' appears in 'the sacred places';[102] for example, at the south door extending its influence into the main body of the church itself, and in a rectangular patch at the base of the exterior altar. In the Church of La Tourette there is a play of surface material in the planes leading up to the altar itself. The majority of the Church is floored in pale concrete panels set to Modulor dimensions, 'opus optimum'. One step up brings the visitor to the level where the monks sit to pray, this is paved in a miraculous watery slate (Figure 2.24). A further step up, the altar is of white stone, the summit being finished

Figure 2.23
Floor beneath seating in
Notre-Dame du Haut,
Ronchamp (1955)

Figure 2.24
Floor of Church.
La Tourette (1959)

in slate. The officiate at the altar in this way experiences those patterns of alternate light and darkness which are such a familiar theme in Le Corbusier's work – its significance of which will be explored in the next chapter.

The contrived crevices of Le Corbusier's Modulor cement 'opus optimum'[103] pavements would send messages of rhythm to the soles and to the eyes, controlling movement almost as in a child's game. Le Corbusier's interest in the eurythmic ideas of his brother Albert, learnt from Dalcroze, should not be underestimated. In the Chapter House of La Tourette the monks lowering their eyes in prayer are greeted with a network of Modulor lines on the floor that continue in the glazing and out into the surroundings. Lying face down on the floor of the Church as they do,[104] they receive the physical imprints of the Modulor lines upon their bodies. Like a living diagram they are in this way drawn into Le Corbusier's radiant web.

2.3   Colour

As Le Corbusier's friend Elie Faure wrote in *Equivalences*, there was a 'mysterious accord between sensuality, sensibility and intelligence' which could be influenced through the orchestration of colour.[105] In his belief 'It is through polychromy that we can introduce into the house the sensational game, coloured epic gentle or violent'.[106] Colour was used symbolically by Le Corbusier[107] to influence mood and to assert or diminish the presence of particular architectural elements. In its initial stages his architecture would share the muted Mediterranean palate and uniform smoothness of his early Purist paintings; see, for example, the drawings prepared for the Villa Baizeau, at Carthage, 1928.[108] Colour, though far more vivid, would be used with equal care in Le Corbusier's later work where light would be used to bring it into his buildings, either reflected off brightly painted surfaces – as at Ronchamp, where light bounces off the red interior of one of the tower to create an intense rosy glow – or by means of coloured glass.

'For me, for twenty years, in my work where colour occupied half of my day, [his mornings spent painting] blue commanded me: blue and green in echo'.[109] Both of these colours were, for Le Corbusier, those of nature and indeed woman, which may explain why they are echoed in the tiles inset into the concrete façade of the nursery of the Unité Marseille. Numerous schedules remain a testament to the extreme care that went into specifying the decorative scheme for this building.[110] In Le Corbusier's later work, large flecks of colour tile were often introduced into the surfaces of the concrete furniture that so often inhabited his buildings. The colours chosen usually seem symbolic, red being used near the fireplace of the Jaoul Maison B and so on. With regard to the colour of concrete Le Corbusier wrote: 'It has been said that the appearance of the cement is dreary, that is to say that its colour is dreary. This is just as false as to say that a colour can be dreary per se, when in fact colours have value only in relation to their surroundings'.[111] Concrete is indeed a very different thing when seen in the blaze of the Mediterranean sun.

In 1932 Le Corbusier developed a colour system for the firm Salubra. It was 'a system which makes it possible to establish a strictly architectural polychromy in the modern dwelling, one in accordance with nature and with the deep needs of each person'.[112] Le Corbusier described the range as a 'keyboard . . . each of us will be touched by such or such a harmony'.[113] Creating harmony through colour and creating harmony through proportion were parallel processes. 'Colour . . . Mister Psychiatrist, is it not an important tool in diagnosis?' he wrote.[114]

2.4   Space

Once more drawing on the ideas of Elie Faure, Le Corbusier observed that 'Proportions provoke sensations; a series of sensations like the melody in music'.[115] A further means to influence the body was through geometry. In his early schemes regulating lines would be used to send harmonious spatial messages to the senses;[116] in his later work the Modulor would assist in this task. Le Corbusier was always keen to stress the links between his system of proportion and that of the body itself, beauty 'acting like sound waves on a resonator'.[117]

Such was his concern to fit his buildings to the needs of the body that he often worked at full scale. Wogenscky recalled that Le Corbusier asked his assistants to draw plans and sections life sized on a large blackboard – 'In this way the loggias of the apartments were designed in their real dimensions. Le Corbusier himself corrected the drawings with chalk. He sculpted the architecture',[118] with thought processes moving 'from the interior towards the exterior', very much with inhabitation in mind.[119] Smaller-scale plans reveal traces of fine lines drawn repeatedly as his pencil point went through the motions of daily life. Heights of surfaces, and sight lines were of paramount importance.[120] In his last book *Nursery Schools*, Le Corbusier recorded twenty-four hours in the life of a child living in the Unité, its captions, like the captions in a child's picture book, evidence of the intense thought that went into its planning at the scale of a child.[121] In the rooftop play space, security and comfort were given through the creation of the low curved walls around the paddling pool offering a rather different sensation to the visceral pleasures of fear and excitement built into the architecture in the form of 'that famous "frightening" inclined wall' that appears beyond (see Figure 6.24).[122]

2.5   Sound

Any discussion of the way in which Le Corbusier's architecture appeals to the body would be incomplete without a mention of sound. This became rudely apparent to me when sitting alone in the stark rectangular box that is the church at La Tourette, not an easy space to understand or to appreciate. So small is the Dominican community there now that they often choose to conduct their prayers in the chapterhouse, meaning that there was no opportunity to hear voices either singing or at prayer while I was there. Therefore when standing in the church I sang out one note. The result was astonishing. The space completely transformed. The sound bounding and rebounding around the hard flat surfaces for about 12 seconds before dissolving into the quiet hum that is the church. 'I admit that I perhaps have a flair for acoustics' wrote Le Corbusier perhaps with some justification.[123] Le Corbusier did not rely entirely on gut feeling in this matter. Rudimentary tests were also brought into play. For example, Richard Moore discovered, in conversation with Saporta, one of Le Corbusier's assistants, that in order to refine the acoustics for the main auditorium for his League of Nations Competition scheme Le Corbusier made a foil tray the same shape in plan as the auditorium, filled it with water and watched the behaviour of waves generated as they moved across it.[124]

The inner ear, its liquid interior responsible for sensations of sound and balance, was yet another part of the human anatomy of great interest to Le Corbusier as sound would play an important role in a number of his more ambitious architectural conceptions, for example Ronchamp where:

> 'They will be able to make incredible music, an unbelievable sound when they have twelve thousand people outside with amplifiers. I said to the priest, "you should get rid of the kind of music played by an old maid on an old harmonium – that's out of tune – and instead have music composed for the church, something new, not sad music, a loud noise, an unholy din"'.[125]

His desire to incorporate sound into his work was not confined to his religious work.[126] For example, he wrote ruefully of his scheme for the Carpenter Centre 'Had the original idea for electronic emissions of sound been incorporated, the synthesis of major arts would have been complete'.[127]

2.6   Conclusion

Le Corbusier sought to revitalize links between the body and the environment. Such ideas underpinned his preoccupation with the 'synthesis of the major arts' – his desire to create a radiant environment, all details of which, space, colour, sound were governed by laws of harmony as he saw it. The plan for the Basilica at La Sainte Baume was to create just such a space but, due to the disapprobation of the Church, it was never built. The nearest Le Corbusier ever came to achieving his goal was when he was commissioned to design the Philips Pavilion (see Figure 1.5) for the Brussels World Fair, site of *The Electronic Poem* – as such it provides a fitting end to this chapter. Here space, colour, image and sound – provided by the composer Edgar Varese – were brought together in the most anthropomorphic of spaces, again it seems loosely based in form upon the *Icône* of Le Corbusier's paintings. Each of those who witnessed *The Electronic Poem* at the Brussels World Fair of 1958 would be thrown into 'a torrent, a mass, a depth of sensations, showing, demonstrating, and perhaps proving something'.[128]

Light, and indeed shadow, were also, of course, of primary importance in his conception of the Philips Pavilion and was of course central to the emotive strength of his buildings in general:

> Light on forms, precise intensity of light, successive volumes, acting on our sensitive being, provoking physical, physiological sensations, which scientists have described, classified, detailed. That horizontal or that vertical,

this sawtooth line broken brutally or that soft undulation, this closed concentric form of a circle or a square, which acts profoundly on us, influences our designs, and determines our feelings. Rhythm, diversity or monotony, coherence or incoherence, marvellous or disappointing surprise, the joyful shock of light or the chill of darkness, calm of a well-lit bedroom or anguish or a roomful of dark corners, enthusiasm or depression.[129]

The body's instinctual response to particular light conditions was also to be exploited and indeed enhanced, as shall be seen in the next chapter.

Notes

[1] Le Corbusier in I. Zacnic, *The Final Testament of Père Corbu: a Translation and Interpretation of Mise au Point* (New Haven, CT: Yale University Press, 1997), p. 120.

[2] Le Corbusier, *The Decorative Art of Today* (London: Architectural Press, 1987), p. 167. Originally published as Le Corbusier, *L'Art décoratif d'aujourd'hui* (Paris: Editions Crès, 1925), p. 169.

[3] Le Corbusier, *Precisions* (Cambridge, MA: MIT, 1991), p. 160.

[4] Ibid., p. 73.

[5] As Plato observed 'rhythm and harmony find their way into the inward places of the soul' resulting in a 'true education of the inner being'. Plato, *The Republic III* in S. Buchanan (ed.), *The Portable Plato* (Harmondsworth: Penguin, 1997), p. 389.

[6] Le Corbusier, *The Decorative Art of Today*, p. 167. Le Corbusier was a great admirer of Faure (1873–1937) who was one of the original members of CIAM, the Congrès Internationaux d'Architecture Moderne. He owned a number of books by Faure, some signed by the author himself. E. Faure, *Equivalences* (Paris: Robert Marin, 1951).

[7] A. Rüegg (ed.), *Polychromie Architecturale: Le Corbusier's Colour Keyboards from 1931 to 1959* (Basel: Birkhäuser, 1997), p. 101.

[8] Le Corbusier, *Precisions*, p. 82.

[9] C. Green, 'The architect as artist' in T. Benton (ed.), *Le Corbusier Architect of the Century* (London, Arts Council, 1987), p. 126.

[10] Le Corbusier, *Precisions*, p. 68.

[11] Le Corbusier, *Oeuvre Complète Volume 6, 1952–1957* (Zurich: Les Editions d'Architecture, 1995), p. 176. Originally published in 1957.

[12] Le Corbusier, *The Marseilles Block* (London: Harvill, 1953), p. 17. Originally published as *L'Unité d'habitation de Marseille* (Mulhouse: Editions Le Point, 1950).

[13] See F. Samuel, *Le Corbusier: Architect and Feminist* (London: Wiley, 2004) for an expansion of this discussion. A brief conversation between the author and the current cleaner of the Maisons Jaoul revealed that she found the house easy to clean, but rather large.

[14] Letter Le Corbusier to his mother, 17 June 1948, Fondation Le Corbusier (hereafter referred to as FLC) R2.4.123.

[15] FLC 30794 in H. Allen Brooks (ed.), *The Le Corbusier Archive, Volumes XVII* (New York: Garland, 1983), p. 510. Hereafter referred to as Allen Brooks, *Archive*.

[16] Le Corbusier, *Oeuvre Complète Volume 5, 1946–1952* (Zurich: Les Editions d'Architecture, 1995), p. 208. Originally published in 1953.

[17] Le Corbusier-Saugnier (Le Corbusier and A. Ozenfant), 'Manuel de l'habitation,' a part of their article 'Des yeux qui ne voient pas . . . II: Les Avions, 'L'esprit Nouveau, 9, June 1921, n.p., cited in M. McLeod (ed.), *Charlotte Perriand: An Art of Living* (New York: Harry N. Abrams, 2003), p. 54.

[18] See Samuel, *Le Corbusier* for an expansion of this topic.

[19] Le Corbusier, *Oeuvre Complète Volume 5*, p. 191.

[20] R. Banham, *The New Brutalism, Ethic or Aesthetic* (London: Architectural Press, 1966), p. 85.

[21] Le Corbusier, *The Radiant City* (London: Faber, 1967), p. 78. Originally published as Le Corbusier, *La Ville Radieuse* (Paris: Éditions de l'Architecture d'Aujourd'hui, 1935).

22 Le Corbusier, *Modulor* (London: Faber, 1954), p. 224. Originally published as *Le Modulor* (Paris: Editions d'Architecture d'Aujour hui, 1950).

23 Christopher Pearson writes of the way in which Le Corbusier distributed gendered art-works within his clients houses, for example in the Villas Stein and Mandrot. 'At the Mandrot villa . . . the association of the female form with passivity and nature and the male form with a more active dominance of its surroundings is more typical of Le Corbusier' masculinist symbology'. C.E.M Pearson, 'Integrations of art and architecture in the work of Le Corbusier. Theory and practice from ornamentalism to the "Synthesis of the Major Arts"' (unpublished PhD thesis, Stanford University, 1995), p. 139.

24 Le Corbusier, *Modulor*, p. 113.

25 K. Silver, *Esprit de Corps: The Art of the Parisian Avant-Garde and the First World* War, *1914–1925* (Princeton, NJ: Princeton University Press, 1989), p. 230.

26 Originally published in 1918. Reprinted in C.S. Eliel (ed.), *L'Esprit Nouveau: Purism in Paris* (New York: Harry N. Abrams, 2001), pp. 157–8.

27 Le Corbusier, *A New World of Space* (New York: Reynal Hitchcock, 1948), p. 16.

28 Ibid., p. 21. See D. Neagele, 'The image of the body in the oeuvre of Le Corbusier' in *Architecture Landscape and Urbanism 9, Le Corbusier and the Architecture of Reinvention* (London: AA Publications, 2003), pp. 16–39.

29 K. Frampton, *Studies in Tectonic Culture: The Poetics of Construction in Nineteenth and Twentieth Century Architecture* (Cambridge, MA: MIT, 1996), p. 153.

30 Le Corbusier, *Precisions*, p. 40.

31 C. Rowe, *The Architecture of Good Intentions* (London: Academy Editions, 1994), p. 60.

32 Dossier Meyer, Doc. 5, 24 February 1926, quoted in T. Benton, *The Villas of Le Corbusier* (London: Yale University Press, 1987), p. 144.

33 Pearson, 'Integrations of art and architecture', p. 140.

34 Le Corbusier, *When the Cathedrals were White: A Journey to the Country of the Timid People* (New York: Reynal and Hitchcock, 1947). p. 14.

35 Stirling wrote 'The rendering which is whitewashed over, has been hand thrown and has an impasto of about 2 inches. This veneer suggests a quality of weightlessness and gives the walls something of the appearance of papier mâché'. James Stirling, 'Ronchamp: Le Corbusier's chapel and the crisis of rationalism', *Architectural Review*, 119:711, March 1956, p. 156.

36 Le Corbusier, *Oeuvre Complète Volume 6*, p. 52.

37 J. Coll, 'Structure and play in Le Corbusier's art works', *AA Files*, 31 (1996), pp. 3–15.

38 See a series of sketches of La Tourette indicate that the façade of the church was conceived as an abstracted woman. FLC 30317 in Allen Brooks, *Archive, Volume XXVIII*, p. 601.

39 Le Corbusier, *The Chapel at Ronchamp* (London: Architectural Press, 1957), p. 25.

40 Ibid., p. 27.

41 Le Corbusier, *Le Poème de l'angle droit* (Paris: Editions Connivance, 1989), section C2, Flesh. Originally published in 1955.

42 Le Corbusier, *Modulor 2* (London: Faber, 1955), p. 148. Originally published as *Le Modulor II* (Paris: Editions d'Architecture d'Aujourd'hui, 1955), p. 154.

43 Le Corbusier, *Le Poème de l'angle droit*, section F3, Offering.

44 Le Corbusier, *Talks with Students* (New York, Princeton: 2003), p. 59.

45 Letter, Le Corbusier to Sert, 26 May 1962 reproduced in E. Sekler and W. Curtis, *Le Corbusier at Work: The Genesis of the Carpenter Centre for the Visual Arts* (Cambridge, MA: MIT, 1978), p. 302.

46 Letter Le Corbusier to Sert, 11 September 1961 quoted in Sekler and Curtis, *Le Corbusier at Work*, p. 164.

47 Ibid., p. 195.

48 Ibid., p. 164.

49 Le Corbusier specified to Sert the best way of getting lines in smooth grainless 'Isorel formwork cut with one of three types of incisions which would result in thin protruding lines in the concrete itself'. Ibid., p. 194.

50 FLC 22144, H. Allen Brooks (ed.), *The Le Corbusier Archive, Volume XXIX* (New York: Garland, 1983), p. 325.

[51] According to Réjean Legault the concrete finish here was the work of the contractor, not the architect. It this was the case it serves Le Corbusier's purpose remarkably well. 'That some monks read the surfaces achieved by means of quasi-industrial techniques as "stigmata of suffering" is only one of the building's many paradoxes.' Réjean Legault, 'The semantics of exposed concrete', in J.L. Cohen, and G. Martin Mueller (eds), *Liquid Stone: New Architecture in Concrete* (Basel: Birkhäuser, 2006), pp. 46–56 (47).

[52] Rowe wrote of La Tourette: 'It is not so much a church with living quarters attached as it is a domestic theatre for virtuosi of asceticism with, adjoining it, a gymnasium for the exercise of spiritual athletes. The figure of the boxer and his punch bag on the terrace of the 1928 project for Geneva has become conflated with the image of Jacob wrestling with the angel.' C. Rowe, *The Mathematics of the Ideal Villa and Other Essays* (Cambridge, MA: MIT, 1976), p. 195.

[53] Le Corbusier, *Oeuvre Complète Volume 5*, p. 204. For further discussion of 'harmonious contrast' see Le Corbusier, *Oeuvre Complète Volume 4*, p. 82.

[54] D. Pye, *The Nature and Art of Workmanship* (Cambridge: Cambridge University Press, 1968), p. 36.

[55] Le Corbusier, *Oeuvre Complète Volume 5*.

[56] Le Corbusier and P. Jeanneret, *Oeuvre Complète Volume 3, 1934–38* (Zurich: Les Editions d'Architecture, 1995), p. 19. Originally published in 1938.

[57] Le Corbusier's handprints and footprints appear prominently with those of his friend Rebutato in a mural on the wall of L'Etoile de Mer, Cap Martin.

[58] I owe this observation to Tim Benton, Paris, 9 December 2006.

[59] FLC 17984 in Allen Brooks, *Archive, Volume XII*, p. 351.

[60] J. Stirling, 'Ronchamp: Le Corbusier's chapel and the crisis of rationalism', p. 161.

[61] See for example FLC 17418 in Allen Brooks, *Archive, Volume VIII*, p. 403.

[62] FLC 15377, ibid., p. 191.

[63] FLC 17889 in Allen Brooks, *Archive, Volume XII*, p. 306. See Le Corbusier's design for a latch for the Facom project of 1936, FLC 28067 in Allen Brooks, *Archive, Volume XIII*, p. 50.

[64] See for example FLC 26425. Allen Brooks, *Archive, Volume XVII*, p. 60. FLC 17408, 17416, 23749 in Brooks, *Archive, Volume XXIX*, p. 399. FLC 25649 in Allen Brooks *Archive, Volumes XVI*, p. 258.

[65] FLC 30411 in Allen Brooks, *Archive, Volumes XXI*, p. 506.

[66] See FLC 1075 in Allen Brooks, *Archive, Volume XXVIII*, p. 8 for the details of the cell.

[67] Sekler notes a 'return to the very fundamentals of pier-and-lintel architecture' that characterizes the boat club at Chandigarh. Sekler and Curtis, *Le Corbusier at Work*, p. 253.

[68] Conversation with Robert Rebutato, Paris, 9 December 2006. Apparently he avoided being drafted into the army because Le Corbusier made the claim that his experiments with prestressed concrete were so important.

[69] These theories are lengthily justified in my PhD thesis. 'Orphism in the work of Le Corbusier' (unpublished, Cardiff, 2000).

[70] Cockle shells also appear in imprint in the hall of the Unité and on Le Corbusier and Yvonne's tomb.

[71] Le Corbusier, *The Radiant City*, p. 8.

[72] Le Corbusier, *Le Poème de l'angle droit* (Paris: Editions Connivance, 1989), section E3, Caracteres.

[73] On the frontispiece of his edition of Rabelais' *Gargantua and Pantagruel*, in the Fondation Le Corbusier, in a note dated 1961, Le Corbusier recorded, as if for posterity, that his brother Albert introduced him to the concept of the four alchemical metals in 1905. He repeats the message inside on page 52.

[74] See Samuel, *Le Corbusier*, p. 128.

[75] M. Krustrup, *I'Illiade Dessins* (Copenhagen: Borgen, 1986), p. 113.

[76] Susan Haskins describes the Magdalene's transition into a Venus figure in Italy during the first half of the sixteenth century, as part of Marcilio Ficino's (1433–99) attempt to merge the work of Plato and the Neoplatonists with both pagan philosophy and Christian religion. S. Haskins, *Mary Magdalene* (London: HarperCollins, 1993), pp. 236–7.

[77] Le Corbusier, *The Chapel at Ronchamp*, pp. 131–3.

[78] FLC 6841 in Allen Brooks, *Archive, Volume XXVI*, p. 70. See also FLC 6852–6, p. 77.

[79] Ibid., FLC 6930, p. 191.

[80] Le Corbusier and P. Jeanneret *Oeuvre Complète Volume 1, 1910–1929* (Zurich: Les Editions d'Architecture, 1995), p. 104.Originally published in 1937. See also Corbusier and P. Jeanneret, *Oeuvre Complète Volume 2, 1929–34* (Zurich: Les Editions d'Architecture, 1995), p. 121. Originally published in 1935.

[81] Le Corbusier and Jeanneret *Oeuvre Complète Volume 1*, p. 100.

[82] Ibid., p104.

[83] M. McLeod (ed.), *Charlotte Perriand: An Art of Living* (New York: Harry N. Abrams 2003), p. 44.

[84] Letter J. Heilbuth to H. Strassova, 23 February 1952, FLC U3.3.4.

[85] Le Corbusier, *The Decorative Art of Today*, p. xxiii.

[86] Ibid., p. 72.

[87] Le Corbusier, *Precisions*, p. 111.

[88] Le Corbusier and Jeanneret *Oeuvre Complète Volume 1*, p100.

[89] Ibid., p. 157.

[90] Late in life Le Corbusier became particularly concerned that his furniture should be available at a price suitable for a mass market. Letter Le Corbusier to Heidi Weber. 15 July 1964, www.steelform.com/de/letter.html, accessed 28 March 2006.

[91] Le Corbusier and Jeanneret, *Oeuvre Complète Volume 1*, p. 104.

[92] Ibid., p. 100.

[93] McLeod, *Charlotte Perriand*, p. 45.

[94] Ibid., p. 46.

[95] Ibid.

[96] Ibid., p. 47.

[97] Ibid., pp. 47–8.

[98] Ibid., p. 48.

[99] Ibid., p. 54.

[100] Benton, *The Villas of Le Corbusier*, p. 71.

[101] Where paving was incorporated, grass was often encouraged to sprout up in between. W. Curtis, *Le Corbusier: Ideas and Forms* (Oxford: Phaidon, 1986), p. 76. See also Benton, *The Villas of Le Corbusier*, p. 144.

[102] Le Corbusier, *The Chapel at Ronchamp*, p. 107.

[103] Ibid., p. 107.

[104] J. Petit, *Un Couvent de Le Corbusier* (Paris: Les Éditions de Minuit, 1961).

[105] 'L'accord mystérieux entre la sensualité, la sensibilité et l'intelligence'. E. Faure, *Equivalences* (Paris: Robert Marin, 1951), p. 18 in FLC. Similar sentiments were expressed by another of his favourite authors, Henri Provensal. 'Les couleurs exercent sur nous une grande influence, due en partie à ce fait que leur perception s'associe à celle d'objets qui nous impressionnent profondément'. H. Provensal, *L'Art de Demain* (Paris: Perrin, 1904), p. 54 in FLC.

[106] Le Corbusier quoted by P. Boudon in *Le Corbusier's Pessac* (Paris: 1936).

[107] L.M. Colli, 'La Couleur qui cache, la couleur qui signale: l'ordonnance et la crainte dans la poètique corbuséenne des couleurs' in *Le Corbusier et La Couleur* (Paris: Fondation Le Corbusier, 1992), pp. 21–34.

[108] FLC 31453 and 31454 in Allen Brooks, *Archive, Volume V*, p. 212.

[109] Le Corbusier 'polychromie architecturale', unpublished preface for the Claviers Salubra, 1932, FLC B1(18), 1, 4. Cited in Colli, 'La Couleur qui cache', p .22.

[110] See for example FLC 25645 in Allen Brooks, *Archive, Volume XVI*, p. 256.

[111] Le Corbusier, *Oeuvre Complète Volume 5*, p. 191.

[112] Le Corbusier, 'Claviers de couleurs' from the trade literature for Salubra reprinted in Colli, 'Le Corbusier e il colore'; I Claviers Salubra,' *Storia dell'arte*, 43 (1981), p. 283.

[113] From the essay 'Architectural polychromy' by Le Corbusier, in Rüegg (ed.), *Polychromie Architecturale*, p. 137.

[114] Ibid., p. 107.

[115] Le Corbusier, *Precisions*, p. 133.

[116] FLC 15589 shows the importance of regulating lines in the composition of the lower reaches of the Pavillon Suisse. FLC 15589 in Allen Brooks, *Archive, Volume VIII*, p. 289.

[117] Ibid., p. 156.

[118] A. Wogenscky, 'The Unité d'Habitation at Marseille' in Allen Brooks, *Archive, Volume XVI*, p. x.

[119] Ibid., p. xi.

[120] See for example FLC 29310 in Allen Brooks, *Archive, Volume XVII*, p. 462.

[121] Le Corbusier, *The Nursery Schools* (New York: Orion, 1968), pp. 34–54.

[122] Ibid., p. 76.

[123] J. Petit, *Un Couvent de Le Corbusier* (Paris: Les Éditions de Minuit, 1961), p. 29.

[124] R.A. Moore, 'Le Corbusier and the *mecanique spirituelle*: an investigation into Le Corbusier's architectural symbolism and its background in Beaux Arts design' (D Phil thesis, University of Maryland, 1979), pp. 183–4.

[125] J. Peter, *The Oral History of Modern Architecture* (New York: Harry N. Abrams, 1994), p. 146.

[126] Electronic sound would be emitted by the Church of Sainte Pierre, Firminy Vert. Le Corbusier proposed to consult Edgar Varese on he the subject. J. Loach 'Church of Saint-Pierre, Firminy-Vert' in Benton (ed.), *Le Corbusier Architect of the Century*, p.253.

[127] Sekler and Curtis, *Le Corbusier at Work*, p. 225.

[128] Le Corbusier, *Precisions*, p. x. Taken from preface to second French edition dated 1960.

[129] Ibid., p. 75.

Light and dark 3

Le Corbusier was not interested in creating blanket uniform lighting conditions. In spite of his dismissal of Caravaggio, he revelled in the drama of chiaroscuro, hence his enthusiasm for the photography of Lucien Hervé. Stating that 'light and shadow reveal form',[1] his buildings need strong directional light for the creation of shadow and for the enhancement of their planes. 'Observe the play of shadows, learn the game... Precise shadows, clear cut or dissolving. Projected shadows, sharp. Projected shadows, precisely delineated, but what enchanting arabesques and frets. Counterpoint and fugue. Great music'.[2] For Le Corbusier light served a number of important practical and symbolic purposes, its choreography subject to endless refinement. However before documenting Le Corbusier's exploitation of light, shadow and reflection through the nuances of architectural detail, it is necessary to explore its meaning.

3.1 Meaning

As a young man Le Corbusier had eulogized about the Sanctuary of the 'Mother of God' at Mount Athos and its 'mysterious relationships of form and colour... *in the rhythm of the controlled light*' describing this as 'a divine calling for the ancient builders!'.[3] Le Corbusier here refers to his masonic sympathies, to his belief that the medieval master builders were party to a secret knowledge, Pythagorean in essence.[4] In Gnostic faiths such as Manichaeism, which focused upon the relationship between the body and the soul, the cosmos was described in terms of the relationship between night and day. According to Hans Jonas the symbolism of light and darkness is 'everywhere in Gnostic literature'.[5] Most usually associated with life and death, it could also symbolise good and evil and, indeed, the 'other world' and 'this world' which was perceived to be dark and imperfect.[6] Le Corbusier was very guarded in what he actually committed to paper lest he inspired the disapprobation of the Catholic Church, but we know that he is very likely to have discussed light in these terms from the correspondence with his flamboyant client for the scheme at La Sainte Baume, Edouard Trouin and the Dominican monk Marie-Alain Couturier, editor of the influential journal *L'Art Sacré*. When eventually Trouin visited La Tourette, he described its lighting as 'Manichaean or Albigensian'[7] reflecting upon its relationship with the lighting planned for his own Basilica where they had tried to 'utilise the sun' to illuminate 'the hyphen between worlds and also the place of union'.[8]

Games of illumination played a significant role in the work of a number of writers much admired by Le Corbusier, most notably André Gide, Edouard Schuré and Guillaume Apollinaire who, in the words of Virginia Spate, used ancient metaphors of light 'revived by nineteenth-century poets to express the primordial unity of all matter and the aspiration of the soul to be reunited with light, the divine source of all being'.[9] Apollinaire believed that the visionary poet had the ability to transcend time and gain contact with the past that lay deep within his subconscious.[10] Only in this way could he become whole. The initiatory journey, based on the story of Orpheus, from darkness into light thus became, for Apollinaire, a metaphor for the poet's own quest for inner wholeness, an idea that, evidence suggests, Le Corbusier shared.

The opposition of light and dark was of profound importance to Le Corbusier's life and work. It provided the focus of Le Corbusier's sign for the 24-hour day which tracks the movements of the sun above and below the horizon – used for example, on the entrance stone of the Unité apartment block at Marseilles (see Figure 1.8). He wrote that 'If, in the course of the mutation of the machine civilisation, I have been able to contribute something, as a person with some rationality and intelligence, as technician, as a thoughtful man, it will be this sign'.[11] It was to be an object of meditation for those 'whose mission it is to see clearly and to lead' and held within it the key to 'habitation . . . knowing how to live! How to use the blessings of God; the sun and the spirit that He has given to men to enable them to achieve the joy of living on earth and to find again the Lost Paradise'.[12]

If meditation upon this figure could produce striking results in the sus-ceptible, then the best way to facilitate the journey to the 'Lost Paradise', the original unity at the end of the Gnostic journey, would be to place the initiate actually within the sign itself to experience its power at first hand.[13] It may well be for this reason, that in section, the route through the Basilica at La Sainte Baume (Figure 3.1) took the form of Le Corbusier's symbol of the 24-hour day (see Figure 1.8). Light would penetrate the complex at the ends of the various 'galleries' to draw the visitor through the upper and lower realms of Le Corbusier's sign to be greeted on emerging from the mountainside by the sun and a panoramic view of the

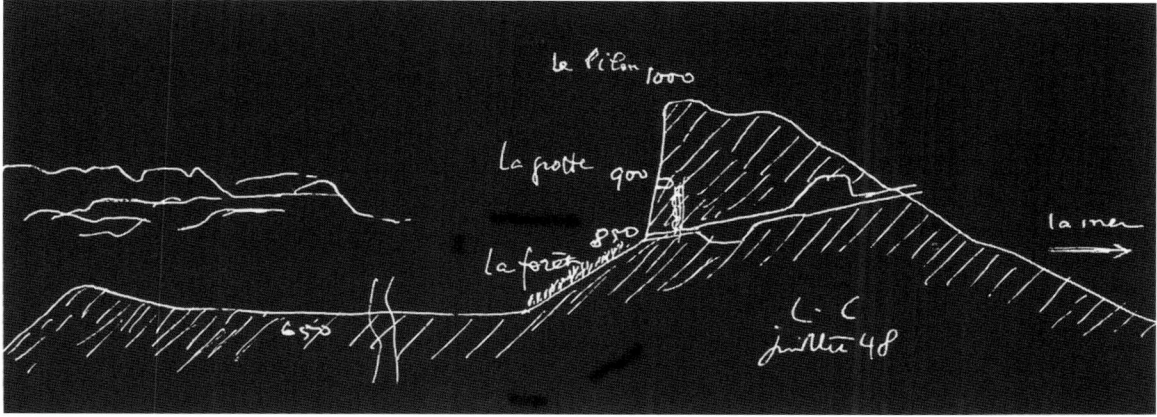

Figure 3.1   Section across Le Corbusier's scheme for the Basilica at La Sainte Baume (c. 1948)

Mediterranean to the south.[14] Like the journey of Orpheus through the underworld, knowledge would be achieved on the route through darkness into light. Knowledge was also to be achieved through engagement with the body – almost synonymous with darkness in Manichaen religion – and with love – a fundamental theme of *The Poem of the Right Angle*.

Le Corbusier and was fully aware that the cult of light'[15] would clearly play a key role in the creation of ascetic order that he so desired:

> Imagine the results of the Law of Ripolin. Every citizen is required to replace his hangings, his damasks, his wall-papers, his stencils, with a plain coat of white ripolin. His home is made clean. There are no more dirty, dark corners. Everything is shown as it is. Then comes inner cleanness . . . When you are surrounded with shadows and dark corners you are at home only as far as the hazy edges of the darkness your eye cannot penetrate. You are not master in your own house. Once you have put ripolin on your walls you will be master of yourself. And you will want to be precise, to be accurate, to think clearly.[16]

Seeing clearly is a theme that repeats and repeats in Le Corbusier's work – the lighting for the Assembly at Chandigarh would, for example allow the members '*To see clearly*, to decide world affairs and to take advantage of the optimism of the sun's rays'.[17] Indeed, slippages of meaning between light and knowledge occur frequently in Le Corbusier's work.[18]

3.2   Windows

With a series of little sketches Le Corbusier demonstrated 'the history of architecture by the history of windows throughout the ages'[19] which he described as a 'struggle for light', almost as though the evolution of humankind could be expressed through the form of its fenestration.[20] His history concludes with the apogee of civilization, the horizontal window, one of his five points of a new architecture and one of the four Corbusian window types that will be discussed here; the pan de verre, the brise soleil and the ondulatoire is discussed later.

Le Corbusier wrote of the function of windows in *Towards a New Architecture*:

> Windows serve to admit light, 'a little, much, or not at all,' and to see outside. There are windows in sleeping cars which close hermetically or can be opened at will; there are the great windows of modern cafés which close hermetically or can be entirely opened by means of a handle which causes them to disappear below ground; there are the windows in dining cars which have little louvers opening to admit air 'a little, much or not at all,' there is modern plate glass which has replaced bottle glass and small panes; there are roll shutters which can be lowered gradually and will keep out the light at will according to the space of their slats.[21]

If a clear span of glass is needed for maximum enjoyment of views, the paraphernalia associated with opening lights can be both cumbersome and obstructive. This may be why Le Corbusier was not happy to allow a normal window to act simultaneously as both light and ventilator: 'a window I made for lighting, not for ventilation'.[22]

3.2.1 Horizontal windows

Le Corbusier was adamant about the benefits of the horizontal window in terms of lighting.[23] Benton writes that: 'The 2.50 metre standard unit which developed during the 1920s was a unit of proportioning, but it was also flexible.[24] Any kind of opening or fixed form could be adopted, whether pivoting on a central point, or side hung or sliding. Minor articulations to accommodate internal partitions need not disrupt the window'.[25] In his opinion the horizontal windows of the Villa Cook (1927) were in reality 'far from being standardized sliding windows, they include four categories: fixed, sliding, casement and centrally hung'.[26] They were constructed out of oak, the sliding windows had bronze runners and their casements, bronze fittings. The drainage holes and pipes to catch condensation that appear so prominently in the La Roche Jeanneret and subsequent houses were here forgotten, meaning that water dripped onto the interior window ledges.[27] No matter who the housing was for the same window type should be used.[28] Apparently, Le Corbusier a model to be produced by Saint Gobain for his villas,[29] but for such schemes as the Ozenfant studio the fenestration had to be made by hand to look mass produced.[30] Anxious to reduce the cost of creating window frames with moving parts,[31] Le Corbusier expended much effort on window refinement, on reducing their complexity and on making them easier to build.[32] 'I have built many of these "ribbon windows", my attention has been drawn to the sills that still do not seem frank to me, to these lintels that still seem expensive to me . . . And further still, the window is the most expensive organ of a house. In addition to its frame, there is the finish all around, very expensive'.[33]

In Ford's opinion Le Corbusier's use of the sliding wood window at the Villa Savoye was a 'curious one' (Figure 3.2).[34] Observing that most of Le Corbusier's contemporaries chose to use steel frames as these were better suited to the creation of simple, seemingly flat, curtains of glass,[35] Ford suggests that Le Corbusier favoured the use of timber at the Villa Savoye as the 'recessed notch at the head, the projecting sill, and the two planes of the sliding window make it possible to see the wall as a series of parallel planes'.[36] He draws upon Colin Rowe's work on the spatial organization of Le Corbusier's buildings to justify his argument that Le Corbusier envisaged space 'as a series of parallel surfaces receding into space'. Richard Weston makes a point that is not dissimilar. In his opinion, the windows of the early villas were designed 'To present the bounding surfaces as "stretched planes" and not gravity bound supporting walls'. Further, window frames were placed at the outer edge of openings so that the glass would appear to be part of a continuous surface.[37] Le Corbusier himself observed that:

> To evoke attention, to occupy space powerfully, a surface of perfect form was necessary first, followed by the exaltation of the flatness of that surface by the addition of a few projections or holes creating a back and forth movement. Then, by the opening of windows (the holes made by windows are one of the essential elements of the reading of an architectural work), by the opening of windows an important play of secondary surfaces is begun, releasing rhythms, dimensions, tempos of architecture inside the house and outside.[38]

Figure 3.2 Sliding wooden window, Villa Savoye (1930)

One of the overriding themes of Le Corbusier's concern with fenestration certainly does seem to have been to find glazing systems that enhanced rather than interfered with the regulating lines governing the proportions of his façades.[39] Occasionally, as Rowe has observed, glass would be used for a façade, not because of its translucent capabilities, but for its 'planar qualities'.[40] An example of this is the north elevation of the Carpenter Centre where, in Curtis's opinion, conscious that the glass would appear as a reflective surface, Le Corbusier designed the whole elevation almost as a skin.[41]

The sliding window was to leave its flimsy beginnings behind in the Unité Marseilles, where it appears at full height, for example giving access to the balcony of the café (Figure 0.3). Here one light remains fixed, without seeming to interfere significantly with the inside–outside flow of space. The glass is not set centrally within the frame. It is set closer to the outside skin than the inner leaf, encouraging still that sense of exterior planarity valued so much in Le Corbusier's earlier schemes.

3.2.2 Glass walls (pan de verre)

During the 1920s Le Corbusier's aim seems largely to have been the simple one of letting as much natural light into his buildings as possible. Yvonne, his wife, complained bitterly of the amount of glass in their apartment at 24 Rue Nungesser et Coli – 'all this light is killing me!'[42] she exclaimed; complaints that he must have taken to heart, as he later observed that his first thoughts on sun shading had come to him in the apartment 'and with good reason!'[43] Le Corbusier's drive for maximum light was facilitated by his brief love affair with air conditioning. In the wry words of John Summerson: 'Le Corbusier is the great apostle of fresh air, so what does he do but advocate that (in certain cases) all windows shall be hermetically sealed – so that mechanically freshened air can be pumped in'.[44] His flawed vision of *respiration exacte*[45] facilitated the development of yet another favourite Corbusian conception, the *pan de verre*, glass wall, glass section or window wall (depending on the translation) giving almost unlimited access to light.

Around 1933 Le Corbusier began experimenting with the use of large moving panels, precursors of the brise soleil, on the façades of his buildings – horizontal louvres, for example, cross the main façades of the Plan Macia for Barcelona (1933). Pivoting panels were also used on the exterior of a projected Lotissement in that same city.[46] By the third volume of the *Oeuvre Complète* Le Corbusier was already admitting to the 'problem'[47] of the transparent envelope in the creation of housing and that 'the hour of doom' was fast approaching for the 'curtain wall',[48] not only because of overheating, but because of his burgeoning desire to give each individual apartment a garden of its own.[49]

3.2.3 Brise soleil

As was often the case, when faced with a problem Le Corbusier turned to the past for inspiration. He found the solution to his overheated façades in the 'loggia which is really a brise soleil, a portico, such as Socrates advocated, which allows the inhabitants of the house to savour the good things in which a Bountiful God dispenses to men', beneficial in that it gave coolness in summer and warmth in winter.[50] It 'was created, from the beginning in order to bring about the "inside–outside" contact between dwelling and nature'.[51] In housing projects such as the Unité, it gave vertical expression to the cellular arrangement within (Figure 3.3). Banham observed that 'however desperate its motivations' the brise soleil were 'one of his most masterly inventions'.[52] For Charles Correa, however,

Figure 3.3
Brise soleil, Unité,
Marseilles Michelet (1952)

they were 'really great dust-catching, pigeon-infested contrivances, which gather heat all day and then radiate it back into the building at night, causing indescribable anguish to the occupants'.[53]

'Positioned according to the sun' the brise soleil would, according to Le Corbusier, help 'to bring rule into architecture'.[54] Apropos of ruminations over whether elements of the brise soleil itself should be mobile he concluded that 'The brise soleil must not be a mechanism but an organ in an organism', responding itself to the sun.[55] In remaining static the brise soleil itself draws attention to its movements. Indeed, if you spend several days in the Unité Marseilles you swiftly become acutely aware of the passage of sunlight, marking time, from one long side of the building to another at around noon. Indeed, it seems particularly apposite that Le Corbusier should have started out, like his father, as a decorator of watches.[56]

Le Corbusier was very particular that the term 'brise soleil' should be used 'not "baffle" which means nothing'. He added enigmatically: 'All modern architecture has a mission to occupy itself with the sun. Brise soleil is therefore the most correct term'.[57] Just why this might be the case is not clear, 'brise' being quite a strong word to do with shattering, breaking or crushing:

> The Earth and Sun dance
> the dance of four seasons
> the dance of the year
> the dance of the twenty
> -four hour day
> the summit and chasm of
> solstice
> the plain of equinox
> The solar clock and
> calendar have given
> architecture the "sun-breaker"
> placed before the glass surfaces
> of modern buildings. An
> architectural symphony[58]

These words from *The Poem of the Right Angle* confirm that, like the horizon line in his diagram of the 24-hour day (see Figure 1.8), the brise soleil was a place where sun met shadow, in Le Corbusier's terms a site of great significance.

Considerable care was taken with the design of the Corbusian brise soleil, the associated glazing and the resultant lighting, as can be seen from the multitude of drawings prepared for the 'loggia' of the Unités at Marseilles and Nantes-Rezé (1952–3).[59] It is significant that this is one of the few details of the latter building that Le Corbusier draws attention to in the *Oeuvre Complète*.[60] As each Unité was subject to individual financial constraints – the budget for Marseilles Michelet was, for example, lavish compared to that of Firminy – such details were rarely transplanted wholesale from one scheme to another.[61] Variations on the same theme feature at La Tourette (Figure 3.4) and the Maison du Brésel, among others.

The brise soleil appears at its most sophisticated on the Carpenter Centre (Figure 3.5), changing in accordance with the orientation of the façade and its curvature.[62] It was not used arbitrarily as decoration, only appearing where it was needed; for example, on the Chancellerie of project for French embassy in Brazil where it was utilized solely on the northern, hot, side of the circular building.[63]

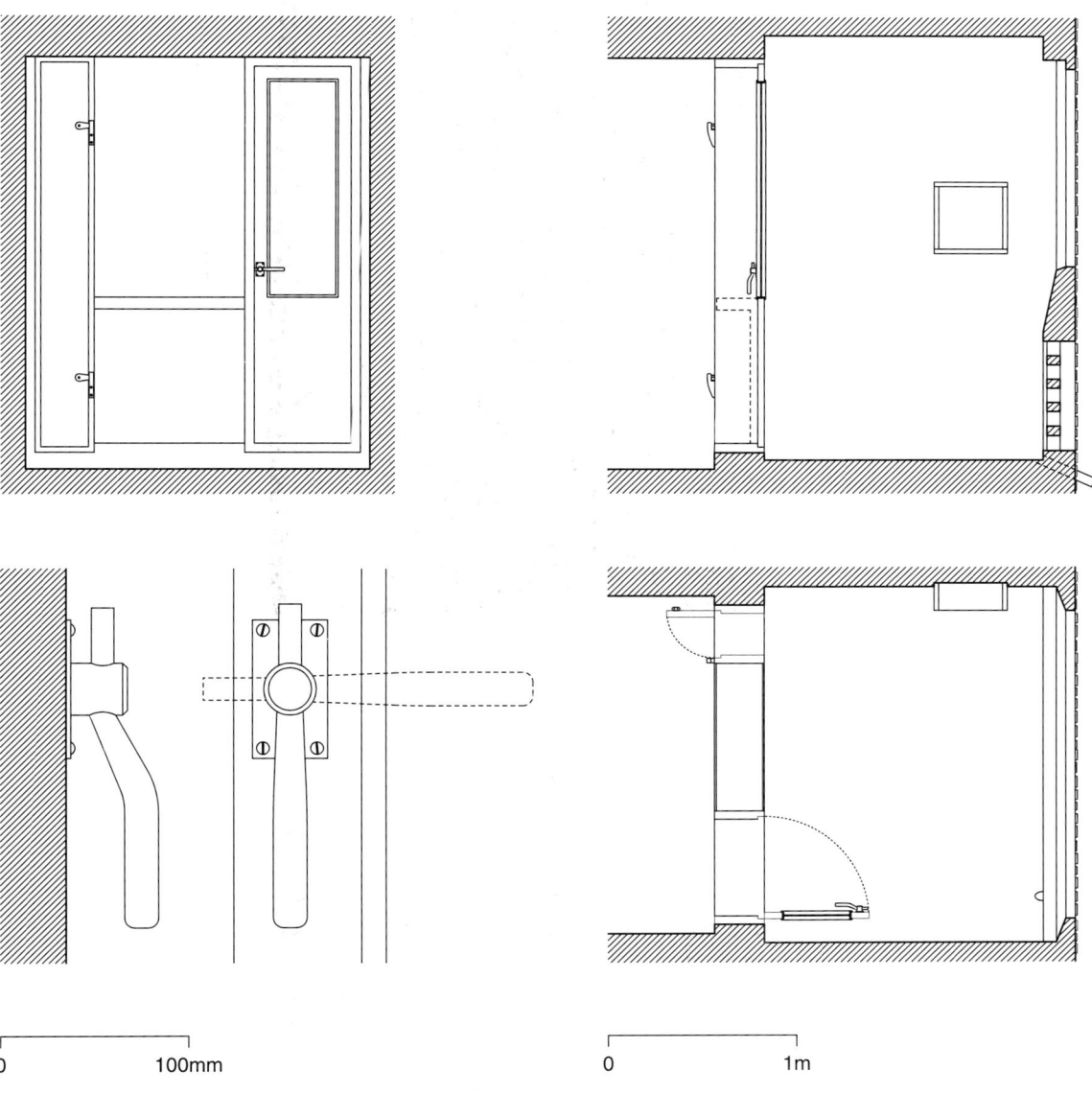

0   100mm

0   1m

Figure 3.4   Cell, La Tourette (1959)

Figure 3.5 Brise soleil, Carpenter Centre, Boston, USA (1963)

3.2.4 Ondulatoires

The ondulatoire, the undulatory glass surface,[64] first made its appearance at La Tourette (Figure 3.6). Le Corbusier wrote that here 'In the garden-court of the cloister, the fenestration is composed of large concrete

Figure 3.6 Ondulatoire, La Tourette (1959)

elements reaching from floor to ceiling perforated with glazed areas and separated from one another by "ventilators"; vertical slits covered by metal mosquito netting and furnished with a pivoting shutter'.[65] In 1956 Le Corbusier asked Iannis Xenakis, a young engineer and composer, to apply the Modulor proportional system to vertical struts of the glazing to make 'proportion, time and space . . . music'.[66] Xenakis describes their development in lengthy technical detail in an essay on the monastery in Volume XXVIII of the Garland series: 'I found out the vertigo of combinatorics in architectural elements, after having experimented with them in music . . .'.[67] A similar system was utilized at, among others, the Assembly of Chandigarh, the Maison des Jeunes at Firminy, the Maison du Brésel, and the Carpenter Centre where, as Curtis observes, 'especially on a curved plane, the ondulatoires allow a direct experience of their rhythm even to the static observer'.[68] I discuss elsewhere the subliminal messages of harmony gleaned through the experience of walking across a Modulor pavement. In my opinion, the ondulatoires would perform a similar function.

Le Corbusier wrote disingenuously that the ondulatoire was invented to save money as the glass could be set directly into frames of concrete.[69] His hostility to window frames is readily apparent in schemes such as La Tourette where concrete and glass are married directly together, expressing an extreme 'poverty'.[70] The basic detail could be reused, but its 'form and biology' needed rethinking in each new situation. A quote from the Builders Specification for the Carpenter Centre reveals exactly what it meant to build such a frameless window.

b) Glazing into concrete and in aluminium jambs –
   1) Prime faces of concrete rabbet with Pecora p-53 primer. Surfaces shall be clean and dry before application.
   2) Set inside and outside wedge shaped neoprene shims, 3" long, approximately 18"o.c. If glass is less than 18" provide two spacers.
   3) Set glass in reglet. Provide 80 durometer setting locks at quarter points.
   4) Insert neoprene spacers between glass face and neoprene shims specified above taking care to centre glass in reglet. Spacers and shims shall be 40 to 50 durameter.
   5) Fill rabbet with butyl caulking compound BC 158 as manufactured by Pecora as shown.
   6) Face exterior with head of polysulfide sealant, sythacaulk, GC-5, gray, non sagging, soft curing, as manufactured by Pecora.[71]

Clearly the provision of such a window was not quite the simple exercise it purported to be.

Since the ondulatoire could not be opened to allow for ventilation, 'aerateurs', opening slots, were provided to allow the ingress of fresh air and protection from insects – an 'Etude d'aérateur' gives an insight into the intricacies of its development[72] as do working drawings for La Tourette (Figure 3.7). The aerateur came in a variety of forms and was not solely used with the ondulatoire. At the Carpenter Centre, because of

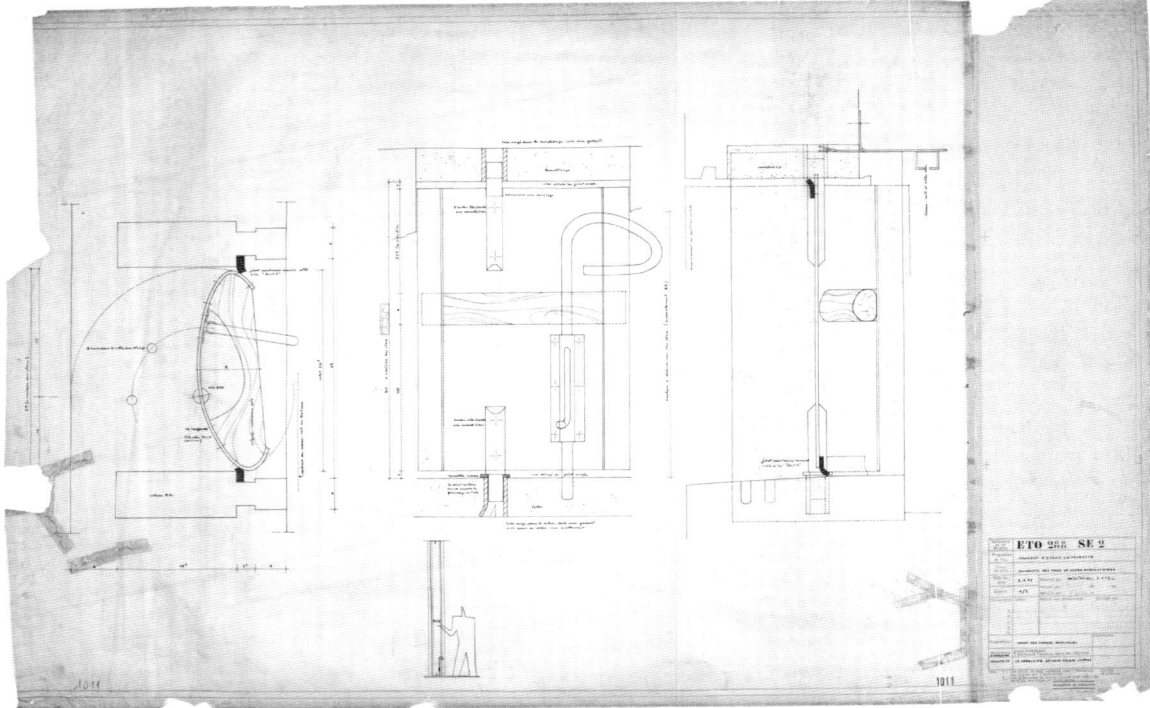

Figure 3.7 Aerateur, La Tourette (1959), FLC 1011

the climate and the nature of local craftsmanship, it was to be made of wood with concrete struts on either side.[73] Apparently Le Corbusier took exception to initial designs completed by an American firm: 'The building is not supposed to have the qualities of an automobile! All those rubber luxuries will be eaten away by dust, fly shit, etc . . .'[74]

3.3 Rooflights

Le Corbusier conceived different rooflights for different purposes. While some were designed with the simple purpose of drawing light into the heart of the building, others were more dramatic, enlisted to frame views of the sky or borrow a shaft of light from the sun.

The early rooflights are often shockingly raw in detail. At the Bestegui apartment, for example, a panel of glass was set into the roof on the same level as the lawn. Le Corbusier called it 'la dalle de verre', glass paving stone, as such it must have contributed to the unnerving feeling of an already surreal design (Figure 3.8).[75] He referred to the 'delicacy' of such details and rightly so, as they must have leaked copiously.

At a pragmatic level Le Corbusier often inserted basic clerestory windows to provide light and ventilation at ceiling height; for example, above

Figure 3.8 De Bestegui apartment, roof garden. Photo from *Oeuvre Complète*

the bar in the Maison du Brésel, or in the ground floor lavatory of the
Pavillon Suisse or the recesses of Jaoul Maison B. These were not
designed to be seen. Here light from the clerestory bounces off the wall
and then is reflected down into the space below, providing a functional
level of lighting in the deeper recesses of the plan.

Certain rooflights seem to have been designed to frame a view of the
sky. In the third level of the curved studios of the Carpenter Centre a circular void frames a 'pure' circle of blue. The interior of its drum is painted
red which as Curtis states 'filters a slightly eery light into the interior'. He
notes that a similar effect is achieved in two fourth floor seminar rooms.
One is painted black and has a small square rooflight lined in green.
The other seminar room is painted white and has a rectangular skylight,
lined in red, set diagonally in the yellow ceiling of the room itself. Curtis
writes that 'the whole becomes a study in the torsional effects of different
coloured surfaces'.[76] In terms of the Le Corbusier's symbolism of colour,
the two rooms would seem to be in direct opposition to one another. In
either case the sky is enhanced as a focus for reflection.

When, to accommodate a tree, Le Corbusier cut out a circle in the
roof of the terrace of the Pavillon Esprit Nouveau, he created another
form of rooflight, albeit open to the elements. At the Shodhan house
an oval hole in the lower slab is echoed by a hole in the parasol roof
above. Curtis writes that 'the sky is glimpsed through both as through
a magnifying lense'.[77] The same forms can be found in the pool in the
garden – a similarity which, as Curtis suggests 'brings the exterior closer'.

Such visual 'puns' are a characteristic of Le Corbusier's architecture, adding greatly to its spatial and narrative complexity.

In a further variety of rooflight the sky is obscured from view and is clearly not a priority. It is, for example, extremely difficult to see the sky through the 'Mitrailette' rooflights over the sacristy at La Tourette (Figure 3.9). Le Corbusier reproduced two pages from a book of images that his client Trouin made to evoke his vision of the Basilica in the section on La Sainte Baume in the *Oeuvre Complète*.[78] In it Trouin included a copy of a sketch that Le Corbusier had drawn of Hadrian's Villa in 1910. Le Corbusier's original annotations to these drawings indicate the presence of what he called 'a mysterious hole' cut into the rock. It seems that he was interested in the way that the sunlight appeared to dazzling effect in the deepest recesses of the vault, an effect that he attempted to recreate in several of his buildings.

Figure 3.9
'Mitraillette' rooflights over the sacristy La Tourette (1959)

Figure 3.10 Interior of pink/red tower over chapel at Notre-Dame du Haut, Ronchamp (1955)

Le Corbusier describes the lighting in the towers of Ronchamp as 'very special' – I would suggest because of a link between light and sound, erotic and spiritual revelation (Figure 3.10).[79] The notion that the Virgin was in some way impregnated through her ear, by the words of God, was celebrated by several medieval poets.[80] Le Corbusier may well be alluding to this intriguing admixture of light and sound. Certainly he believed profoundly in the power of musical harmony to bring us closer to the divine. Through its earlike form, the tower acts as a receiver of sound. The word of God enters Mary's body in the form of light – indeed, one of the towers is lined in red to reinforce the bodily theme. Simultaneously ear and vagina, open to spiritual or erotic connotations.

Highly directional rooflights would play a pivotal role in the spatial composition of La Tourette, as Colin Rowe has observed of 'those three, twisting, writhing, and even agonized light sources' that illuminate the Chapel of the Holy Sacrament (Figure 3.11) that 'cause a quite independent and equally powerful moment of convolution'.[81] With memorable imagery Rowe writes of the way that the cannons 'seem to quiver like the relics of a highly excruciating martyrdom'; as such they invite a visceral response in the manner described in the last chapter.[82]

Just as the brise soleil would mark the passage of the sun through the day, Le Corbusier was interested in using his sacred architecture

Figure 3.11 Rooflights over the Chapel of the Holy Sacrament, La Tourette (1959)

as a calendar, marking key events of the religious year through light. The examples are numerous. Xenakis recalled that 'pentagonal prisms of concrete' were set into the terraced roof of the sacristy of La Tourette 'tilted in such a way as to let the sun at the equinoxes pass into the principal nave by way of a slit in the church's concrete wall along the length of the sacristy'.[83] He added that 'There, Le Corbusier added a final touch by imagining, beneath this slit, a slightly inclined plane, like and invitation to the light. Thus was the church joined to the cosmos like pyramids and other sacred edifices'.[84]

Le Corbusier also intended to introduce a small funnel into the roof of the church of Saint Pierre, Firminy, positioned so that it would focus a shaft of light onto the altar on Easter morning.[85] Such games were not confined to specifically sacred space. Le Corbusier himself wrote of the ceiling of the Assembly Hall at Chandigarh that it had been 'designed to reflect the summer sun, to receive the winter sun and to reflect the sun of the equinoxes onto the interior surfaces of the hyperboloid'.[86]

While cosmological considerations were clearly at the forefront of Le Corbusier's thought, practicality was still an issue. Xenakis made a study of the Church at La Tourette and, using a light meter, discovered that it would be too dark. This realization led Le Corbusier to create the vertical slit in the north-east corner of the church and a 'partial slit' between the ceiling and walls of the nave. They also went through a number of iterations in solving the problem of glare in the chair stalls.[87]

3.4   Reflection

The idea of reflection ties in with Le Corbusier's interest in oppositions. Reflection provides an important means of accessing light, but it also creates possibilities for spatial games, in the early houses achieved by a rather literal use of mirror, for example the slice of mirror that appears beneath the curve of the ramp at the Villa La Roche. This reflects the curve of the ramp above, making it appear as a complete half circle.[88] A similar effect would be achieved with the cupboards of Villa Church which, because of the mirror set around the adjoining window, appear to sweep past it (Figure 3.12).[89] Flanked by cupboard doors of aluminium the overall effect would have been one of shimmering and light, with some of the flickering sense of mystery and transparency inherent in his Purist paintings.

The reflective qualities of water were also ripe for exploitation by Le Corbusier. He wrote of the pilotis for the League of Nations being 'multiplied by their reflection'.[90] At the other end of his career the pools at Chandigarh were designed specifically with reflection in mind.[91] Yet Le Corbusier did not limit himself to the use of real water to achieve

Figure 3.12   Interior of Villa Church (1929)

the subtle and varied lighting effects associated with reflection. The floor of the entrance hall of the Assembly building would be polished, reflecting and doubling the long lines of pilotis, the effect being that of a forest or some ancient temple.[92] The highly polished slate floors that occur in a number of his later schemes serve a very similar purpose. The floor of the altar of the Church of La Tourette (Figure 3.13) is aqueous in the extreme as is the floor of its contemporary, the Maison du Brésel discussed in Chapter 7.

Le Corbusier's one-time client, Charles de Bestegui, did not like electric light, desiring only to have candles in his home because he believed they gave off 'living light'.[93] It seems to me that there is a similar distinction in Le Corbusier's work. Daylight is living light. Artificial light is not, and therefore needs rather different treatment. Although within the Basilica of La Sainte Baume 'electric light' would play 'a symphony of shadow, of half-light and of light which could be extraordinary',[94]

Figure 3.13
Floor of the Church at La Tourette (1959)

electric light would not suffice at the altar, which would itself, according to Le Corbusier, be 'lit by the rays of the sun guided by mirrors' in a manner learnt from the ancient Egyptians.[95] He and Trouin would go to great lengths to make sure that real sunlight fell here on the altar, presumably because of its symbolic significance. Additionally, Le Corbusier took a great deal of care with the electric lighting of his schemes, electricity itself having its own unique place in the symbolism of his work.

3.5   Artificial lighting

Reflection also played an important part in Le Corbusier's approach to artificial lighting[96] – see for example a lighting drawing for the Pavillon des Temps Nouveaux, Paris 1937 (Figure 3.14).[97] Banham has noted how, by 1930, with the design of the Villa Savoye, Le Corbusier had started to use the ceiling as a reflecting service, with tubular lamps hung

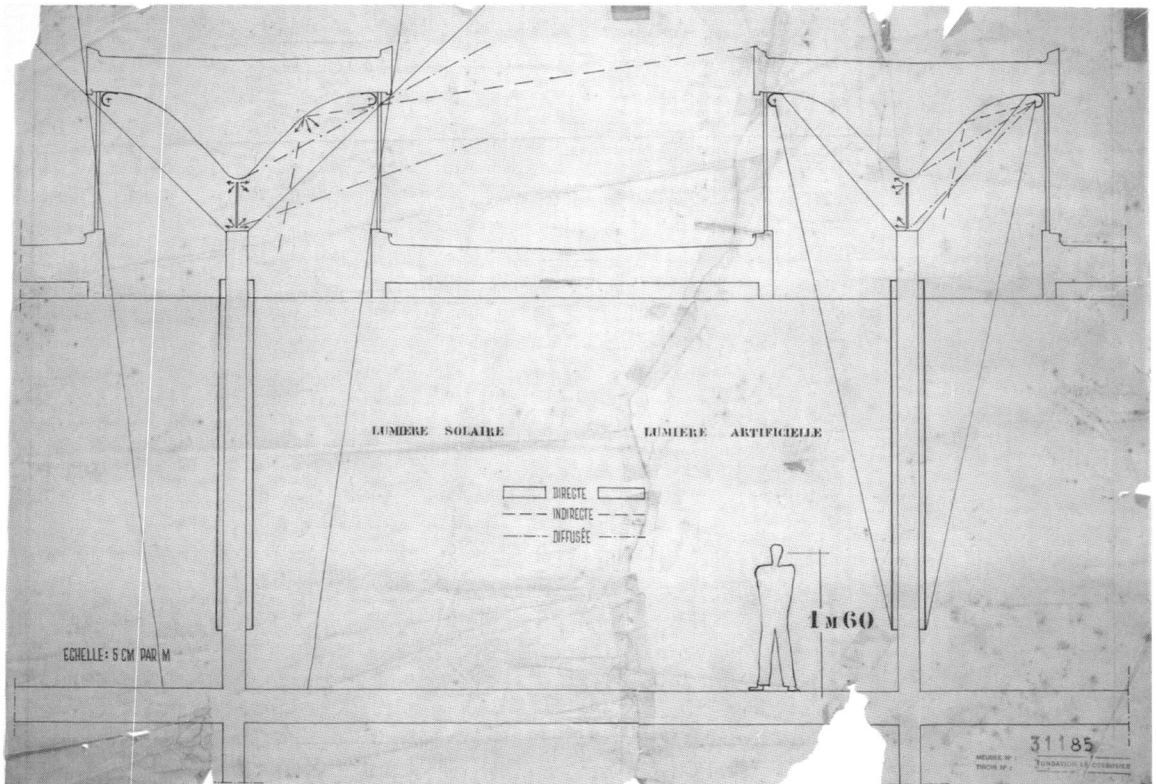

Figure 3.14   Lighting drawing for Pavillon des Temps Nouveau (1937), FLC 31185

below in an inverted trough in 'a condition analogous to his intentions in daylighting – what use is a window, if not to light the walls?'[98] At the other end of his career the lighting system for the Carpenter Centre was similarly designed to accentuate the purity of its structure. Building on the same principles used at the Villa Savoye, the underside of its floors were to be painted white and used as a reflector. These too were to be lit by a trough, this time discontinuous.[99]

Le Corbusier maintained a fondness for uplighters throughout his career.[100] Such lighting makes a space feel cavernous and atmospheric and would therefore be particularly effective in the vaulted houses. Uplighters were also often used at the ground piloti level, making the building above appear to be floating on a cushion of light, as at the Pavillon Suisse.[101] Their use in the exterior chapel at Ronchamp would contribute to its mystique and to its drama when seen from a distance at night.[102] 'Fosses pour projecteurs', trenches for lighting, were created at the feet of the piloti of the Unité Marseilles to light up the cavernous undercroft (Figure 3.15). They add greatly to the sensation of mystery anticipated in a photo of an early model of the scheme (Figure 3.16).[103] The pilotis disappear beneath the glowing glass panels hinting at the presence of a possible underworld.

Immense care was taken with the design of the light fittings for schemes such the Pavillon Suisse and the Unité. Drawings show the evolution of extremely totemic, curved metal luminaires, linear in elevation but highly sculpted in section, for the Marseilles Unité (Figure 3.17).[104] It seems that 'off the peg' solutions were very rarely used although an 'Etude de lampe' (1956) in Volume XXVIII of the Garland Series

Figure 3.15 Lights in hall at base of pilotis, Unité, Marseilles Michelet (1952)

Figure 3.16 Photo of model of Unité, Marseilles Michelet (1952) from Le Corbus-ier, Special Edition L'Homme et L'Architecture, 12–13 (1947), p. 5

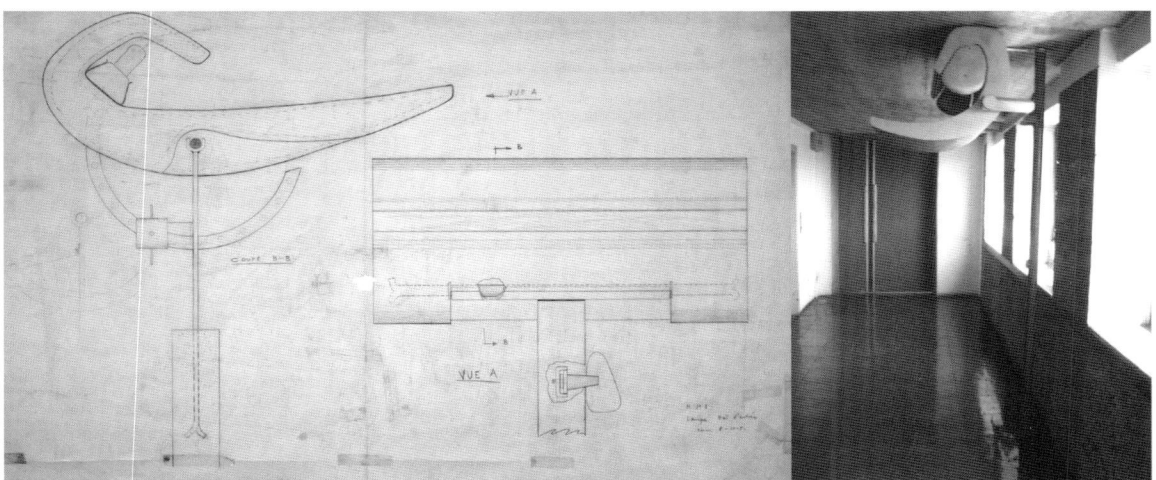

Figure 3.17 Lamps, Unité, Marseilles, Michelet (1952), FLC 29271

suggests the development of a whole series of lamp types.[105] Like Le Corbusier's handles, handrails and other fixings the lights were very often organic in form, smooth metal curves that cup the light, reminiscent of the hands of Icône in Le Corbusier's paintings of that name (see Figure 2.4).[106]

Particular care was taken with lighting at the Cabanon where the wall-mounted lights have a cover that can be rotated to direct the light upwards or downwards, in its form a reminder of his sign of the 24-hour day. The table is lit by a lamp of Le Corbusier's own fabrication, made from a frame that once held bombs to be dropped from an aircraft and found by Le Corbusier on the beach below the house.[107] Sheathed in paper, he would indubitably have enjoyed the significance of reusing a machine of death as a means of illumination (Figure 3.18).

One element of Le Corbusier's architecture that has always struck me as particularly curious are the wall-mounted light fittings which consist of a piece of metal tubing, in the region of a metre long, projecting stiffly at right angles out of the wall. A socket is fixed at the end of the tube containing one rather bare and lonely looking bulb. This detail occurs in some of the early buildings, for example, over the ramp of the Villa La Roche (Figure 3.19) and, more significantly, above the dining table in his own home at 24 Rue Nungesser et Coli (Figure 3.20). It is a very strange detail which could be justified by one of two motivations – the

Figure 3.18 Lamps in the Cabanon (1950)

Figure 3.19
Ramp through gallery of
Villa La Roche (1925)

first a very strong desire in Le Corbusier to retain the untouched integrity
of the vault above – the second an interest in the shadows cast by
such a thing. This type of light fitting occurs in close proximity to major
windows (there is another one in the gallery of the Maison La Roche).[108]
As a result, light cast upon the tubular fitting projects a linear shadow
that tracks across the wall at different times of day like an enormous
sun dial. Certainly, as Banham has noted, the appearance of ceiling or
wall-mounted naked bulbs is so frequent in the work of Le Corbusier,
that 'one is forced to suppose that this nudism of the light-source must
have been programmatic'.[109]

Figure 3.20
Dining table, penthouse,
24 Rue Nungesser et Coli
(1934)

3.6 Conclusion

The experience of varied forms of light would form an integral part of the initiatory route, to be discussed more fully in Chapter 5. 'The rhythm of the controlled light' would instil the body with a sense of harmonious proportion, while at the same time, acting as a metaphor for a journey into knowledge. In Le Corbusier's early schemes he concerned himself with the moral and hygienic benefits of providing maximum light, leading to spaces the creation of that are almost abusive in their levels of lux. However, in his later work his approach to natural lighting became more subtle allowing him to combine the practical with the philosophical in a rather more convincing way.

Notes

[1] Le Corbusier, *Textes et dessins pour Ronchamp* (Paris: Forces Vives, 1965).

[2] Le Corbusier, *The Chapel at Ronchamp* (London: Architectural Press, 1957), p. 47.

[3] Le Corbusier, *Journey to the East* (Cambridge MA: MIT, 1987), p. 183. Originally published in 1966.

[4] F. Samuel, *Le Corbusier: Architect and Feminist* (London: Wiley Academy, 2004), pp. 107–8. For further information on this subject see F. Samuel, 'Orphism in the work of Le Corbusier with particular reference to his unbuilt scheme for a basilica and city at La Sainte Baume (1945–1959)' (unpublished PhD thesis, Cardiff, 2000), pp. 18–21 and p. 96. More recently and more extensively the issue of Masonry in the work of Le Corbusier has been explored by Jan Kenneth Birksted, ' "Beyond the clichés of the hand-books": Le Corbusier's architectural promenade', *The Journal of Architecture*, 11:1 (2006), pp. 55–132.

[5] H. Jonas, *The Gnostic Religion* (Boston, MA: Beacon Press, 1963), p. xvi. Originally published in 1958.

[6] Ibid.

[7] Letter Edouard Trouin to Le Corbusier 24 August 1960, FLC 13 01 186.

[8] 'Perret' Document with no FLC number found interleaved in E. Trouin [Louis Montalte pseud.], *La Basilique Universelle de la Paix et du Pardon/La Saint Baume* (Levallois Perret: Imprimerie Schneider, Fres et Mory, 1948), FLC 13 01 402.

[9] V. Spate, *Orphism: the Evolution of Non-figurative Painting in Paris in 1910–14* (Oxford: Clarendon, 1979), p. 63.

[10] Ibid., p .62.

[11] From introduction to Le Corbusier, *When the Cathedrals were White: A Journey to the Country of the Timid People* (New York: Reynal and Hitchcock, 1947), p. xvii. Originally published 1937.

[12] Ibid.

[13] M. Eliade, *Images and Symbols* (London: Harville Press, 1961), p. 53.

[14] Le Corbusier, *Oeuvre Complète Volume 5, 1946–1952* (Zurich: Les Editions d'Architecture, 1995), p. 25. Originally published in 1953. There are parallels in Henry Plummer's description of La Tourette. H. Plummer, 'Masters of Light, First Volume: Twentieth Century Pioneers', *Architecture and Urbanism Extra Edition* (November 2003), pp. 246–8. Mary McLeod has noted that for the regional syndicalists, a group with which Le Corbusier was involved, the Mediterranean sun represented the 'the essence of France's classical heritage; both rational thought and spiritual joy' represented by the sun god Apollo (also worshipped under the names Pan and Orpheus), whose role in Le Corbusier's work is highly significant. The sun god Apollo may have had additional significance for this reason. Mary McLeod, 'Urbanism and utopia: Le Corbusier from regional syndicalism to Vichy' (D.Phil thesis, Princeton, 1985), p. 245.

[15] Le Corbusier and P. Jeanneret, *Oeuvre Complète Volume 2, 1929–34* (Zurich: Les Editions d'Architecture, 1995), p. 121. Originally published in 1935.

[16] Le Corbusier, *The Decorative Art of Today* (London: Architectural Press, 1987), p. 188, originally published as Le Corbusier *L'Art décoratif d'aujourd'hui* (Paris: Éditions Crès, 1925).

[17] Le Corbusier, *Precisions on the Present State of Architecture and City Planning* (Cambridge, MA: MIT, 1991), p. 161.

[18] See T. Willmert, 'The ancient fire, the hearth of tradition: combustion and creation in Le Corbusier's studio residences', *arq*, 10, 1 (2006), pp. 57–78.

[19] Le Corbusier, *Precisions*, p. 53.

[20] Le Corbusier and Jeanneret, *Oeuvre Complète Volume 2*, p. 121.

[21] Le Corbusier, *Towards a New Architecture* (London: Architectural Press, 1982). Originally published as *Vers une Architecture* (Paris: Crès, 1923), p. 112. In the Villa Cook the more expensive plate glass was use for all the visible windows. Le Corbusier and Jeanneret even offered to pay the extra expense themselves when the client balked at the price. T. Benton, *The Villas of Le Corbusier* (London: Yale University Press, 1987), p. 158.

[22] Le Corbusier, *Precisions*, p. 54.

23 Le Corbusier and P. Jeanneret *Oeuvre Complète Volume 1, 1910–1929* (Zurich: Les Editions d'Architecture, 1995), p. 129. Originally published in 1937. See also Le Corbusier, *Precisions*, p. 55.

24 The problems that Le Corbusier had in evolving the windows into units of proportion are discussed in T. Benton, 'Pessac and Liège revisited: standards dimensions and failures', *Massilia*, 3 (2004), pp. 64–99.

25 Benton, *The Villas of Le Corbusier*, p. 12.

26 Ibid., p. 158.

27 Ibid.

28 Le Corbusier and Jeanneret, *Oeuvre Complète Volume 1*, p. 77.

29 Le Corbusier, *Precisions*, p. 95. See also Benton, *The Villas of Le Corbusier*, p. 12.

30 W. Curtis, *Le Corbusier: Ideas and Forms* (Oxford: Phaidon, 1986), p. 57.

31 Le Corbusier and Jeanneret, *Oeuvre Complète Volume 2*, p. 121.

32 See Benton, *The Villas of Le Corbusier*, p. 12 for a description of the continual problems experienced by Le Corbusier with the use of metal windows.

33 Le Corbusier, *Precisions*, p. 54.

34 E.R Ford, *The Details of Modern Architecture* (Cambridge, MA: MIT, 1990), p. 243.

35 Timber windows were posited for the Maison Planeix as a cost cutting measure which may explain their use at the Villa Savoye. Benton, *The Villas of Le Corbusier*, p. 134.

36 Ford, *The Details of Modern Architecture*, p. 241.

37 R. Weston, *Materials, Form and Architecture* (London: Laurence King, 2003), p. 163.

38 Le Corbusier, *Precisions*, p. 73.

39 Ibid.

40 C. Rowe, *The Mathematics of the Ideal Villa and Other Essays* (Cambridge, MA: MIT, 1976), p. 167.

41 E. Sekler and W. Curtis, *Le Corbusier at Work: The Genesis of the Carpenter Centre for the Visual Arts* (Cambridge, MA: MIT, 1978),p. 21.

42 C. Jencks, *Le Corbusier and the Tragic View of Architecture* (London: Allen Lane, 1973), p. 100.

43 Le Corbusier, *My Work* (London: Architectural Press: 1960), p. 107.

44 J. Summerson, *Heavenly Mansions* (New York: Norton, 1963), pp.190–1.

45 'The possibilities brought complementary solutions: inside the buildings is introduced the so called "exact airing", i.e. the circulation of clean fresh air, continually in movement and of normal temperature . . . ' Le Corbusier and Jeanneret, *Oeuvre Complète Volume 2*, p. 121.

46 Ibid., p. 199.

47 Le Corbusier and P. Jeanneret, *Oeuvre Complète Volume 3, 1934–38* (Zurich: Les Editions d'Architecture, 1995), p. 35 Originally published in 1938.

48 Le Corbusier, *Oeuvre Complète Volume 7, 1957–1965* (Zurich: Les Editions d'Architecture, 1995), p. 217. Originally published in 1965.

49 See D. Hawkes, *The Environmental Imagination* (London: Taylor and Francis, 2006) for a further discussion of Le Corbusier's approach to environmental issues.

50 Le Corbusier, *Oeuvre Complète Volume 5*, p. 95.

51 Le Corbusier, *Oeuvre Complète Volume 7*, p. 217.

52 R. Banham, *The Architecture of the Well-Tempered Environment* (London: Architectural Press, 1969), p. 158.

53 C. Correa, 'Chandigarh: the view from Benares' in H. Allen Brooks (ed.), *The Le Corbusier Archive, Volume XXII* (New York: Garland, 1983), pp. x.

54 Le Corbusier, *Oeuvre Complète Volume 5*, p. 95.

55 Le Corbusier, *Sketchbooks Volume 2* (London: Thames and Hudson, 1981), sketch 53.

56 I owe this observation to Inge Linder-Gaillard.

57 Sekler and Curtis, *Le Corbusier at Work*, p. 194.

58 Le Corbusier, *Le Poème de l'angle droit* (Paris: Editions Connivance, 1989), section B4, Mind. Originally published in 1955.

59 See for example H. Allen Brooks (ed.), *The Le Corbusier Archive, Volume XVI* (New York: Garland, 1983), p. 467. Hereafter referred to as Allen Brooks, *Archive*.

60 Le Corbusier, *Oeuvre Complète Volume 5*, p. 170.

[61] I am grateful to Tim Benton for his thoughts on this matter. Conversation with author, 9 December 2006.

[62] Letter 8 June 1960. Quoted in Sekler and Curtis, *Le Corbusier at Work*, p. 95.

[63] Le Corbusier, *Oeuvre Complète Volume 7*, p. 19.

[64] Ibid., p. 32.

[65] Ibid.

[66] Le Corbusier, *Modulor 2* (London: Faber, 1955), p. 321. Originally published as *Le Modulor II* (Paris: Editions d'Architecture d'Aujourd'hui, 1955).

[67] I. Xenakis, 'The Monastery of La Tourette' in H. Allen Brooks (ed.), *The Le Corbusier Archive, Volume XXVIII* (New York: Garland, 1983), pp. xi–xii.

[68] Le Corbusier, *Oeuvre Complète Volume 7*, p. 100.

[69] Ibid.

[70] Ibid., p. 53.

[71] Building Specification, section 12, p.7 in the possession of J.L. Sert quoted in Sekler and Curtis, *Le Corbusier at Work*, p. 203.

[72] See for example FLC 27982 in Allen Brooks, *Archive, Volume XXVIII*, p. 44.

[73] Sekler and Curtis, *Le Corbusier at Work*, p. 198.

[74] Letter Le Corbusier to Sert , 11.6.1961 quoted in Sekler and Curtis, *Le Corbusier at Work*, p. 196.

[75] Le Corbusier and Pierre Jeanneret, *Oeuvre Complète Volume 2*, p. 55.

[76] Seckler and Curtis, *Le Corbusier at Work*, p. 32.

[77] Curtis, *Le Corbusier: Ideas and Forms*, p. 210.

[78] Le Corbusier, *Oeuvre Complète Volume 5*, p. 30.

[79] Le Corbusier, *Oeuvre Complète Volume 6* (Zurich: Les Editions d'Architecture Zurich, 1976), p. 20.

[80] Gregory of Nyssa (d. 394) posited the idea that Mary conceived Jesus on hearing the words of the angel. M. Warner, *Alone of All her Sex: The Myth and Cult of the Virgin Mary* (London: 1976), p. 37.

[81] Rowe, *The Mathematics of the Ideal Villa*, p. 192.

[82] Ibid., p. 187.

[83] Xenakis, 'The Monastery of La Tourette', pp. xii.

[84] Ibid.

[85] J. Loach 'Church of Saint-Pierre, Firminy-Vert' in T. Benton (ed.), *Le Corbusier Architect of the Century* (London: Arts Council, 1987), p. 253, Owing to the shifting position of Easter day, this detail does not work in the scheme as realised. Author conversation with Yves Metthaud 26 April, 2007.

[86] Le Corbusier, *Oeuvre Complète Volume 7*, p. 91.

[87] Xenakis, 'The Monastery of La Tourette', pp .xii.

[88] Mirror was used to give the appearance of a continuous sweep of shiny timber cupboard doors in the living room of Ville d'Avray. Le Corbusier and Jeanneret *Oeuvre Complète Volume 1*, p. 203.

[89] Curtis, *Le Corbusier: Ideas and Forms*, figure 83.

[90] Le Corbusier, *Precisions*, p. 48.

[91] Le Corbusier, *Oeuvre Complète Volume 5*, p. 142.

[92] See image in Sekler and Curtis, *Le Corbusier at Work*, p. 252.

[93] Charles de Bestegui to Robert Baschet in *Plaisir de France*, March 1939 quoted in M. Tafuri, ' "Machine et mémoire": the city in the work of Le Corbusier', H. Allen Brooks (ed.), *The Le Corbusier Archive, Volume X*, (New York: Garland, 1983), p. xxxi. Stephen Sartorelli trans.

[94] Le Corbusier, *Oeuvre Complète Volume 5*, p. 25.

[95] H.F., 'Le Plateau Provencal de La Sainte Baume: abritera-t-il un jour une église rupestre?', *Le Monde*, 5 July 1948, p. 3.

[96] See Benton's detailed description of the lighting for the Villa La Roche. Benton, *The Villas of Le Corbusier*, p. 65.

[97] FLC 31185 in H. Allen Brooks (ed.), *The Le Corbusier Archive, Volume XIII* (New York: Garland, 1983), p. 552.

[98] R. Banham, *The Architecture of the Well-Tempered Environment* (London: Architectural Press, 1969), p. 151.

[99] Sekler and Curtis, *Le Corbusier at Work*, p. 184.

[100] Allen Brooks, *Archive, Volume XVI*, pp.105 and 107.

[101] FLC 15495 and FLC 15528 in Allen Brooks *Archive, Volume VIII*, pp. 245 and 260.

[102] See illustration in Le Corbusier, *The Chapel at Ronchamp* (London: Architectural Press, 1957), p. 49.

[103] See FLC 25280 in Allen Brooks, *Archive, Volume XVI*, p. 94.

[104] FLC 26367, 26369 in Allen Brooks *Archive, Volume XVII*, pp. 30–1 and FLC 27844, p. 337.

[105] FLC 2629 in Allen Brooks *Archive, Volume XXVIII*, pp. 49–53.

[106] Similar light fittings were proposed for the Sukhna Dam, Chandigarh. FLC 6354, Correa, 'Chandigarh: the view from Benares', p. 486.

[107] This story, like a number of other significant anecdotes, has been passed from word of mouth to the guides of the Roquebrune Office de Tourisme, October 2006.

[108] This light does not appear in early photos of the La Roche gallery, but Le Corbusier remained friends with Raoul La Roche for the rest of his life and presumably suggested this improvement to his home.

[109] Banham, *The Architecture of the Well-Tempered Environment*, p. 148.

Framing

4

I commissioned from you a 'frame for my collection'. You provided me with a 'poem of walls'.[1]

The idea of framing is absolutely central to Le Corbusier's design philosophy. Le Corbusier thought continually in terms of frames – frames to house people, frames to house views, frames to house his special collection, frames to store utilitarian things, frames to extend into the environment drawing the influence of nature within. These frames, often proportioned to the Modulor, might be solid, diaphanous or implied – 'A thought which reveals itself without word or sound, but solely by means of shapes which stand in a certain relationship to one another'.[2] For Le Corbusier the creation of frames gave him an opportunity to accentuate and celebrate his very particular view of space. In the opinion of Rowe 'the ability to charge depth with surface, to condense spatial concavities into plane, to drag to its most eloquent pitch, the dichotomy between the rotund and the flat is the absolutely distinguishing mark of Le Corbusier's later style'.[3] Detail would play an intrinsic role in such games of perception, the subtlest of nuances continually used to reinforce the presence or absence of spatial depth, of frames to house views, objects and indeed space.

4.1 Views

Le Corbusier's interest in the framing of views would receive extreme expression with his designs for the Bestegui apartment in Paris. The photographs in the *Oeuvre Complète* reveal a roof space, almost hermetically sealed from the panorama of Paris that surrounded it (Figure 2.22).

Here the Arc de Triomphe appears like an ornament on a bourgeois mantelshelf in a room carpeted in grass. Having been denied views of the city in the roof garden above the visitor would discover the whole drama of the city via a revolving periscope on the floor below.[4] Apparently the apartment had no electric lighting. Electricity was instead used to trundle lines of hedges back and forth, disclosing or restricting views accordingly. In a letter to another client, Madame Meyer, Le Corbusier revealed the type of experience he had had in mind 'by means of sliding screens one can cut oneself off completely . . . rather as in the paintings of Carpaccio . . . '.[5]

One of the most straightforward uses of the architectural frame is to pull the exterior environment into the confines of a building. Possibly the best known of all Le Corbusier's frames is that on the north-west façade of the Villa Savoye, the view that greets the visitor at the very end the ramped route to the rooftop (Figure 4.1). Here minimal detail around the opening diminishes the barrier between the space of the roof garden and the space beyond. Benton writes of two 'complementary' explanations for its existence.[6] Originally it formed the window of the master bedroom 'in one real sense, the heart of the house', but when, for economic reasons, this room was moved down a floor, the window remained providing the 'point of rest at the end of the promenade architecturale'. Benton observes that 'both meanings are superimposed and are "there" '.[7]

Of all Le Corbusier's window types the horizontal window is perhaps the most successful in bringing the environment into the interior of the building, as it gives access to the horizon in a long unbroken panorama, much as a person would experience it in the open air.[8] 'I see reflections

Figure 4.1 Window of solarium Villa Savoye (1930)

on the water, I see beautiful boats sail past, I see the Alps, framed as in a museum, panel by panel', wrote Le Corbusier of his own beleaguered entry for the League of Nations competition.[9]

Unlike the horizontal window, the square window provides one intense prospect – in the case of the 'baraque' adjoining the Cabanon, of the sea beyond. Here Le Corbusier could sit at his desk and think, staring at the horizon (Figure 4.2). The other Cabanon windows are similarly focused. Such a window is not about movement, it is about

Figure 4.2 Window of Le Corbusier's desk at the Cabanon (1950)

being static.[10] Le Corbusier had two other desks – the first in a tiny dark cellule, built to the same Modulor proportions as the Cabanon itself within the depths of his atelier at Rue de Sèvres, the second an enclosed box set within his studio at 24 Rue Nungesser et Coli, tucked in against a mansard of glass brick (Figure 4.3). In both of these he denied himself any view except that of his interior reality. A spirit of self-restraint governs the design of his Paris desks, one that does not extend itself to the Cabanon, built late in life, built for relaxation and built, presumably, when he felt that he had earned the view. Le Corbusier painted the backs of the shutters at the Cabanon so that, when they were closed, images of female divinities would be revealed in place of the view of the sea, each intimately connected in his mind with the other – the view, the water cherished within its containing niche.[11]

Figure 4.3
Le Corbusier's desk in penthouse, 24 Rue Nungesser et Coli (1934)

Movable partitions to save space appear in a number of Le Corbusier's housing schemes.[12] The Maison Loucheur would be transformed by day and by night with beds in the walls and by sliding panels that would open the parents' bed to the main room.[13] Other examples are the mobile partitions and hidden beds featured in the Petite Villa au bord du Lac Leman (1925)[14] and the 'mobile partition wall' that subdivides the children's bedroom of Unité.[15] Of particular note are the innumerable oak shutters, windows and doors in the Maisons Jaoul, particularly Maison B which is less boxy than A. Here each space can be transformed from a dark cocoon into being almost totally open – with various states in between – through the strategic use of moving timber parts (Figure 4.4).

The necessary corollary of the partition, or the plane, is the gap – another type of frame. The strategic use of the gap is absolutely characteristic of Le Corbusier's approach to detail. He always built gaps into his work where otherwise a less than happy joint would have occurred, for example at the junction between an orthogonal concrete balustrade and a circular column, as at the Mill Owners' Building and on the ramp up to entrances of the Maisons Jaoul. Perhaps his favourite trick was the use of the shadow gap, used primarily at the junction between exterior walls and floors, eliminating the need for skirtings in the process. While hiding the inevitable cracks that develop in such areas, the shadow gap, as used for example beneath the rubble wall of the Pavillon Suisse, makes the building appear to hover. On the roof of the Unité a simple concrete

Figure 4.4 Shutters in Maison Jaoul B (1955)

Figure 4.5
Concrete bead at ankle
height on roof of Unité,
Marseilles Michelet (1952)

bead confirms the horizontal whatever the fall of the flat roof beneath it
(Figure 4.5), providing a tidy and uniform datum level for games of proportion. At the Heidi Weber Haus in Zurich the enamel panels are fixed
to the steel structure with a shadow gap all around, again emphasis-
ing their independence from the structure as a whole. Where expansion
joints, to alleviate cracking, proved to be necessary – as they were across
the entire Unité block – they were celebrated both within and without.
Le Corbusier would always make a feature of such a detail rather than
hide it away (see Figure 0.1). On the Unité roof Le Corbusier expanded
the joint, lining it with a fillet of glass which accentuates, through contrast,
the beauty of the surrounding concrete and created a shimmering frame
for the view of the sea beyond.[16]

As dark paint would boldly outline the elements of his paintings,
shadow would boldly outline the elements of his architecture. However,
Le Corbusier would sometimes invert this relationship, picking out the

Figure 4.6   Stairwell Villa Savoye (1930). Photo from Le Corbusier's *Oeuvre Complète*

forms of his architecture in light instead of shadow. He enjoyed creating gaps around seemingly structural elements, allowing a halo of light to seep in at the edges, simultaneously refuting their load bearing capabilities. This can be seen most clearly around the stair well of the Villa Savoye (Figure 4.6) and between the roof and walls at Ronchamp where 'A horizontal crack of light 10 cm wide will amaze' (see Figure 2.16).[17]

4.2   Objects

The framing of objects within the home received a similar degree of attention. As part of the move towards ascetic simplicity, mentioned above, Le Corbusier wanted to cleanse the home of unsavoury nooks and crannies. In a similar way he railed against old forms of wardrobe and bureau 'that complicate our existence by preventing the rational organisation of households',[18] his ultimate aim being to liberate 'our spirit' from this 'hodgepodge of furniture'.[19] Creating a feeling of 'calm' within the home through the use of unified seating and storage solutions would become a central tenet of his design for interiors.[20] The new furniture equipment would leave 'a maximum of unencumbered space in every room, and only chairs and tables to fill it'.[21] Ever conscious of the passage of time he wrote: 'I have saved a considerable amount of space: one can move around easily; gestures are rapid and exact; storage automatic.

These are minutes gained, every day; precious minutes'.[22] He even went so far as to argue that his 'entirely new thesis in the matter of furnishing'[23] would save so much space that dwellings could become smaller, their rents decreased and cities reduced in size.[24]

Storage, for Le Corbusier, was anything but a dull subject. 'Try to imagine the new dwelling... Every object is stored as in a jewel case; some equipment comes forward on ball bearings, your clothing is spread out before your eyes, etc.'[25] Here is another example of the theatricality Le Corbusier applied to the most mundane of events. Your sock drawer would glide out to meet your hand. Objects 'appear'. Items of equipment 'come forward', as if by themselves, in a manner reminiscent of space age fantasy.

On the balcony of the Villa La Roche, flanking the main triple height hall, a wide shelf presents a working surface along the top of the unit which holds two rows of books (Figure 4.7). Usually, large and small books are stored on shelves of the same depth – here one shelf, intended for the storage of large books protrudes forward beyond the others, but remains flush with the overarching work surface above. The books are held in a De Stijl composition of projecting and receding planes, nurtured

Figure 4.7
Shelf library, Villa La
Roche (1925)

tenderly through working drawings,[26] simultaneously addressing issues of practicality and artistic aspiration.[27]

Central to Le Corbusier's conception of the new furniture equipment were 'Standard casiers, suitable to receive all domestic things'.[28] *Casier* means box, compartment, drawer – an intentionally ambiguous word, most usually used for pigeonholes. Although designed as types[29] the casiers themselves would be individually customized – 'sliding panels in sheet metal, in plywood, in marble, in plate glass, in aluminium etc.' – and would be installed allowing 'a taste for simplicity or opulence'.[30] In the 'Apartment for a young man' at the Brussels Exposition (1935) slate appeared on the interior of one of the casier doors, a convenient blackboard for a rendition of Le Corbusier's theories of the Radiant City (Figure 4.8).[31] Yet Arthur Rüegg writes of the casiers at the 1929 Salon d'Automne that 'Engineered like chemists' display cases, these units have so many screw holes in the sliding frames alone that the celebrated flexibility of the "equipment" was in truth practically nonexistent'.[32]

Figure 4.8
'Apartment for a young man' at the Brussels Exposition (1935)

Internal fixtures and fittings would often echo the buildings that enveloped them. Colin Rowe wrote of the table at the entrance of the Villa Savoye that 'floating in the space and cantilevered from its column' it was 'a miniature recapitulation of the idea of the house itself'.[33] Le Corbusier's Bat'a boutique (1935), was clearly conceived as a large casier, the showcases within it being boxes within a box.[34] At the Maison du Brésel the pigeonholes provide in miniature a version of the overall block itself, building and furniture conceived as one. In his pursuit of order Le Corbusier envisaged apartments slotting into the frames of his buildings, like a wine bottle into a rack or just as a hand would push the drawer of a filing cabinet into place (Figure 4.9)– their inhabitants, as Rowe wryly commented 'mildly idiosyncratic ingredients of bureaucratic existence'.[35]

Casiers would take a variety of configurations. They appear, for example, as partitions in the plans of buildings such as the Villa Stein de Monzie at Garches, 1927. Often they were amalgamated into low walls, dividing the otherwise free-flowing space, as in the bedroom on display at the Salon d'Automne 1929, which is separated from the bathroom.[36] Casiers would also house service elements, freestanding, for example in the hall of the Pavillon Suisse[37] or reconfigured into soundproofing party walls.[38] Additionally they could form part of the window wall as in Cité de Refuge where they would give it a sensation of depth.[39] They could also be set into masonry[40] as were 'les casiers encastrés', literally the embedded casiers of the Unité, Marseilles (Figure 4.2).[41]

Here, in an early study, Le Corbusier drew two inverted pyramids in the side wall of the brise soleil (Figure 4.11)[42] – these would evolve into the niches which would act as the 'tuning fork of proportion' for the building as a whole.[43] One such casier, in the form of the window, was captured at the base of the Unité. Entitled 'Le Modulor', it is in many ways the conceptual heart of the scheme[44] and is based on early studies made for his

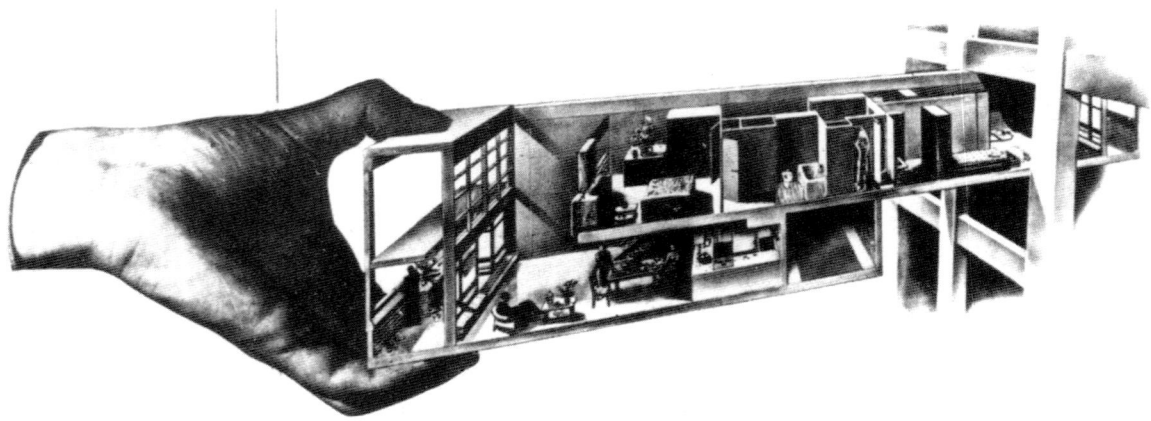

Figure 4.9   Unité apartment slotting into its frame

Figure 4.10
Embedded casier in side
of brise soleil, as used
today. Unité, Marseilles
Michelet (1952)

system of proportion (Figure 4.12 and 4.13).[45] Le Corbusier's interest in depth and relief would receive further expression in the embossed hiero-glyphs of the Unités. Indeed it seems quite possible that Le Corbusier favoured this relief technique, not only because it lent itself to the plas-tic qualities of concrete, but because it drew attention to the issue of space.

The niche, the embedded casier, often designed for the display of 'objects that provoke a poetic reaction' became a standard part of Le Corbusier's constructional vocabulary, the intention, I would suggest, to create a window on to another kind of reality. In *The Decorative Art of Today* Le Corbusier wrote with regret of the lack of art in the home. This he believed to be a 'collective fact with great social consequences'.[46] Art was 'a radium, a potential of the mind, a concentrated power'.[47] Like the buildings of the Radiant City, at a small scale each individual work of art had the power to 'radiate and evoke poetic emotion'.[48] They would

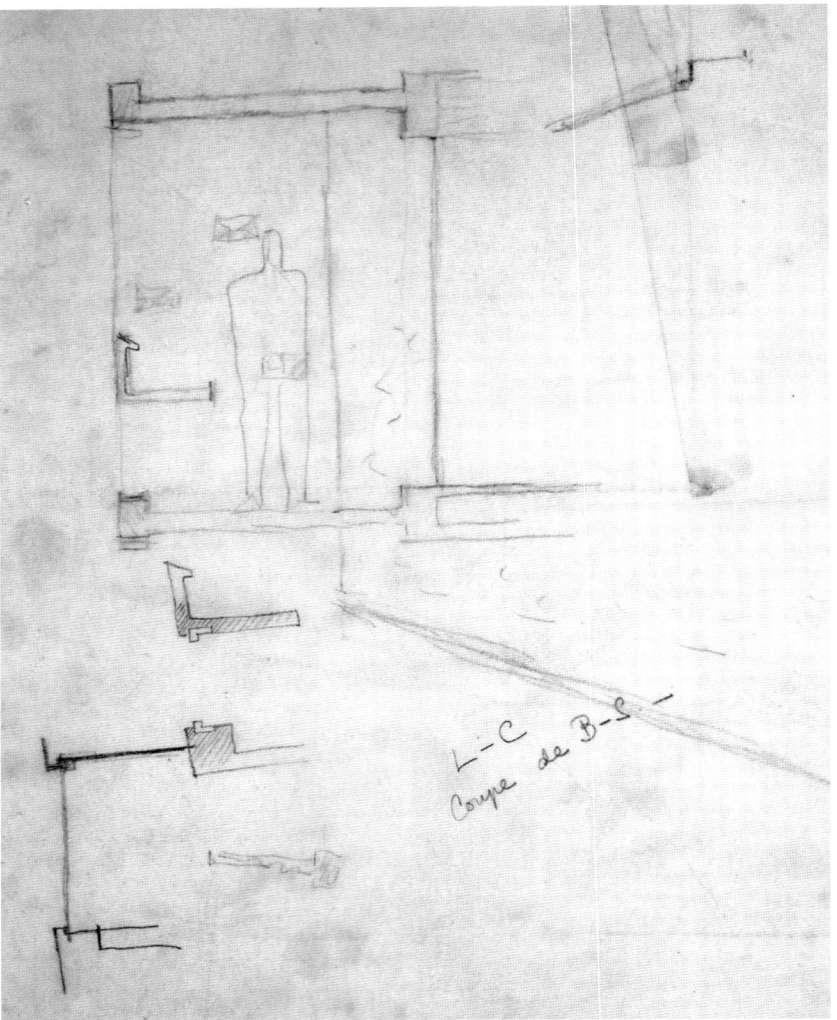

Figure 4.11 Sketch of brise soleil, Unité, Marseilles Michelet (1952), showing inverted pyramids set into side wall, FLC 27213

facilitate that process of transformation that Le Corbusier hoped would take place within the inhabitants of his buildings: 'We are now ready to bring into our home, in the exceptional conditions of architectural calmness, the work of art that will make us think or meditate'.[49] In one image of the Pavillon d'Esprit Nouveau in the *Oeuvre Complète* a casier containing pots of plants is placed in significant juxtaposition with the framed Léger painting (Figure 4.14) which is behind it. The echoes between the two spaces, one painted, one real, gives the space within the casier an illusionistic feel. This photograph appears next to a passage devoted to the 'double life' of art, the 'mirror' of life. 'The work of art, this "double

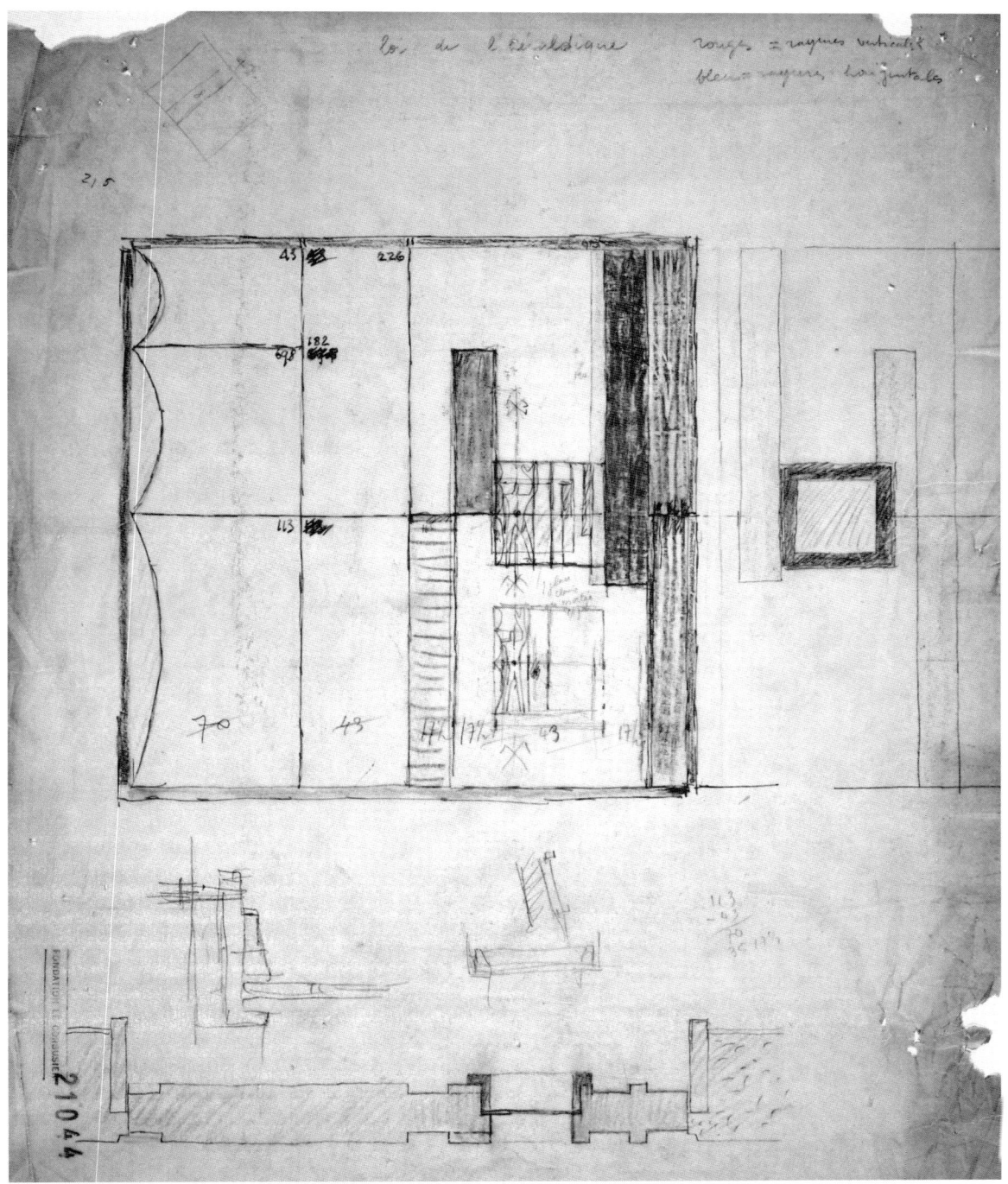

Figure 4.12 'Le Modulor', Unité, Marseilles Michelet (1952), FLC 21044

Figure 4.13 'Le Modulor' at ground level, Unité, Marseilles Michelet (1952)

Un casier (peinture Léger)

Figure 4.14 Casier in Pavillon d'Esprit Nouveau (1925)

life" of a human being existent or disappeared, or unknown; this mirror of a sincere individual passion, this hour of profound exchange; this confession of a kinship, these eloquent words and without detour spoken in the absolute of private conversation; perhaps a *Sermon on the Mount*'.[50] Leading on from Le Corbusier's statement my suggestion is that the casier, its form, its detail and its contents, in this case, might potentially form part of the work of art too.

According to Arthur Rüegg, during the early part of his career, Le Corbusier had a 'passion' for analysing and organizing into new groupings objects that he discovered while out collecting. His aim was, in Rüegg's words, 'to recognize "series," to create "unities" that transcend time and space'.[51] This can be seen from a close analysis of the niche above the fireplace (Figure 4.15) at 24 Rue Nungesser et Coli as it is represented in the *Oeuvre Complète*.[52] Here contained within the depth of the wall can be seen three of what Le Corbusier called 'objects that provoke a poetic reaction':

Figure 4.15   Niche over fireplace penthouse, 24 Rue Nungesser et Coli (1934). Photo from Le Corbusier's *Oeuvre Complète*

I mean all the objects with which we maintain a constant communication, companion objects which might also be poetic objects. We may feel like collecting them, and they will seem to us to be contemporary, although in actual time, they certainly are not. This anachronism must not be measured by the scale of time. It arises only in the gap between things utterly different in spirit. What we mean by contemporaries, at this level of perception, are objects with sister souls. So objects originating in any time and place whatsoever may aspire to this brotherly communion. Books are full of persuasive fairy tales, iconography, because of this. Artificially created by the agile fingers of man, these objects can be endowed with meaning by nature in its turn . . . [53]

The frame of the niche is virtually nonexistent. There is no bead around the opening, no sill. The objects sit as if within the wall. Evoking the household gods – the lares and penates of the villas in Pompeii, visited by Le Corbusier as a young man – they would reinforce what was, for him, the sacred nature of domestic space.

4.3 Space

For Le Corbusier the window was clearly a frame whose depth and limits presented infinite possibilities for spatial sleight of hand. Reference should be made to images of the Parthenon included in *Towards a New Architecture*, entitled 'The audacity of the square mouldings' in which shadows create a great sensation of depth and layering (Figure 4.16).[54]

THE PARTHENON

The audacity of the square mouldings ; austerity and nobility.

Figure 4.16
'The audacity of square mouldings' from *Towards a New Architecture*

During his early travels Le Corbusier was much impressed by the contours and glazes of the 'exquisite niches of Islamic interiors'.[55] Using tools of perspective, texture and colour, and the judicious choice and positioning of frames, he would, increasingly, play games with the perceived depth of window reveals. Daniel Naegele has written of various Corbusian strategies for perspective games, their intention being to provoke 'thoughtful, experiential, engaged perception'.[56] For example, a small window set into rough wall in the Villa aux Mathes of 1935 was to have a wide chamfer on its exterior with 'glacis cement' on its reveals, literally glazed cement.[57] Here the exterior chamfer seems to have been more about expressing the depth of the wall rather than the absorption of light. In this case the chamfered edges are even and symmetrical, like a one point perspective with a central vanishing point, a truncated pyramid.[58] In the south wall at Ronchamp the perspective is skewed and the chamfers uneven (Figure 4.17).[59] Here the colour of the reveals works with the paintings on the glass to create a story in the manner of Le Corbusier's *Poem of the Right Angle* where text, colour and imagery combine to create meaning. The sweep of space from interior to exterior provided by the openings is barely obstructed by the minimal frames. The viewer sees the window head on, but the chamfers reveal the window as though experienced from an entirely different position. The shift in perspective causes a heightened awareness of geometry in the viewer whilst creating an unnerving sensation of dynamism and tension.

Figure 4.17   Chamfered windows south wall of Notre-Dame du Haut, Ronchamp (1955)

Figure 4.18
Chamfered windows of
pilgrims' house,
Notre-Dame du Haut,
Ronchamp (1955)

The coloured exterior reveals of the windows of the pilgrims' house pull in views of the chapel itself (Figure 4.3). As at Pessac where colour was used to create illusions of space, colour was here used to heighten the spatial and narrative power of the frame. Le Corbusier observed of the wall of windows in the Unité: 'The coloured transparent or translucent glazing, consisting of small panes with accentuated frames, creates subtle plastic play'.[60] Curtis writes of the 'flanges of colour in Le Corbusier's paintings' which he likens to the coloured sound absorbent curtains glimpsed through the glass of the Carpenter Centre. These flanges can be seen with great clarity, for example, in *Femme à la fenêtre de Georges*, 1943 (Figure 4.19) and they are a repeated characteristic of his painted work.[61]

On the exterior of the pilgrims' house at Ronchamp the white render of the window flanges extends out onto the surface of the reinforced concrete into which they are set.[62] The same effect was achieved within the chapel itself, on the wall adjacent to the choir gallery where, as James

Figure 4.19   Le Corbusier, *Femme à la fenêtre de Georges*, 1943

Stirling observed, 'the whitewash on the splayed reveals of the opening returns on to the purple wall to a distance of 3 inches' resembling, in his mind 'the painted window surrounds of houses around the Mediterranean coast'.[63] Such tricks add to the impression of multiple planes and giving the wall an extreme depth of the wall, contributing to the distorted sensation of space within the whole.

In the *Oeuvre Complète* there is an image of the exterior chapel of Ronchamp where the figure of the Madonna, installed in her niche, can

Figure 4.20 Open air gathering of pilgrims at Notre-Dame du Haut, Ronchamp (1955). Photo from Le Corbusier's *Oeuvre Complète*

be seen half in sun and half in shade (Figure 4.20). Attention is drawn to her by the spike of an open umbrella. 'Observe the play of shadows', wrote Le Corbusier.[64] Working drawings indicate that it was his specific intention that she should be bisected into zones of light and shadow (Figure 4.21).[65] In representing her like this Le Corbusier seems to be suggesting that Mary has a dual aspect, a notion that is given further substance when we consider that the statue of the Virgin is fixed on a pivot in the niche, so that she can be turned, to face outward, towards nature, or inward, towards the church. Le Corbusier was fully aware that Mary was represented through the colour blue; instead he chose to colour the reveals of her box in red, green[66] and yellow, re-emphasizing his cherished vision of a more carnal or natural Mary, Mary Magdalene.

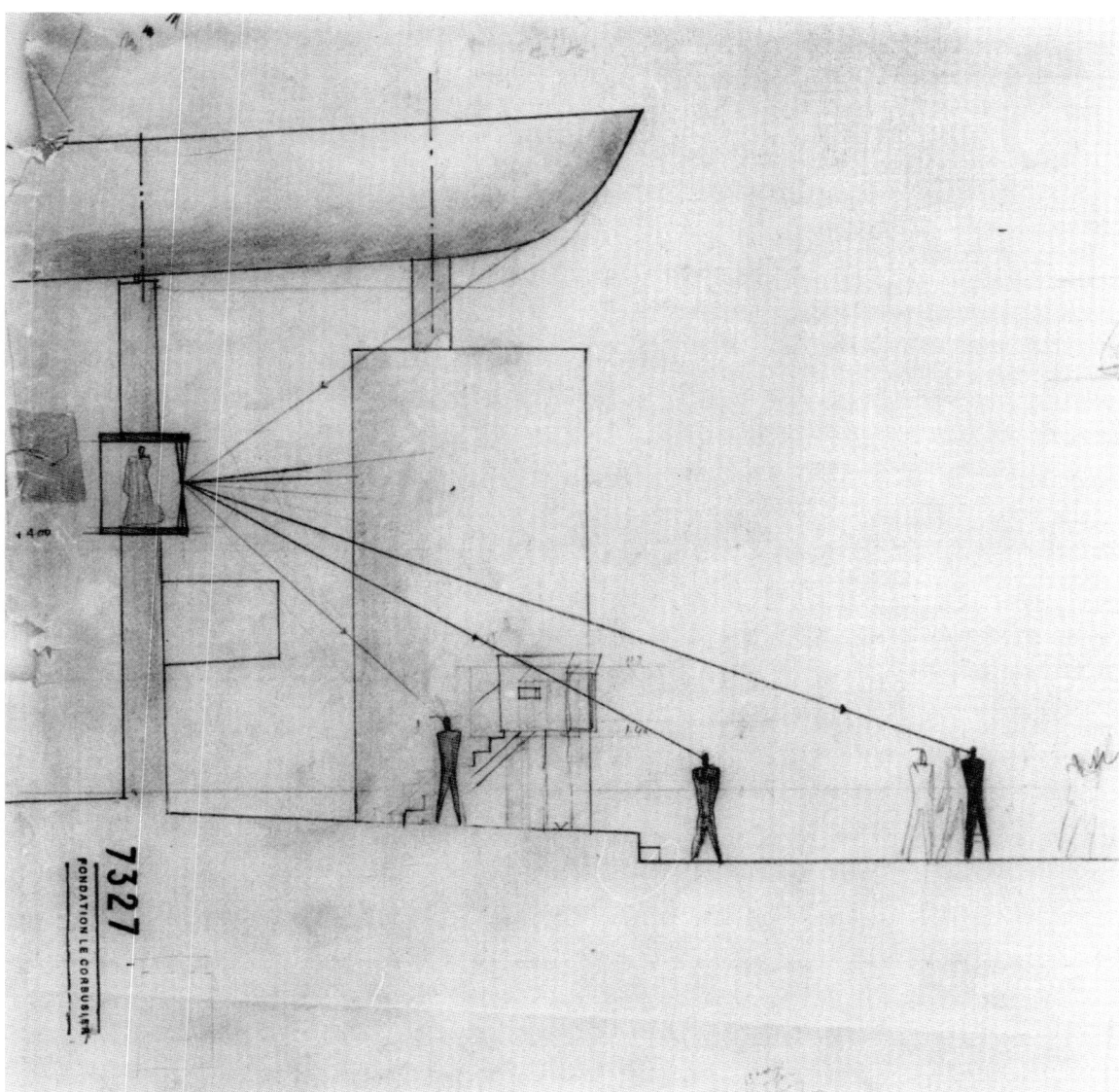

Figure 4.21 Section through niche Notre-Dame du Haut, Ronchamp (1955) indicating extent of shadow over figure of Virgin

As a natural corollary of his interest in subtractive space Le Corbusier was, at times, prepared to celebrate blankness, the blank panel on the façade of the Villa Schwob in La Chaux de Fonds 1916, being an early case in point (Figure 4.22). It is not an accidental blankness – it is a blankness celebrated and framed in render. Rowe writes of the north wall of La Tourette, itself largely blank,[67] that it is 'a summation of an institutional programme'[68] that compels the visitor to enter the 'perceptual intricacies'

Figure 4.22 Exterior of Villa Schwob (1917) Charles Edouard Jeanneret (Le Corbusier)

of the building itself.[69] As well as providing a focus for meditation the blank panel – the negation of the frame – exists as a static counterpoint to the shifting spaces and games of meaning that are so characteristic of Le Corbusier's architecture.

Jerzy Soltan wrote disdainfully of working in offices ' "after Corbu" time' when 'Any void, any hole, began to be glorified as INEFFABLE SPACE with no real understanding of its meaning'[70]. From this statement it can be inferred that the framing of ineffable space must have been a common subject of discussion between Le Corbusier and his assistants and that the frames and voids in his work were fraught with intention. In the words of Le Corbusier, 'I have not experienced the miracle of faith, but I have often known the miracle of inexpressible space, the apotheosis of plastic emotion'.[71]

4.4 Conclusion

Le Corbusier's frames could be heavily emphasized or minimally detailed. A heavy frame creates a full stop in space, an event or a ritual. A minimal frame creates spatial flow – a unity between the frame and that which is being framed. Chamfers, the internal flanges of the frame, can add to the effect of difference, unity or illusion. This must have been why he took such care with the framing of his own paintings and indeed the covers of his books.

The casier that frames and highlights ineffable space is, in essence, the casier that holds two glasses and a bottle of pastis set into the wall of a Unité apartment. It is typical of Le Corbusier that he should treat the storage of everyday objects like a religious rite. Drawing attention to the sacred nature of even the most basic of activities fits in with his obsession with 'knowing how to live'. Emblematic of order, the casier remains one of the essential building blocks of Le Corbusier's architecture confirming and reaffirming the links between all things.

Notes

[1] Dossier La Roche, Doc 506 bis, 24 May 1926 quoted in T. Benton, *The Villas of Le Corbusier* (London: Yale University Press, 1987), p. 71.

[2] Le Corbusier, *Towards a New Architecture* (London: Architectural Press, 1982), p. 187. Originally published as *Vers une Architecture* (Paris: Crès, 1923).

[3] C. Rowe, *The Mathematics of the Ideal Villa and Other Essays* (Cambridge, MA: MIT, 1976), pp. 196 and 200.

[4] Benton, *The Villas of Le Corbusier*, p. 213.

[5] Quoted in W. Curtis, *Le Corbusier: Ideas and Forms* (Oxford: Phaidon, 1986), p. 76.

[6] See sketches of development of window onto lake, Villa Le Lac Vevey, which started as a pergola between house and lake. H. Allen Brooks (ed.), *The Le Corbusier Archive, Volume II* (New York: Garland, 1983), p. 22. Hereafter referred to as Allen Brooks, *Archive*.

[7] Benton, *The Villas of Le Corbusier*, p. 11.

[8] K. Frampton, *Studies in Tectonic Culture: The Poetics of Construction in Nineteenth and Twentieth Century Architecture* (Cambridge, MA: MIT, 1996), p. 144.

[9] Le Corbusier, *Precisions on the Present State of Architecture and City Planning* (Cambridge, MA: MIT, 1991), p. 48.

[10] Similar windows would be included within the timber end façades of Project Roq et Rob, also looking over the sea at Cap Martin, 1949. FLC 18801, Allen Brooks, *Archive, Volume XIX*, p. 114.

[11] Le Corbusier, *Oeuvre Complète Volume 5, 1946–1952* (Zurich: Les Editions d'Architecture, 1995), p. 63. Originally published in 1953.

[12] See for example the Réorganisation Agraire. Le Corbusier and P. Jeanneret, *Oeuvre Complète Volume 2, 1929–34* (Zurich: Les Editions d'Architecture, 1995), p. 188. Originally published in 1935.

[13] Le Corbusier and Jeanneret, *Oeuvre Complète Volume 2*, p. 95.

[14] Le Corbusier and P. Jeanneret *Oeuvre Complète Volume 1, 1910–1929* (Zurich: Les Editions d'Architecture, 1995), p. 74. Originally published in 1937.

[15] Le Corbusier, *Oeuvre Complète Volume 5*, p. 210.

[16] See FLC 27035 for an early less elegant version of this detail. Allen Brooks, *Archive, Volume XVII*, p. 333.

[17] Le Corbusier, *The Chapel at Ronchamp* (London: Architectural Press, 1957), p. 95.

[18] Le Corbusier, *Precisions*, p. 111.

[19] Ibid., p. 115.

[20] Le Corbusier and Jeanneret, *Oeuvre Complète Volume 2*, p. 46. He had experienced such spaces before as a youth when he sketched the interior of a house in Tŭrnovo showing built in furniture window seat and windows as a kind of unity. Le Corbusier, *Journey to the East* (Cambridge, MA: MIT, 1987), p. 63. Originally published in 1966.

[21] Le Corbusier and Jeanneret, *Oeuvre Complète Volume 1*, p. 104.

[22] Le Corbusier, *Precisions*, p. 111.

[23] Le Corbusier and Jeanneret, *Oeuvre Complète Volume 2*, p. 42.

[24] Ibid., p. 122.

[25] Le Corbusier, *Precisions*, p. 115.

[26] FLC 15245 in Allen Brooks, *Archive, Volume I*, p. 548.

[27] Benton, *The Villas of Le Corbusier*, p. 68.

[28] Le Corbusier and Jeanneret, *Oeuvre Complète Volume 2*, p. 42.

[29] FLC 19353 in, Allen Brooks, *Archive, Volume 1*, p. 591.

[30] Le Corbusier, *Precisions*, p. 113.

[31] Le Corbusier and P. Jeanneret, *Oeuvre Complète Volume 3, 1934–38* (Zurich: Les Editions d'Architecture, 1995), p. 122. Originally published in 1938.

[32] A. Rüegg, 'Transforming the bathroom: Perriand and Le Corbusier, 1927–57' in M. McLeod (ed.), *Charlotte Perriand: An Art of Living* (New York: Harry N. Abrams, 2003), p. 117.

[33] C. Rowe, *The Architecture of Good Intentions* (London: Academy Editions, 1994), p. 60.

[34] Allen Brooks, *Archive, Volume XII*, p. 357.

[35] Rowe, *The Architecture of Good Intentions*, p. 66.

[36] Le Corbusier and Jeanneret, *Oeuvre Complète Volume 2*, p. 47.

[37] I. Zacnic, *Le Corbusier: Pavillon Suisse: The Biography of a Building* (Basel: Birkäuser, 2004), p. 219.

[38] Le Corbusier and Jeanneret, *Oeuvre Complète Volume 2*, p. 194.

[39] Ibid., p.108.

[40] Le Corbusier, *Precisions*, p. 113.

[41] Le Corbusier, *Oeuvre Complète Volume 5*, p. 208.

[42] FLC 27213 in Allen Brooks, *Archive, Volumes XVII*, p. 409.

[43] Le Corbusier, *Oeuvre Complète Volume 5*, p. 231.

[44] FLC 25307 in Allen Brooks, *Archive, Volume XVI*, p. 109.

[45] FLC 21044 in Allen Brooks, *Archive, Volume XV*, p. 215.

[46] Le Corbusier, *The Decorative Art of Today* (London: Architectural Press, 1987), p. 187. Originally published as Le Corbusier, *L'Art décoratif d'aujourd'hui* (Paris: Editions Crès, 1925).

[47] Ibid., p. 181.

[48] Le Corbusier, *Modulor 2* (London: Faber, 1955), p. 266. Originally published as *Le Modulor II* (Paris: Editions d'Architecture d'Aujourd'hui, 1955).

[49] Le Corbusier, *Precisions*, p. 115.

[50] Author's translation. Le Corbusier and Jeanneret *Oeuvre Complète Volume 1*, p. 106.

[51] A. Rüegg, 'Marcel Levaillant and "La Question du Mobilier"', in S. Von Moos and A. Rüegg (eds), *Le Corbusier Before Le Corbusier* (New Haven, CT: Yale, 2002), p. 128.

[52] See also sketch of niche to appear in Pavillon des Temps Nouveaux, FLC 718 in Allen Brooks, *Archive, Volume 13*, p. 413.

[53] Le Corbusier, *Talks with Students* (New York, Princeton: 2003), p. 70.

[54] Le Corbusier, *Towards a New Architecture*, pp. 204–5.

[55] Le Corbusier, *Journey to the East*, p. 62.

[56] D. Naegele, 'Photographic illusionism and the "new world of space"' in M. Krustrup (ed.), *Le Corbusier, Painter and Architect* (Nordjyllands: Arkitekturtidsskrift, 1995), p. 85.

[57] Allen Brooks, *Archive, Volume XII*, p. 519.

[58] The truncated pyramid appears as a motif in the floor of Villa Schwob, 1917, indicating that he was already playing spatial games at that time.

[59] See photograph of windows in the north wall behind the choir gallery. Le Corbusier, *The Chapel at Ronchamp* (London: Architectural Press, 1957), p. 13.

[60] Le Corbusier, *Oeuvre Complète Volume 6, 1952–1957* (Zurich: Les Editions d'Architecture, 1995), p. 188. Originally published in 1957.

[61] R. Ingersoll, *A Marriage of Contours* (Princeton, NJ: Princeton Architectural Press, 1990), pl. 25.

[62] J. Stirling, 'Ronchamp: Le Corbusier's chapel and the crisis of rationalism', *Architectural Review*, 119:711 (1956), p. 160.

[63] Ibid., p. 156.

[64] Le Corbusier, *The Chapel at Ronchamp*, p. 46.

[65] In an earlier drawing FLC 7286, the box is completely cast in shadow.

[66] These are the colours that Mary Magdalene appears in effigies at La Sainte Baume.

[67] Rowe, *The Mathematics of the Ideal Villa*, p. 186.

[68] Ibid., p. 188.

69 Ibid., p. 192.
70 J. Soltan, 'Working with Le Corbusier' in Allen Brooks, *Archive, Volume XVII*, pp. ix–xxiv (p. xiv).
71 Le Corbusier, *Modulor* (London: Faber, 1954), p. 32. Originally published as *Le Modulor* (Paris: Editions d'Architecture d'Aujourd hui, 1950).

Elements of the architectural promenade

5

Le Corbusier was always keen to emphasize the fact that his architecture was built around a series of unfolding views, encompassing and celebrating the movements of the body. 'Architecture is interior circulation more particularly for emotional reasons: the various aspects of the work – a symphony whose music never leaves us – are comprehensible in proportion to the steps which place us here, then take us there, permitting our eyes to feast on the walls or the perspectives beyond them, offering up the anticipation or surprise of doors which reveal unexpected space . . .'[1] Just as a film director creates a feeling of suspense, or a writer draws out the end of a book in order to render the conclusion all the more satisfying, the architect can choreograph a route to create maximum drama. In these cases it is the small details that are of the utmost importance in contributing to the sense of anticipation.

The focus of this chapter is on the major route from front door to roof garden although, in many cases, the promenade begins well beyond the building – in the case of the Villa Stein de Monzie at Garches the promenade starts as the car passes the gatehouse.[2] In Le Corbusier's early schemes his spatial exploits were somewhat laboured. Banham wrote of the Cité de Refuge's entrance sequence (Figure 5.1): 'With a literal-mindedness that is either pedestrian or poetic according to one's viewpoint, Corbu offers a distinct and separate built volume for each named function of the sequences (or very nearly so)'.[3] However, as Le Corbusier grew in both skill and knowledge his architecture became vastly more subtle. Curtis, for example, describes the experience of walking through the Carpenter Centre, in terms of layering, dissolving and dematerialization – 'Concrete experienced as dense mass a moment

Figure 5.1
Entrance, Cité de Refuge
(1933)

before now dematerialises into thin planes'.[4] The volumes of the promenade cease to be discrete beads lined upon a string, instead becoming overlapping entities.

Le Corbusier wrote of the way in which 'new experiences could be made'[5] through detailing. These would form part of the unfolding experience of the 'architectural promenade'.[6]

> You enter: the architectural spectacle at once offers itself to the eye. You follow an itinerary and the perspectives develop with great variety, developing a play of light on the walls or making pools of shadow. Large windows open up views of the exterior where the architectural unity is reasserted . . . Here, reborn for our modern eye, are historic architectural discoveries: the pilotis, the long windows, the roof garden, the glass façade. Once again we must learn at the end of the day to appreciate what is available.[7]

Tim Benton refers to the Atelier Ozenfant as Le Corbusier's 'first exercise in the contrived and deliberately tortuous *promenade architecturale*'.[8] In his opinion 'the progress from the ground floor, up the external staircase, back along the landing, into an internal hallway, up a different flight of stairs, to emerge in the atelier facing away from the big windows, reflects Le Corbusier's desire to cram experience into a small space'.[9]

Like entry into a cult, the experience of art was, for Le Corbusier, one of initiation: 'the mystery is not negligible, is not to be rejected, is not futile. It is the minute of silence in our toil. It awaits the initiate. The initiate is the man of greater strength who will explain . . . one day'.[10] An entire narrative would be present within his architecture for those with eyes that see, for those who understood how to live – *savoir habiter*. 'For a finished and successful work holds within it a vast amount of intention, a veritable world, which reveals itself to those who have a right to it: that is to say, to those who deserve it'.[11]

The Jacobs ladder, the route from earth to heaven, was never far from Le Corbusier's thoughts.[12] It is a topos that appears repeatedly in his architecture in the form of a route from darkness to light on the main promenade from front door to roof. However, the daily experience of light would be rather different. At Garches the main living areas were full of what James Stirling called 'an even intensity of light',[13] while the accommodation and circulation were less bright. This means that the inhabitant moving around the building would experience rhythms of darkness and light on a continuous basis rather than the climax of light experienced on the main promenade.

Within each building there are numerous sub routes which muddy, or enrich, the storyline, depending on your perspective. The multiple routes of La Tourette are particularly impenetrable. Here the ultimate route must surely be up on to the roof – Le Corbusier's initial plan for the project – yet it is a journey rarely experienced by any of its inhabitants. Believing that that this destination was almost too beautiful, too distracting from religious life, he restricted access to the top of the building.[14] Instead, Le Corbusier created sub-routes expressive, it seems, of the inner turmoil and darkness of monastic existence. Rowe has observed of La Tourette that 'there is a movement from the brilliance and lateral extension of the refectory and chapter house, through more somber tonality of the library and the oratory, up to the relative darkness and lateral closure of the cells'.[15] Such gradations could be ascribed to reasons of practicality, overheating and glare, but, as was seen in Chapter 3, Le Corbusier was fully aware of the symbolic significance of light in all its forms and it is hard to believe that he could resist utilizing its potential in such cases.

Le Corbusier's promenade encompasses space, light, colour, texture, sound and all the other factors that such an ingenious mind could bring to the subject. While I wish to emphasize the holistic nature of the experience, my aim is to analyse the detail of individual events that are most directly implicated in its creation; doors, staircases and ramps, provide passage for the body on the major route up through the building – places of transition and indeed transformation.

5.1   Doors

The motif of the open book, like the open door, appears in Le Corbusier's painted and graphic work with great frequency – it also appears on one of the altar stones at La Tourette. The left-hand side of the book flat, the right-hand side curved as if held by an invisible right hand.[16] In the same way Le Corbusier always painted doors open with the hinge on the right. The cover opens to reveal a softer interior, the beginning of a story, the opening of the hands (Figure 5.2).

Always keen to emphasize the different types of 'architectural sensation' afforded by doors, Le Corbusier wrote:

> To the young student, I should ask: How do you make a door? What size? Where do you put it? . . . I want reasons for that. And I should add: Hold on: do you open a door? Why there and not elsewhere? Ah, you seem to have many solutions? You are right, there are many possible solutions and each gives a different architectural sensation. Ah, you realize that different solutions are the very basis of architecture? Depending on the way you enter a room, that is to say depending on the place of the door in the wall of the room, the feeling will be different. That is architecture![17]

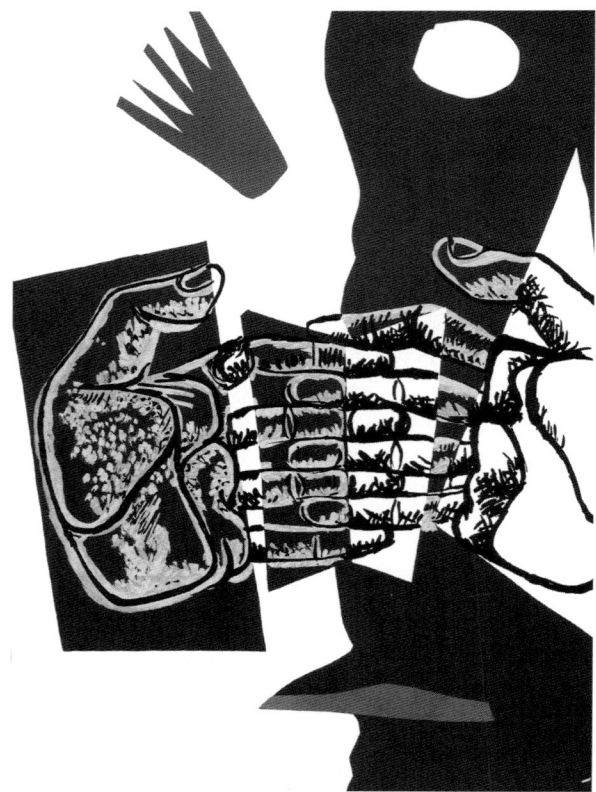

Figure 5.2
Section A5, *The Poem of the Right Angle* (1955)

The door marks the point of transition between two realities, expressed in these words from *The Poem of the Right Angle*:

It is through the doors of
open eyes that looks
exchanged have led to
the flash of communion.[18]

Section F.3 'offering (the open hand)' of *The Poem of the Right Angle* is depicted as an open door, an invitation to another world (Figure 5.3).[19] It cuts the wall in two *longitudinally*, drawing attention to its role as boundary between the two realms.

In *Precisions* Le Corbusier wrote of a twilight walk in La Plata when he came upon a door into a property. 'Just realize the *architectural fact* of this little door set into the wall. The other architectural fact of the door cutting the wall in two'.[20] This longitudinal division of space is reflected in Le Corbusier's doors, which often have two very different faces. The door from the hall to the living room in the penthouse

Figure 5.3
'La main ouverte'. Section
F3, *The Poem of the Right
Angle* (1955)

at 24 Rue Nungesser et Coli provides a case in point. One side, facing into the living room, is black, the other side cream, as befits the spaces to which they were dedicated. When this vast pivoting door is opened it provides an enveloping wing of transitional space to guide the visitor in (Figure 5.4).[21] Seen in plan the trajectory of the door swing brings to mind Le Corbusier's sign of the 24-hour day (see Figure 1.8). Certainly the diurnal movement of the sun is implicated in its contrasting faces. 'Try to look at the picture upside down or sideways. You will discover the game', he wrote.[22] Obsessed by the idea of equilibrium, Le Corbusier may have appreciated the way that the pivoting door made so clear the principals of action and reaction. Pushing the door one way, would result in an opposing movement in the other direction.

Clearly a reason for making either side of the door in different materials would be a desire to retain the integrity of the room when the door was shut. A clear illustration of this is provided by the door of the solarium of the Bestegui apartment, which was clad in stone, like the walls into which it was set, seemingly to give an immaculate uniform finish when closed. Here 'the stone door recloses itself into the solarium'.[23] Nothing would provide a distraction from the grass, the four walls and the play of clouds, the 'summit' of the house an 'aedicule' which is 'perhaps a moving plastic event' (see Figure 2.22).[24]

Not only did Le Corbusier frequently make the wall and door of a uniform colour and material to preserve the integrity of the wall, he also designed simple linear handles to be as unobtrusive as possible; for example, the timber bars that form the handles of the pivoting doors at the Heidi Weber Haus (Figure 5.5). In his earlier work cupboard handles, such as those in 24 Rue Nungesser et Coli, took the form of a hole, lined at the back with a metal plate, minimal in the extreme (Figure 5.6). Such fittings assist in the illusion that the door is actually a wall.

Le Corbusier was fond of the curved lines of a ship's doors accessed by stepping over a high threshold. These were used whenever function would allow, usually for access to minor spaces, for example the door to the neighbouring café from the Cabanon (Figure 5.7), or into sundry bathrooms, but occasionally for more major spaces, such as the roof deck of the Heidi Weber Haus (Figure 5.8). While such doors say much about Le Corbusier's enthusiasm for nautical architecture, I believe that they also say much about his desire to preserve the wall as a consistent plane. The frame of a ship's door is a hole punctured into a steel wall, retaining much of its structural integrity. It is necessary to step up over the threshold to enter the room. Utilizing Colin Rowe's analogy between space and water,[25] the frame of a ship's door holds space in, much as it does water. The frame of an ordinary door necessitates the removal of wall at its base, eroding its consistency in a fundamental way. In Chapter 3 I discussed Le Corbusier's enthusiasm for creating facades like stretched planes and the way in which he used detail to contribute to this overall effect. The use of the ship's door assists with the creation of similarly planar interior façades. On the roof of the Heidi Weber Haus

Figure 5.4   Door between hall and living room, penthouse, 24 Rue Nungesser et Coli (1934)

Figure 5.5   Handles of the timber pivoting doors at the Heidi Weber Haus, Zurich (1968)

Figure 5.6   Cupboard door handles, studio of penthouse, 24 Rue Nungesser et Coli (1934)

Figure 5.7   Door from Cabanon into next door café, L'Etoile de Mer owned by the Rebutato family who were good friends of Le Corbusier's (1950)

Figure 5.8
Door onto the roof of the
Heidi Weber Haus, Zurich
(1968)

it helps to retain the integrity of the box in which it sits in the way that a normal door would never do.

Yet at other times Le Corbusier created doors that would deny enclosure. One of the fundamental skills of architecture is an ability to vary the degree of transparency of thresholds depending on whether spaces that blur together or remain separate are desired. Even the most minimal of doors can register as a threshold through careful detailing. One of the more minor doors beneath the Unité provides a case in point (Figure 5.9). Here Le Corbusier achieved a vast double height expanse of glazing with the most rudimentary of joints. Rather than providing a glazed door within one plane of glass, the glazing of the door itself protrudes into the hall while its clerestory is set back, the junction between the two negotiated by a kind of glass beam that, while providing welcome stiffness to the composition, gives the threshold a tangible presence (Figure 5.10). Although all the elements of the composition are transparent, the glass beam and the concrete reveals contrive to make a frame, a gateway, an event (Figure 5.11). Sometimes there is no door, only a suggestion of a door, made by a frame, as onto the bridged entrance of La Tourette, or into the Mill Owners' Building at Ahmedabad (Figure 5.12). In spite of the light touch exercised by Le Corbusier in these situations, the effect on the division of space is emphatic.

The design of the entrance space itself does, of course, impact on the reading of the door's importance. Even in the earliest houses, where the doors themselves are very understated, for example at the Maison La Roche, the act of entry through, even a secondary door,[26] is celebrated

Figure 5.9
Door into lift lobby of
Unité, Marseilles Michelet
(1952)

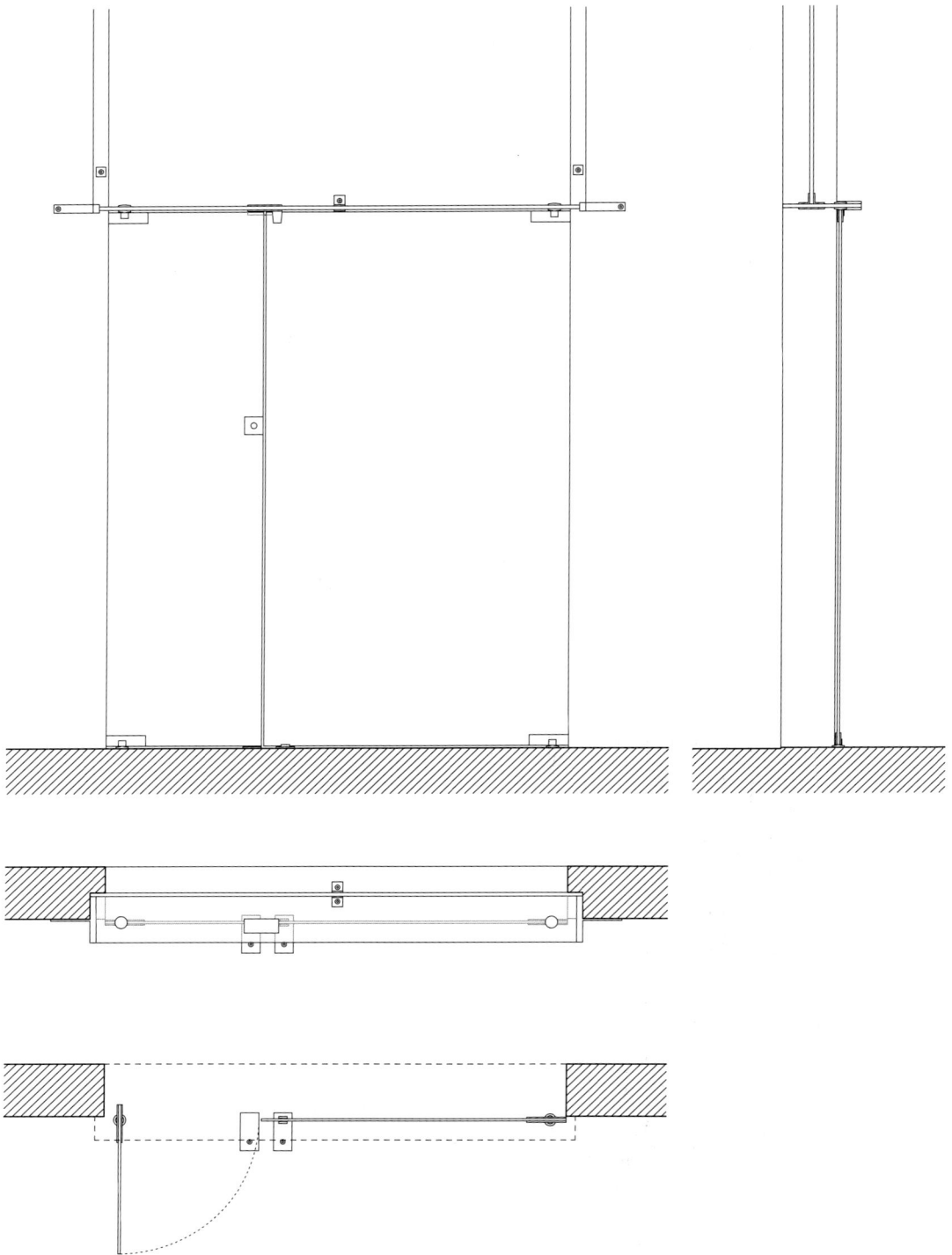

Figure 5.10 Drawing of door into life lobby of Unité, Marseilles Michelet (1952)

Figure 5.11
Detail of door into lift lobby
of Unité, Marseilles
Michelet (1952). Photo
author

Figure 5.12
Bridged entrance to Mill
Owners' Association
Building, Ahmedabad
(1954)

Figure 5.13
Door, Maison La Roche
(1925)

through the careful choreography of doormat and canopy (Figure 5.13), cantilevered at an angle to welcome visitor or, as at the Villa at Vaucresson (1922), protected by a balcony. The space of entry becomes still more tangible in his late work, for example the main entrance of the Carpenter Centre, designed as two pairs of glass doors set within a concrete box, itself set within the glazed south wall of the foyer. The box creates a tiny lobby affording visitors a feeling of liberation as they enter into the hallway itself.[27]

Pivoting doors became particularly prevalent in Le Corbusier's late work – partly I would suggest – because of the symbolic possibilities inherent within them and partly because, when open, they encourage a feeling of spatial flow. The pivoting door invites a bisected view and a rather special view of space, like that in the paintings of Piero della Francesca, much loved by Le Corbusier (whose knowledge

Figure 5.14 Piero della Francesca, *Flagellation* (1455–60)

of art history was profound). The structure of such paintings as the *Flagellation*, or the *Annunciation* – encompassing contrasting views both near and far (Figure 5.14) – is repeated, for example, in Le Corbusier's photographs of his own apartment at 24 Rue Nungesser et Coli (see Figure 4.15) and, indeed, through the frames of his pivoting doors – painting, photograph and building serving to reinforce the importance of events within. Thomas Schumacher has observed that: 'the genre [of the annunciation] . . . almost invariably uses a split screen; the angel is on the left and the Virgin is on the right. And while the figures of these compositions consistently oppose each other, creating a binary tension, the frame often holds the same tension. Left/right, inside and outside, then/now, near/far, all are in opposition, expressing the hinge of History that Christian doctrine attaches to this event'.[28] In Schumacher's belief Le Corbusier used this format so frequently in his architecture and its representation that it is likely that it held some kind of significance for him. It is indeed possible that Le Corbusier's enjoyment of both pivoting windows and doors, hinged off centre, was linked to his appreciation of this spatial format.

The pivot of the door of 24 Rue Nungesser et Coli is not central, presumably to prevent it from obstructing the route too greatly. However, at the Heidi Weber Haus, the pivots do occur at the midpoint of the door, allowing traffic through in either direction. Given Le Corbusier's interest in the use of movable partitions, pivoting doors also had a clear use in that they facilitated the opening of large areas of space. While I have never seen the pivoting panel that leads from the monastery itself into the Church at La Tourette (Figure 5.15) opened to its fullest extent, the experience of passing through the small wicket door set within it

Figure 5.15
Door into Church, La
Tourette (1959)

is itself so extraordinary that one can only wonder what the experience of opening the larger door might be like (Figure 5.16). Built of bronze, and strongly evocative of military machinery – the wing of a plane or the wall of a tank – it is defensive in the extreme.[29] The minor door is so small that it makes the larger door as a whole seem disproportionately huge.[30] Yet some effort is required even to pull open the small inner door and step over the threshold into the church before it swings shut with an emphatic boom that echoes through the church for several seconds,

Figure 5.16
Door into church at
La Tourette (1959)

the archetypal sound of a prison door closing as if forever. In Chapter 2 I discussed a range of door handles designed to attract the hand and rouse the senses. The handle of the door into the Church at La Tourette is rather different – a rectangular hole at the back of which is a facetted push plate, a network of geometric lines in a kind of inverted pyramid (Figure 5.17). To pull the door shut it is necessary to grasp the inner leaf of the hole, an action both precarious and uncomfortable. Like everything at La Tourette there is nothing easy about this door, it perplexes and confounds, impenetrable yet inviting contemplation, it adds greatly to the drama of the route to which it is integral.

Similar drama, this time on a domestic scale, can be found at 24 Rue Nungesser et Coli where a timber door – the door from Le Corbusier's dining room to his bedroom – is attached to a large casier wardrobe on casters.[31] When Le Corbusier went to bed – assuming that he closed his door – he would have to push the whole wardrobe and door into

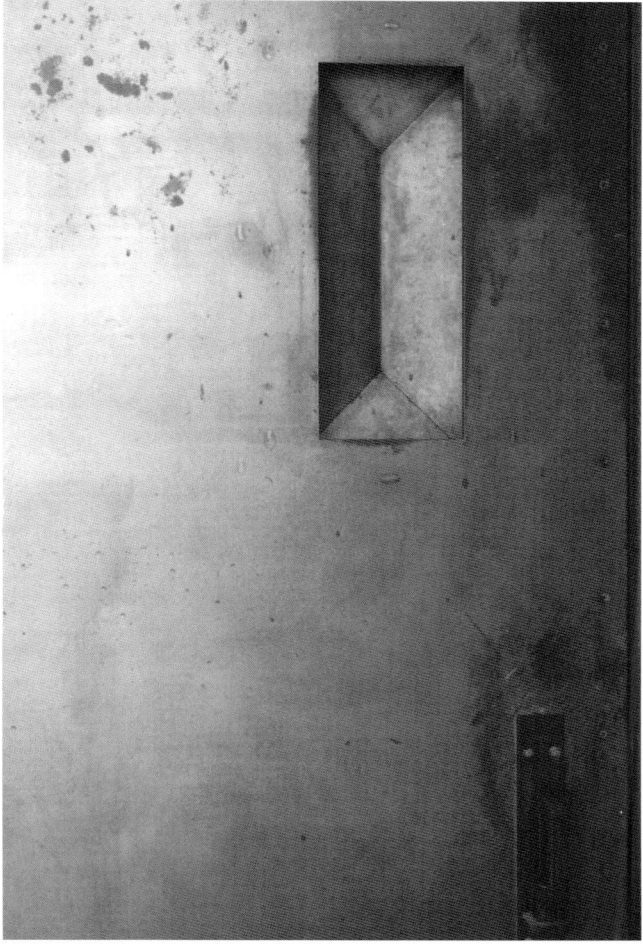

Figure 5.17
Handle of door into
Church, La Tourette (1959)

Figure 5.18
View from bedroom side
of door between bedroom
and dining space,
penthouse, 24 Rue
Nungesser et Coli (1934)

the shut position. This action, now accompanied by much rumbling of tired casters on a well-worn tiled floor, would have been highly physical resulting in a decisive clunk as the door hit the frame, more reminiscent of a door into a castle or a cave, than of a modern block of flats, the whole contributing a sense of security and isolation to the bed itself (Figures 5.18 and 5.19). When open, the door and wardrobe offer a degree of privacy to the bed beyond, while affording the diners at the table a prime view of the well known bidet (discussed in the next chapter) to which Yvonne Le Corbusier took such offence.

Although a concrete framed building with minimal non-load bearing partitions, the flat, described by Peter Carl as a 'museum cave', feels anything but flimsy.[32] Close inspection of the thresholds between the key spaces reveals why this is the case. The frames of the vast doors, often surmounted by a shelf, are given a depth quite disproportionate to the lightweight walls that they inhabit, as such they create a space of transition that allows the free flow of space when open (Figure 5.20). Once closed, door and wall become a unified plane, more solid in appearance than the flimsy wall itself which is allowed to recede into the shadows (see Figure 5.4). This is clearly the case with the pivoting door between hall and living room.

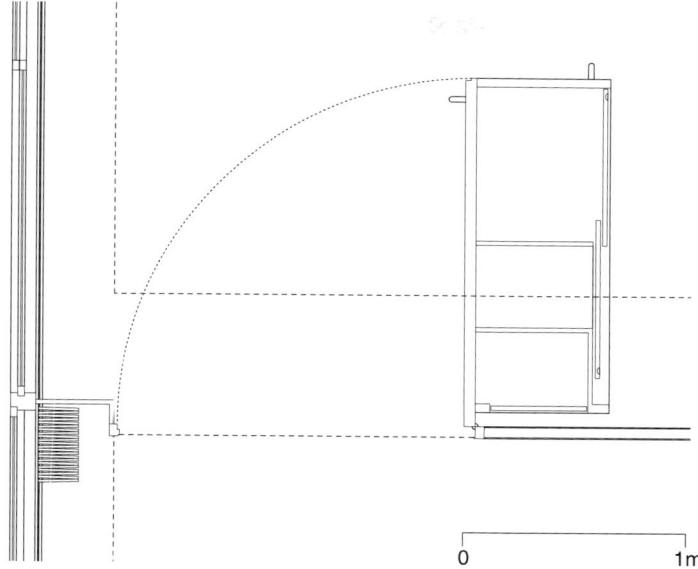

Figure 5.19
Drawing of door between
bedroom and dining
space, penthouse, 24 Rue
Nungesser et Coli (1934)

0   1m

Figure 5.20   Detail of frame of door between hall and living room penthouse, 24 Rue Nungesser et Coli (1934)

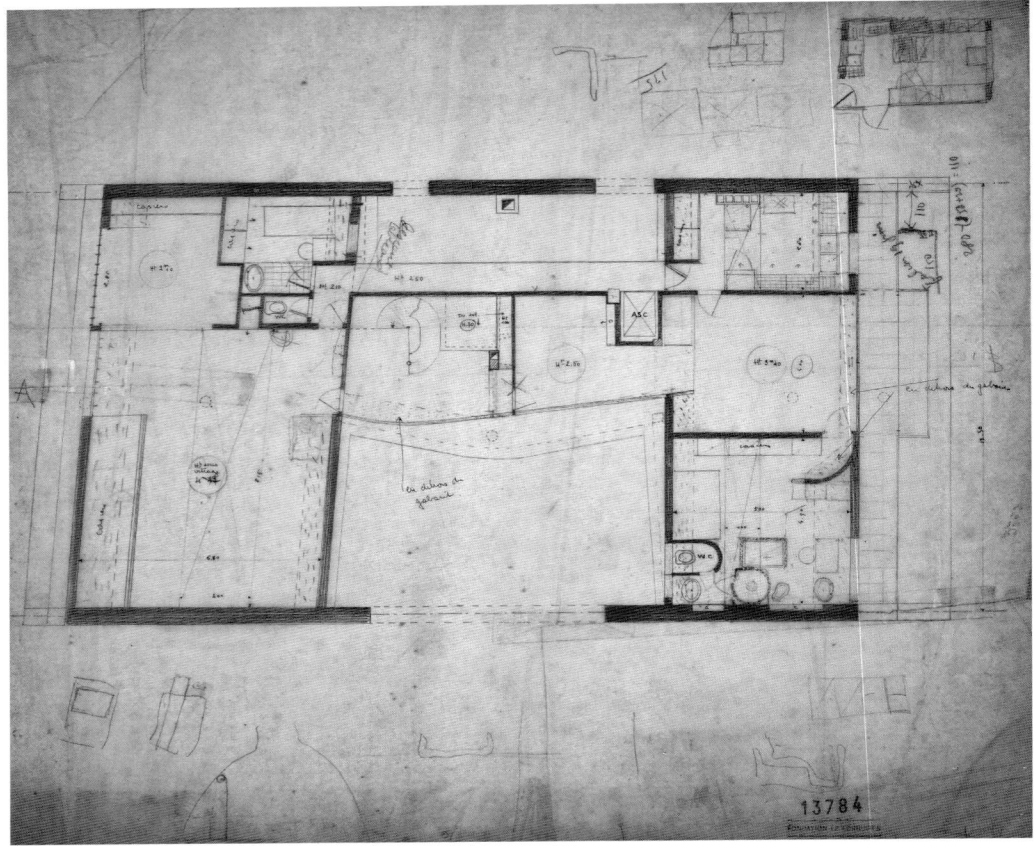

Figure 5.21 Sketch showing one of the ways Le Corbusier thought of making a transition space between the bedroom (lower right-hand side) and the dining space penthouse, 24 Rue Nungesser et Coli (1934), FLC 15653

Developmental drawings indicate that Le Corbusier also wanted to make more of the threshold between the dining room and his and Yvonne's bedroom – indeed, in one drawing Le Corbusier introduced a small curved lobby between the two rooms (Figure 5.21).[33] However he seems to have discovered that the solution to this conundrum did not lie so much in plan, as in section, where manipulations at the higher level of shelf, shadow, frame and vault give an strong sensation of depth. In addition, the door itself is extreme in width as it is attached to the large rolling casier.

Various Corbusian doors take the tapered shape of an aeroplane wing. They are wider at the hinge or pivot and narrow at the side where the handle occurs. The complex form reduces the materials and therefore the weight of the door, but also makes it more sculptural and responsive to touch. When the door is open, the narrow stile is less obstructive to a flow of people and of space than a wider stile would have been. Between the main hall and theatre of the Maison du Brésel the door is hinged at what

Figure 5.22   Door between the main hall and theatre of the Maison du Brésel (1957)

is usually the pivot point in Corbusian doors (Figures 5.22 and 5.23).[34] This may well be to allow latecomers into the theatre while minimizing disturbance, but it also means that the door does not impinge on the theatre space in any way.

Like the door into the auditorium of the Maison du Brésel, the enamel, bronze and cast iron processional entrance at Ronchamp (2770 mm by 2770 mm) is itself set within a frame within a glazed frame (Figure 5.24).[35] The arrangement of both doors in plan is strikingly similar to an image in *The Poem of the Right Angle* (Figure 5.25) accompanied by these words:

Between the poles reigns the tension
of fluids the scores
of opposites are settled an
end to the hatred of irreconcilables is
proposed union ripens
the fruit of confrontation.[36]

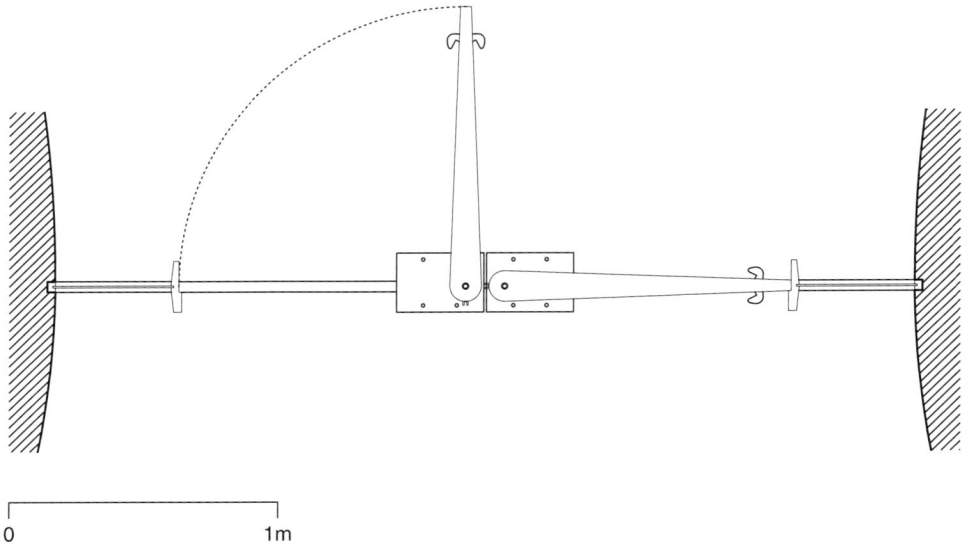

0   1m

Figure 5.23   Door between the main hall and theatre of the Maison du Brésel (1957)

Figure 5.24
Ceremonial door at
Notre-Dame du Haut,
Ronchamp (1955). Photo
author

Figure 5.25
Drawing from Le
Corbusier, Section A5,
Milieu, *The Poem of the
Right Angle* (1955)

The amorphous shape that occupies the pivotal position at the centre of the two poles is itself tapered like the door of the Maison du Brésel and may have provided the inspiration for its form and meaning.

The exterior and interior finishes of the Chapel at Ronchamp are continuous so the ceremonial door announces its presence as threshold while, perhaps paradoxically, allowing the flow of space from outside in (Figure 5.26). A gap between the door and the walls of the

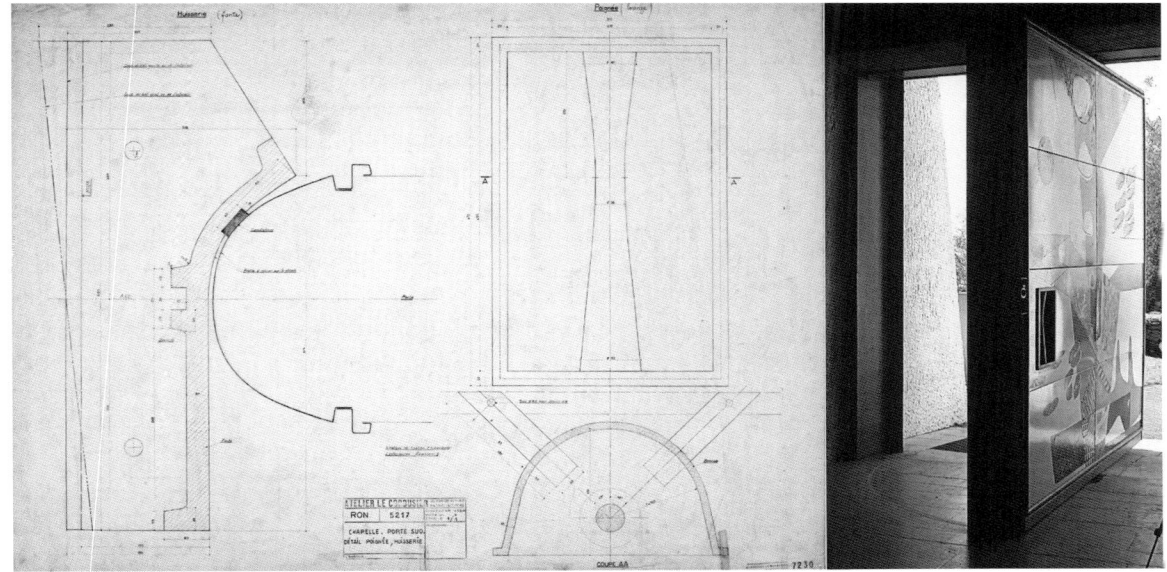

Figure 5.26 Working drawing of ceremonial door at Notre-Dame du Haut, Ronchamp (1955), FLC 07230 and photo of docr open

building prevents the door from brutally subdividing its sweeping masonry curves while, in strong light, providing it with a halo of light. Anything but self-effacing, the Ronchamp door announces itself in a variety of ways: through the extreme contrast between its colourful shiny enamel surfaces and the surrounding walls, through the way that it is set deep within the monumental wall, through the presence of its independent frame, through its dramatic and large handle, through the smooth panel of stone at its base and through the choreography of the elements around it, the holy water stoop and so on. It is adorned with symbols which form the subject of an entire book by Mogens Krustrup.[37] More recently Jan Birksted has argued that the 'FF' symbols on the door have their origins in Le Corbusier's involvement in Masonry.[38] The enamel door of the assembly at Chandigarh is similarly loaded with what Vikramaditya Prakash describes as an 'Edenic subtext'.[39] What seems so significant is the fact that Le Corbusier chose to adorn these highly important doors in this way, the practice of ornamenting doors with magical talismans being ancient in the extreme.[40] What better way to apprise the neophyte on the initiatory architectural promenade of the meaning of the quest?

This discussion would be incomplete without the mention of a far less ostentatious, but equally significant door – the one that marks the entry into Le Corbusier's Cabanon at Cap Martin. Here the front door is of plain timber that slides into a pocket on the right-hand side of the entry (Figure 5.27). Behind it is a screen that swings on hinges with a

Figure 5.27   Front door of Cabanon (1950)

Figure 5.27   (Continued)

wooden bolt highly reminiscent of Japanese architectures. The Cabanon was a 'magical place'[41] for Le Corbusier, encompassing, in many ways, a microcosm of his theories. The rituals of entry here are abbreviated but intense. The clue is the keyhole, the escutcheon which is vastly oversized for the door – more suitable for treasure chest or a mansion, both of which are implicated in the architecture of this tiny wooden hut. 'Sometimes there is a door: one opens it – enters – one is in another realm, the realm of the gods, the room which holds the key to the great systems. These doors are the doors of the miracles'.[42]

5.2   Stairs and ramps

Just as he evolved a limited variety of door and window types, Le Corbusier devised a limited variety stair and ramp types to be reused and refined across his career (Figure 5.28).[43] These include the spiral, the dogleg, the cantilevered stair, each of which would play an integral role in the spiritual promenade. The handrails similarly come from a limited family of types, subject to some change across his career. In early schemes, the same type of stair case is never allowed all the way up an entire building. In larger schemes, such as the Unité, a whole panoply of stair types give access to the upper recesses of the roof garden – one, almost a ladder, feather light – another, solid concrete.[44] Occasionally

Figure 5.28 Stair, penthouse 24 Nungesser et Coli. Stair Maison des Jeunes, Firminy. Fire stair Unité, Marseilles

stairs and ramps are duplicated in a way that at first seems unnecessary; why, for example, did Le Corbusier need to build a ramp in the picture gallery of Villa La Roche when there was a perfectly good stair nearby? Why is there an exterior stair from ground floor to the first floor of the Ozenfant studio as well as an interior stair? Why is there an internal stair at the Heidi Weber Haus as well as an external ramp? It seems likely that functional considerations, of fire, services and so on, may well have come into play, the auxiliary stairs serving a pragmatic role, Sancho Panza to the quixotic promenade.

The spiral, for Le Corbusier associated with the shells, the coils of the inner ear, nature and the golden section, was a repeated motif in his work (*Nature morte géométrique*, Figure 5.29). It erupts into his paintings as it does in his architecture, most clearly through his schemes for the Museum of Unlimited Growth. The spiral, repeating the same archetypal course, yet progressing with each cycle, was central to his conception of evolution. It may be for this reason that it occupies such a significant role in his work.

Spiral stairs are problematic for architects because they create an awkward spatial detritus around them. When Le Corbusier uses spirals he gives them space to breath, allowing them to be admired for their sculptural qualities. In his words 'the spiral, pure vertical organ, is inserted freely into the horizontal composition'.[45] An examination of the exterior stair up to the first floor of Ozenfant's studio provides a case in point (Figure 5.30). Here the spiral has solid banisters but leads to a balcony with railings. The minimal nature of the balcony reinforces by contrast the solid sculptural nature of the spiral itself.[46]

The curved dogleg, rising to a landing, turning 180 degrees and rising to the next floor, became Le Corbusier's favoured stair form in the early

Figure 5.29
Le Corbusier, *Nature morte géométrique et racine* (1930)

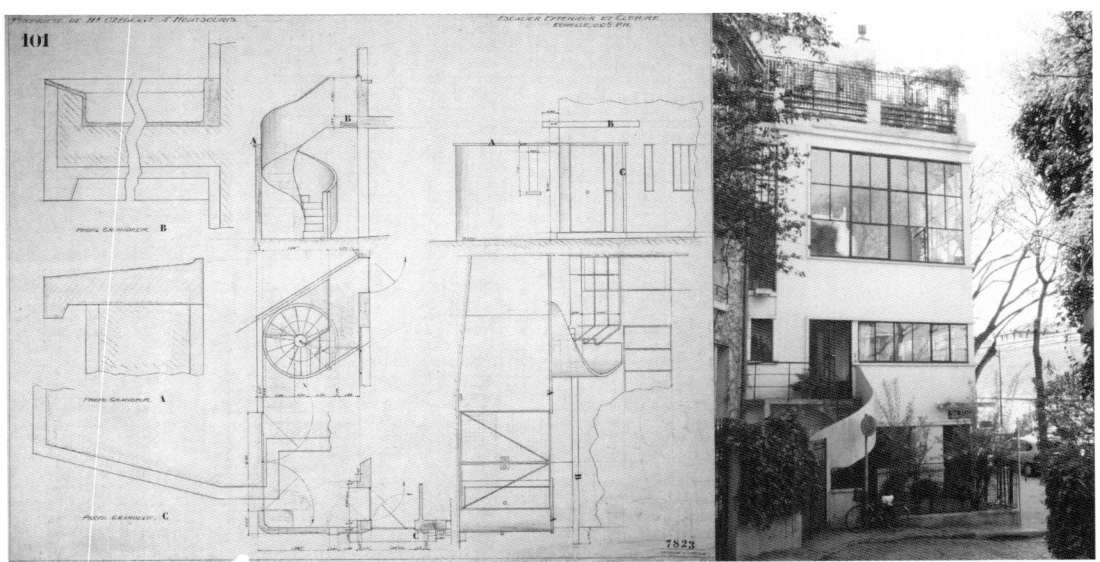

Figure 5.30   Exterior stair of Ozenfant Studio (1924), FLC 07823

years perhaps because it followed the movement of the body round the newel post at each landing, much as the ground plan of the Villa Savoye[47] was famously built in accordance with the movements of a car[48] yet it also seems to ape the forms of Le Corbusier's Purist paintings, inviting comparisons between his buildings and his art. The same stair type was used, to a larger scale, in Le Corbusier's League of Nations project and in his scheme for Centrosoyus in Moscow, 1928.[49]

A further stair, a variation of the dogleg, is one in which the treads cantilever out from either side of concrete slab.[50] This type of stair, the discrete stand alone tower, also finds clear expression in, among innumerable other examples, the early Maison Planeix, the fire stair for the Unité, the heart of Jaoul Maison B and the Heidi Weber Haus (Figure 5.31). Here, through its detailing, it is clearly set apart from its surroundings. At the Heidi Weber Haus the feeling of drama is further accentuated by the use of natural light which flows down the sides of the stair column accentuating its separation from the building as a whole. Looking upwards, the light is so intense that it appears that the stair continues up into the sky. The first tread of each flight is separated conspicuously from the main structure. Its purposeful precariousness sends messages of alarm to the visitor. It is not a stair to be mounted lightly. The railings are

Figure 5.31
An example of a cantilevered staircases – the Heidi Weber Haus (1968)

very minimal, formed out of steel ribbons, there are no hard corners, only sweeping curves to greet the hand. They do little to engender feelings of security.

For want of a better name one of Le Corbusier's stair types could be called precarious. The precarious stair is steep. It is made of thin concrete or steel and has the appearance of folded paper. It is usually supported on a diagonal beam hidden in the shadows or cantilevered off a wall. If any, its railings are very minimal. Ronchamp has three, for example built on the north façade.[51] The stair up to the pulpit is particularly unnerving, especially if negotiated under the eyes of an entire congregation (Figure 5.32). Here the space between the ground and the first tread seems to symbolize a separation between earthly and spiritual realms (Figure 5.33). It begs comparison with Le Corbusier's description of the 'balanced silence' of the pulpit where the 'two quiet oblique lines' of the handrail and the stone book rest are 'fused in the perfect movement of a spiritual mechanics'.[52] A further precarious stair occurs on the roof of the Unité Marseilles. Here the passage onto the stair is mediated by a step of the roughest concrete. The metalwork itself is almost shockingly hand wrought (Figures 5.34 and 5.35).

While Le Corbusier was capable of designing parapets that would assuage the severest case of vertigo (for example, that on the roof of the Unité Marseilles, see Figure 0.1) at times he revelled in the dramatic possibilities represented by the experience of great heights. Benton writes of the Atelier Ozenfant: 'In countless later projects, Le Corbusier built in a final stage of the progress around the house which reaches the level of danger – the steep spiral stairs on the roof of the Villa Stein or the first project for the Villa Savoye, the exposed and parapet-less roofs of the La Roche gallery wing – all these seem prepared as tests for the intrepid

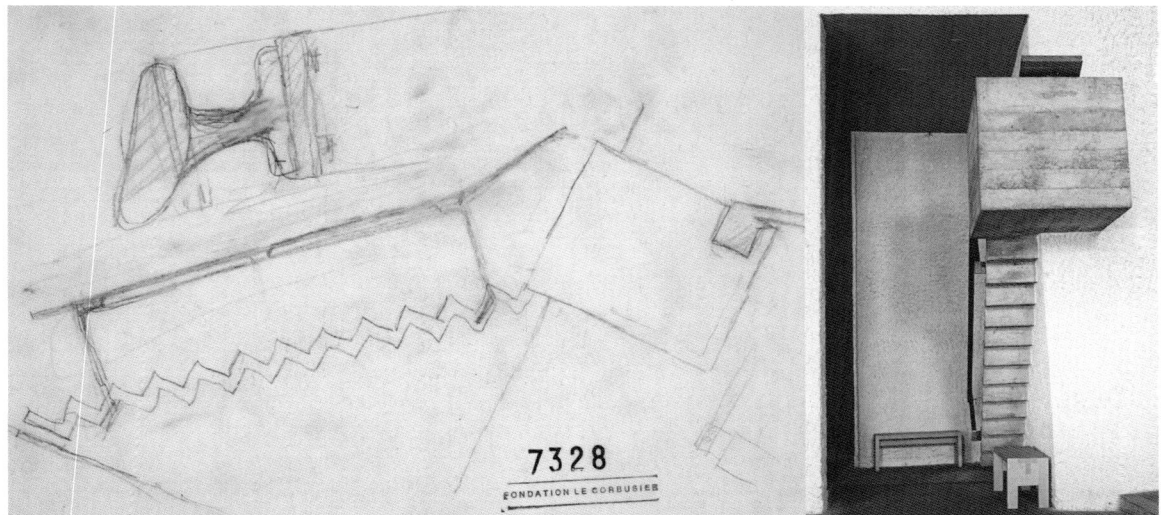

7328

FONDATION LE CORBUSIER

Figure 5.32   Stair up to pulpit, Notre-Dame du Haut, Ronchamp (1955)

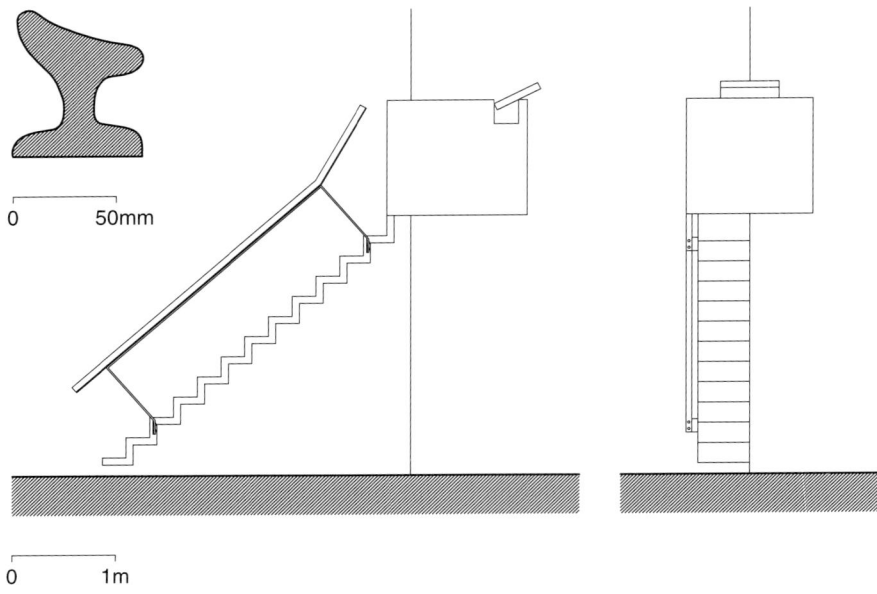

0   50mm

0   1m

Figure 5.33 Drawing of stair up to pulpit, Notre-Dame du Haut, Ronchamp (1955)

Figure 5.34
Stair up lift shaft on roof of
Unité, Marseilles Michelet
(1952)

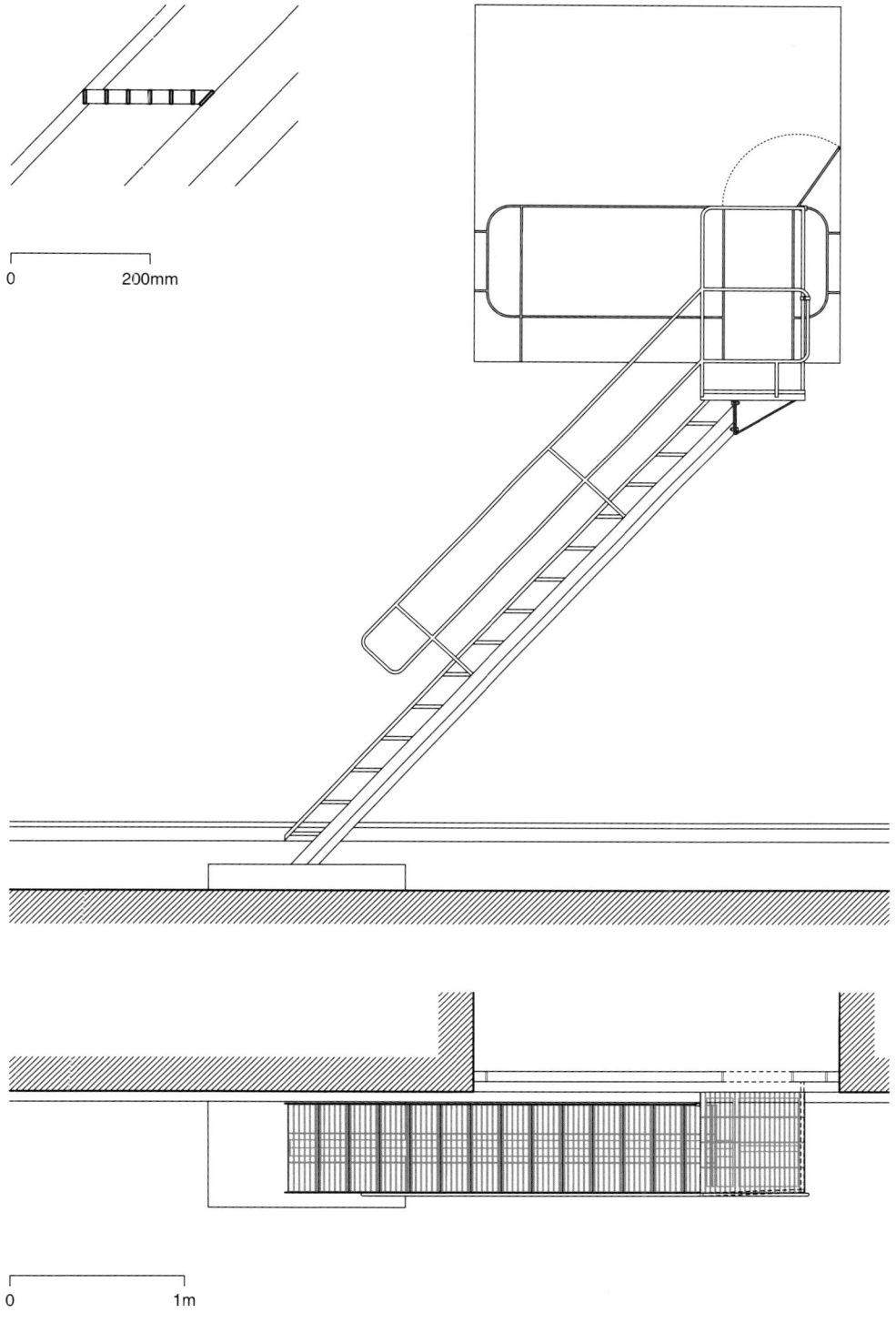

0   200mm

0   1m

Figure 5.35   Stair up lift shaft on roof of Unité, Marseilles Michelet (1952)

Figure 5.36
Bridge over to entrance of
La Tourette (1959)

client and his visitors'.[53] Stairs could be rendered daunting through the solidity or flimsiness of their materials; through the presence, absence, solidity and height of handrails and risers and of course through their position in space.

Stairs at their most theatrical can be found on the Maison Plainex where the visitor traverses bridges and towers. The bridge, a place of transition between one mode of existence and another, is a theme that appears repeatedly in Le Corbusier's work. At Nantes Rezé, the Unité is accessed by a bridge across water – encouraging the visitor to enter a more contemplative mood before entering the building itself. La Tourette is itself accessed across a bridge, although not across water (Figure 5.36). A beautifully simple bridge appears at one of the entrances to the pilgrim's house at Ronchamp (Figure 5.37). Here the concrete staircase is detached from the building and the residual space between is closed over by a grating. The solution is both practical – allowing for the cleaning of shoes and removing the necessity of a cumbersome and dirty mat well – and exciting, in that it enhances the experience of entering into the building. The solidity of steps gives way to the flimsiness of the grating resulting in recognition of the transition that has taken place.

Timber stairs, such as those within the Unité apartment, were designed with the same sensual curves as Le Corbusier's door handles (see Figure 5.39). Like the 'precarious stairs' they are open and lightweight, but their timber construction, reduced pitch and situation within a limited space gives them a softer, less daunting feel. They are so minimal in appearance that they make little impact on the spaces that they sit within. A heavier stair would make the already narrow apartment feel a great deal more claustrophobic. Apparently these stairs were designed with

Figure 5.37
Bridge into Pilgims house
at Notre-Dame du Haut,
Ronchamp (1955)

different age groups in mind, the gap in the tread providing a hand hold for a toddler on all fours, the low rail on the left providing support for a child, and that on the right, for an adult. The experience of the body, of whatever size is paramount.

Just as the relationship of door and wall is significant, so is the relationship between stair and floor. There are stairs that preserve the integrity of the floor and there are stairs that do not. In general, Corbusian stairs occupy a discrete role in his buildings. Le Corbusier described the spiral stair up to the roof of the Bestegui apartment as 'a screw like staircase which does not touch the floor. If it touches it, it will break it'.[54] Very often the first tread is given separate treatment to the rest of the stair strengthening its role as a threshold.

As with doors, the specific treatment of each stair registers the degree to which Le Corbusier wanted it to be noticed. The visual impact of a stair could be influenced by a variety of means, not just its size. The stair would be more striking if it was built of a material other than the walls that framed it – a clear example being the main stair of the Heidi Weber Haus where high drama is achieved by setting concrete against timber.

In Maison B of the Jaoul Houses the stair is a sculptural element that traverses the building from top to bottom, at every level integrating with furniture, seats and the other paraphernalia of life, yet set apart from the walls by a gap in the standard Corbusian manner (Figure 5.38). In the hall

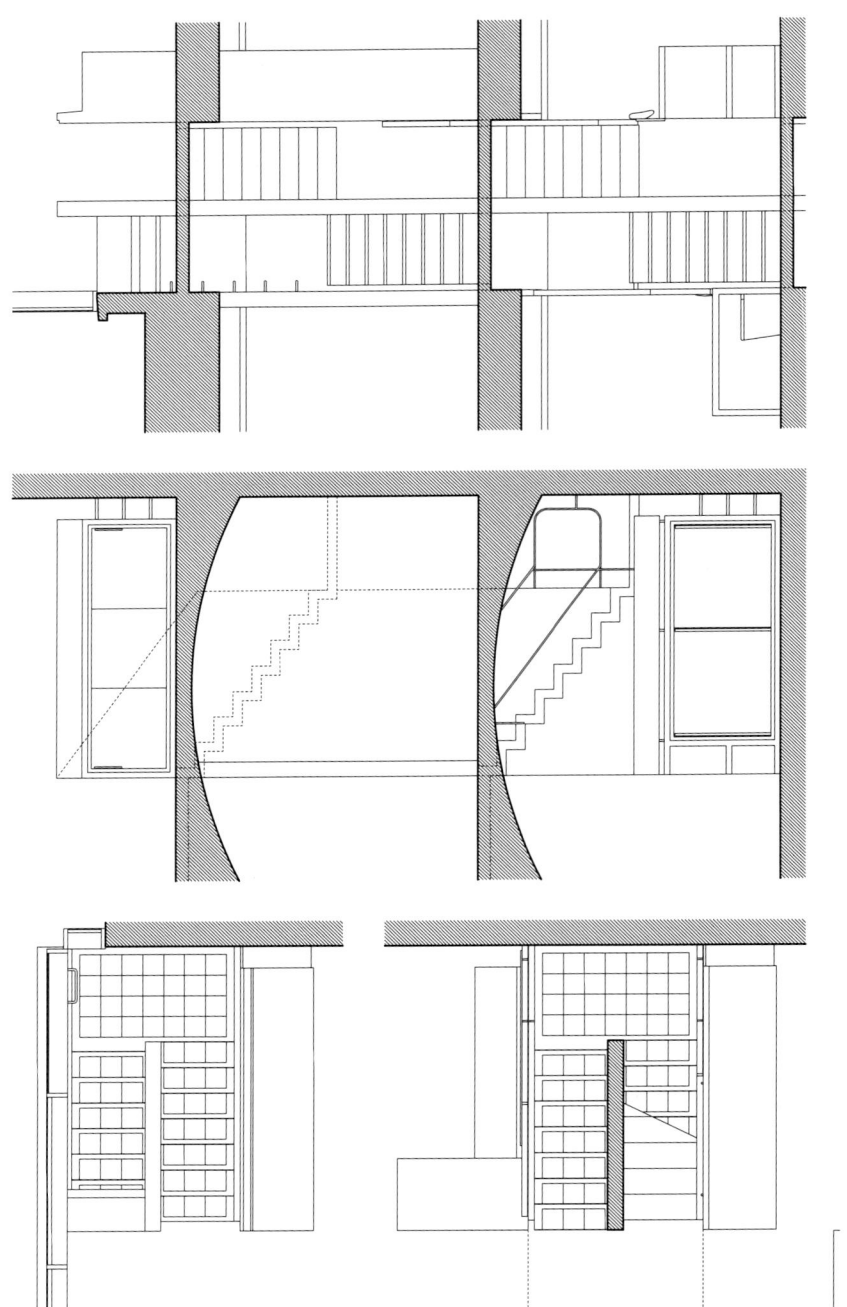

Figure 5.38 Drawing of stair Jaoul Maison B (1955)

0 — 1m

Figure 5.39 Stair within apartment Unité,
Marseilles Michelet (1952)

Figure 5.40 Stair from hall of
Jaoul Maison B (1955)

it has a flat ribbon rail that is very light and inconspicuous allowing the
pale jagged line of the side of the risers and treads to contrast unim-
peded with the black wall behind it, giving them a very strong presence
(Figure 5.40). The stair is very much part of the hall itself. At first floor
level the stair is enclosed within walls that fall away at second floor giving
a feeling of release into space and light (Figure 5.41).

Solid stairs and handrails were of course used where Le Corbusier felt it necessary to break up space and vice versa. Clearly, stairs
were given metal rails in order to minimize differentiation between the
space they sit in and the stair itself (tubular in early schemes – flat
ribbons later). Solid concrete parapets are provided to maximize that
differentiation. Frequently, as on the roof of the Villa Stein-de-Monzie
(Garches) a stair will have one light and one solid balustrade clearly indicating with which space it is affiliated (Figure 5.42). In complete contrast,
as at the first floor level of the Villa Savoye, the stair is enclosed, but
the sculptural form of the enclosure has a deep influence on the surrounding space and contributes greatly to the drama of the stair itself
(see Figure 4.6).

On the roof garden of the Bestegui apartment Le Corbusier played
with the sense of scale by building double height steps next to single
height steps (see Figure 3.8). Together they appear like the seating in an
amphi-theatre awaiting a performance.[55] Scale is of course a vital issue in

Figure 5.41 Stair Jaoul Maison B (1955)

Figure 5.42 Rear terrace. Villa Stein-de-Monzie, Garches (1928). Photo from Le Corbusier's *Oeuvre Complète*

all this. In latter days schemes the Modulor would play an important role in the experience of stairs and indeed ramps.[56] Curtis, for example, notes that the staircases and ramp of the Carpenter Centre were designed with great concern for the Modulor. The width of the stairwell was 1.83 m on plan (the height of the standard 6-foot modulor man). The treads

Figure 5.43 Ramp. Carpenter Centre, Boston, (1963)

themselves were 1.40 m wide, 17 cm high and 33 cm deep – 'the distance from the bottom step to the wall opposite it was set at 2.26 meters (the height of the upraised arm of Modulor man)'. Curtis notes that most of these dimensions came from the 'blue scale' though some were from the 'red scale',[57] but 'the Modulor was not used slavishly in this or other details'. The railings marked 'fer plat' or flat iron were, for example, 7 cm wide, a non-Modulor dimension.[58]

It is my hypothesis that Le Corbusier thought in terms of routes which provided an initiation into the Orphic powers of number like that experienced by Panurge in Rabelais' *Gargantua and Pantagruel*, lovingly transcribed by Le Corbusier – down to the last step – into his own sketch-book.[59] If this was so it would seem to be particularly important that the stairs and ramps should be carefully proportioned to the Modulor. According to Curtis, who writes of the ramp of the Carpenter Centre, this is largely the case (Figure 5.43): 'To experience the "promenade archi-tecturale", with the ramp grooves, intervals, and ratios of pilotis and other elements slipping by was also directly to perceive the kinaesthetic spatial rhythms of an architectural music – the bars and notes of Le Corbusier's "architecture acoustique".'[60]

Benton charts the evolution of one of Le Corbusier's first ramps, that of the Villa La Roche (see Figure 3.19), in some detail in his book *The Villas of Le Corbusier*.[61] He describes it as a 'curiously random migration of forms and functions and displacement of concepts'. The ramp was originally covered in rubber, but the client, a great aficionado of Le Corbusier's work, complained of its slipperiness, as well he might as it is extremely steep.[62] Despite these teething problems the ramp became, of course, another typical element of Le Corbusier's architec-tural language. Much of what I have written about Le Corbusier's use of stairs is also applicable to his treatment of ramps which he seems to have valued for their highly sculptural qualities. Through their presence they draw attention to the promenade architecturale – they are built for viewing as well as being viewed.

At the Villa Savoye the ramp runs right through the house from ground floor to the rooftop Solarium, passing from inside to outside en route. The ramp receives extreme expression in the design for the Centrosoyus in Moscow (1927) where it travels a full eight storeys to the roof, like a vast colon.[63] In the early villas, as Benton observes, the spiral stair formed the 'service artery passing right up through the house'. This motif would 'recur with a similar meaning, carrying the biomorphic analogy, whether arterial or arboreal, to quite specific conclusions'.[64] Ever fond of envisaging his architecture in terms of biological metaphor, the 'Staircases become free organs'[65] the highly complex 's' shaped stair in an early scheme for Pavillon Suisse, for example, doubled back almost like a digestive tract divulging its contents into the lobby (Figure 5.44).[66] The smooth contours

Figure 5.44   Ground floor stair. Pavillon Suisse (1933)

Leading from the 17th level (the classrooms of the Nursery School in Marseille) to the 18th (the roof), this ramp–a joyous stampede–up they go! And on the roof, everything is a burst of light and forms.

Figure 5.45 Ramp in nursery school, Unité, Marseilles Michelet (1952)

of Le Corbusier's ramp would in many ways be more in keeping with their biological antecedents than the jagged form of his stairs. Le Corbusier wrote of the ramp leading from the seventeenth level, the classrooms of the nursery school in the Unité Marseilles (repeated in Unité Firminy) to the eighteenth – the roof – as 'a joyous stampede – up they go! And on the roof, everything is a burst of light and forms' (Figure 5.45).[67] The ramp, as depicted in his book *Les Maternelles* appears deliberately dark and constrained rendering the exterior world all the more dazzling by contrast.[68] There is no better way to express the gushing impulse of rebirth.

Le Corbusier also favoured sloping floors, in themselves a vast ramp, for example that projected for the Church at Firminy Vert. A wide sloping-plane also formed ramp entry and exit to the scheme for the French embassy at Brasilia.[69] At Ronchamp he allowed the contours of

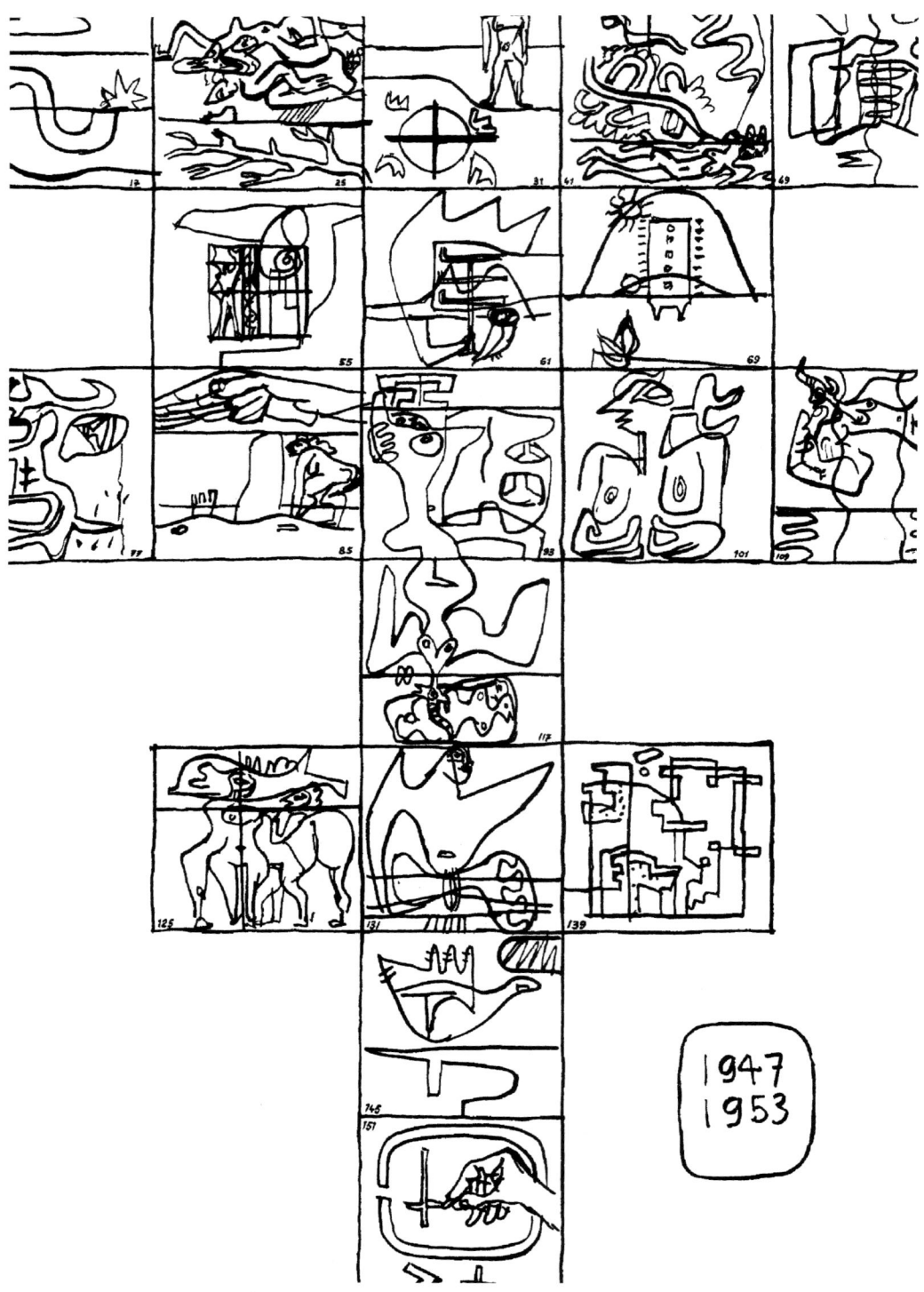

Figure 5.46 Iconostasis, *The Poem of the Right Angle* (1955)

the land to flow untouched through the building, presumably to indicate his respect for nature but the sloping site also contributes to the hierarchy of functions within and provides a fitting end to the promenade that begins at the gate below the pilgrim's houses.

5.3   Conclusion

Each discrete element of the promenade architecturale was designed to promote an engagement with the building and its meaning, an initiation through architecture to Le Corbusier's way of thinking. Rowe makes the highly astute observation of Garches that 'There are statements of a hierarchical ideal; there are counter statements of an egalitarian one'.[70] At the same time, I would suggest, there is a conflict between a hierarchical promenade architecturale and the use of unhierarchical type detail. There is no crescendo in ingenuity, complexity or richness of materials as you move up through the building. In fact the opposite could be said to be the case, a vast amount of care being taken on the design of the entrance and its associated spaces. The same tension is implicit in the iconostasis of the *The Poem of the Right Angle* which is read from the top and finishes at the base although its tree like form suggests a reading which is diametrically opposite (Figure 5.46). Such paradoxes are integral to Le Corbusier's work and contribute vastly to its potency.

Notes

[1] Le Corbusier, *Talks with Students* (New York, Princeton: 2003), p. 46.

[2] W. Curtis, *Le Corbusier: Ideas and Forms* (Oxford: Phaidon, 1986), p. 81. Benton observes that in one of the earlier versions of the scheme a concrete triumphal arch spanned the driveway at lodge level. T. Benton, *The Villas of Le Corbusier 1920–1930* (London: Yale University Press, 1987), p. 181.

[3] R. Banham, 'La Maison des homes and La Misère des villes; Le Corbusier and the architecture of mass housing' in H. Allen Brooks (ed.), *The Le Corbusier Archive, Volume XXI* (New York: Garland, 1983), p. xiii. Hereafter referred to as Allen Brooks, *Archive.*

[4] E. Sekler, and W. Curtis, *Le Corbusier at Work: The Genesis of the Carpenter Centre for the Visual Arts* (Cambridge, MA: MIT, 1978), p. 18.

[5] Le Corbusier and P. Jeanneret, *Oeuvre Complète Volume 2, 1929–34* (Zurich: Les Editions d'Architecture, 1995), p. 16. Originally published in 1935.

[6] Le Corbusier and P. Jeanneret *Oeuvre Complète Volume 1, 1910–1929* (Zurich: Les Editions d'Architecture, 1995), p. 60. Originally published in 1937. Translation from Benton, *The Villas of Le Corbusier*, p. 43.

[7] Ibid.

[8] Ibid., p. 37.

[9] Ibid.

[10] Le Corbusier, *The Decorative Art of Today* (London: Architectural Press, 1987), p. 181. Originally published as Le Corbusier, *L'Art décoratif d'aujourd'hui* (Paris: Editions Crès, 1925).

[11] Ibid., p. 32.

[12] For example 'Jacob's ladder which Charlie Chaplin climbs in the Kid'. Le Corbusier and Jeanneret *Oeuvre Complète Volume 1*, p. 136. See also, Le Corbusier *Poésie sur Algier* (Paris: Editions Connivances, 1989), p. 8. Originally published in 1950.

[13] J. Stirling, 'Garches to Jaoul: Le Corbusier as domestic architect in 1927 and 1953' in Allen Brooks, *Archive, Volume XX*, p. xi.

[14] J. Petit *Un Couvent de Le Corbusier* (Paris Les Éditions de Minuit, 1961), p. 28.

[15] C. Rowe, *The Mathematics of the Ideal Villa and Other Essays* (Cambridge, MA: MIT, 1976), p. 195.

[16] C. De Smet, *Le Corbusier Architect of Books* (Baden: Lars Müller, 2005), p. 116.

[17] Le Corbusier, *Precisions on the Present State of Architecture and City Planning* (Cambridge, MA: MIT, 1991), p. 73.

[18] Le Corbusier, *Le Poème de l'angle droit* (Paris: Editions Connivance, 1989), section D3, Fusion. Originally published in 1955.

[19] Ibid., section F3, Offering.

[20] Le Corbusier, *Precisions*, p. 228.

[21] 'Thus the cemetery binds the city to the plain and makes for it a gateway of reverie.' Le Corbusier, *Journey to the East* (Cambridge MA: MIT, 1987), p. 70. Originally published in 1966.

[22] Le Corbusier, *The Chapel at Ronchamp* (London: Architectural Press, 1957), p. 47.

[23] 'La porte de pierre se referme sur le solarium'. Le Corbusier and Jeanneret, *Oeuvre Complète Volume 2*, p. 54.

[24] Ibid.

[25] Of the League of Nations Rowe writes 'If we could attribute to space the qualities of water, then his building is like a dam by means of which space is contained, tunnelled, sluiced, and finally spilled into the informal gardens alongside the lake.' Rowe, *The Mathematics of the Ideal Villa and Other Essays*, pp. 175–6.

[26] FLC 15125, Allen Brooks, *Archive, Volume I*, p. 489.

[27] Sekler and Curtis, *Le Corbusier at Work*, p. 26.

[28] T. Schumacher, 'Deep space shallow space' *Architectural Review*, 181:1079 (1987), pp. 37–43.

[29] Galvanized iron plate shingles were fixed to the north façade of 'the little house' for his mother at Vevey to protect it from the elements. 'This useful armour looks very attractive. Just at that time commercial aviation was developing, with its cockpits of corrugated aluminium. Without meaning to be so, the little house was right up to date.' Le Corbusier, *Une Petite Maison* (Zurich: Editions d'Architecture, 1993), p. 4. Originally published 1954. In the opinion of Robert Rebutato La Tourette was to have a Roman character. The bronze door certainly fulfils this role. Conversation with author, 9 December 2006.

[30] The Basilica of Peace and Pardon at La Sainte Baume was designed specifically as a response to the end of the Second World War. It is possible that the door of the Church at La Tourette refers to traumas and transformations of war, so much alive in the minds of the people of France at that time.

[31] Le Corbusier, *The Decorative Art of Today*, p. 148.

[32] P. Carl, 'Le Corbusier's penthouse in Paris: 24 Rue Nungesser et Coli', *Daidalos*, 28 (1988), pp. 65–75.

[33] FLC 13784 in Allen Brooks *Archive, Volume XI*, p. 231.

[34] See FLC 12612 in Allen Brooks *Archive, Volumes XXVIII*, p. 179 for the working drawings.

[35] Le Corbusier, *The Chapel at Ronchamp*, p. 107.

[36] Le Corbusier, *Poem of the Light Angle*, section A5, Milieu, p. 45.

[37] M. Krustrup, *Porte Email* (Copenhagen: Arkitektens Forlag, 1991).

[38] J.K. Birksted, '"Beyond the clichés of the hand-books"': Le Corbusier's architectural promenade, *The Journal of Architecture*, 11:1 (2006), pp. 55–132.

[39] V. Prakash, *Chandigarh's Le Corbusier: The Struggle for Modernity in Postcolonial India* (Ahmedabad: Mapin, 2002), p. 74.

[40] A 1962 sketch of the Villa Savoye reveals Le Corbusier thinking of ways that the original villa could be much improved by the inclusion of one such enamel door. Villa Savoye sketch 22.7.1962, ink on vellum, Henry Urbach Architecture Gallery.

[41] R. Rebutato, 'Après-midi tranquille au Cabanon Témoinage', Le Corbusier Moments biographiques, Fondation Le Corbusier, Paris, 8–9 December 2006.

[42] Le Corbusier, *Modulor 2* (London: Faber and Faber, 1955), p. 71.

[43] At Pessac Le Corbusier experimented with using standard formwork for both exterior and interior stairs. T. Benton, 'Pessac and Liège revisited: standards dimensions and failures', *Massilia*, 3 (2004), pp. 64–99.

[44] Le Corbusier, *Oeuvre Complète Volume 5, 1946–1952* (Zurich: Les Editions d'Architecture, 1995), p. 214. Originally published in 1953.

[45] Le Corbusier, *Precisions*, pp.135 and 138.

[46] FLC 7823, Allen Brooks, *Archive, Volume 1*, p. 436.

[47] Le Corbusier and Jeanneret, *Oeuvre Complète Volume 2*, p. 24.

[48] Le Corbusier and Jeanneret *Oeuvre Complète Volume 1*, p. 186.

[49] Ibid., p. 209.

[50] J. Stirling, 'Garches to Jaoul', p. x.

[51] FLC 7204, Allen Brooks, *Archive, Volume XX*, p. 41.

[52] Le Corbusier, *Towards a New Architecture* (London: Architectural Press, 1982), p. 151. Originally published as *Vers une Architecture* (Paris: Crès, 1923).

[53] Benton, *The Villas of Le Corbusier*, p. 37.

[54] Le Corbusier and Jeanneret, *Oeuvre Complète Volume 2*, p. 57.

[55] Ibid., p. 55.

[56] Sekler and Curtis, *Le Corbusier at Work*, p. 182.

[57] Le Corbusier, *Oeuvre Complète Volume 5*, pp. 178–9 for an explanation of the red and blue scales.

[58] Sekler and Curtis, *Le Corbusier at Work*, p. 182.

[59] Discussed extensively in F. Samuel, 'Le Corbusier Rabelais and Oracle of the Holy Bottle,' *Word and Image: A Journal of Verbal/Visual Enquiry*, 17:4 (2001), pp. 325–38.

[60] Sekler and Curtis, *Le Corbusier at Work*, p. 182.

[61] Benton, *The Villas of Le Corbusier*, p. 59.

[62] Ibid., p. 71.

[63] FLC, 15791 in Allen Brooks *Archive, Volume IV*, p. 60.

[64] Benton, *The Villas of Le Corbusier*, p. 143.

[65] Le Corbusier and Jeanneret, *Oeuvre Complète Volume 1*, p. 87.

[66] FLC CU 2557, 14.1.1931 in I. Zacnic, *Le Corbusier: Pavillon Suisse: The Biography of a Building* (Basel: Birkäuser, 2004), p. 110.

[67] Le Corbusier, *The Nursery Schools* (New York: Orion, 1968), pp. 72–3.

[68] See working drawings in Allen Brooks *Archive, Volume XVI*, p. 75 and 266.

[69] Le Corbusier, *Oeuvre Complète Volume 7, 1957–1965* (Zurich: Les Editions d'Architecture, 1995), p. 14. Originally published in 1965.

[70] Rowe, *The Mathematics of the Ideal Villa*, p. 12.

Rituals 6

The theme of the dwelling as a sacred space runs through Le Corbusier's work from the earliest times.[1] As an old man he wrote in *Mise au Point*:

> For fifty years now I have been studying 'Everyman', his wife and children. One preoccupation has concerned me compulsively; to introduce into the home a sense of the sacred; to make the home the temple of the family. From that moment on, everything changed. A cubic centimetre of housing was worth gold, represented possible happiness. With such an idea of dimension and purpose, today you can build a temple to meet family needs beside the very cathedrals . . . [2]

Rituals form being an integral part of Le Corbusier's domestic architecture, as well as his religious architecture, his aim was to draw attention to the small, but highly significant acts of daily life and to make people think about their meaning. In the words of André Wogenscky, 'using an "infinity of tact", he designed "an envelope around man and woman . . . encompassing all their gestures, their movements and their acts . . . their thoughts" '.[3]

For Le Corbusier, a window 'behind which a man stands' is not just a window it 'is a poem of intimacy, of the free consideration of things'.[4] He was desperately aware of the fragility of life and the limits of his own time on earth – which lead to a fascination with death and, I would suggest, a desire to create architecture as *momento mori*. The acts of washing, cooking and eating, the focus of this chapter, are given ceremonial significance through their position and their details.

His framing of domestic events endows them with the quality of archetype creating links with the 'eternal stories' of the past that were forever in his mind. Increasingly these would include those of Catholicism. Before moving to a discussion of ritual in a domestic setting, it is therefore important to be aware of the extent of Le Corbusier's interest in ritual in the more orthodox context of the Church.

6.1   Altars

Annotations to Le Corbusier's own copies of the journal *L'Art Sacré* indicate that he gave much thought to the ways in which he could revitalize the ceremonies of the Church with architecture. Evidence of Le Corbusier's fascination with liturgical choreography and its accoutrements is provided by the iconostasis of *The Poem of the Right Angle* (see Figure 5.46). The iconostasis originated in the Byzantine era as a small wall, a threshold or fence that separated the sanctuary from the nave, the sacred from the secular, hence the appropriateness for this term for *The Poem* which is all about the meeting of the sacred – the vertical line, with the terrestrial – the horizontal; the iconostasis became the place of display of icons and indeed, in the case of Le Corbusier, the place of display of his own *Icône*, right at its very centre.

A similar stratification occurs at La Tourette where the 'high altar' separates the laypeople and the monks' choir, the relationship between the two being very important to the Dominicans. In fact, as Xenakis recalls, the original design for the altar was too tall, causing an unacceptable degree of separation between the two communities. It was originally conceived 'like a place for terrible sacrifices. It was too dramatic, too Aztec. Christ sacrificed himself, as did Dionysus [Orpheus], but the drama had to remain internal and luminous'.[5] As a result, the altar was reduced in size, separated, by just a few steps from that of the monks, on one side, and that of the community and was designed to be equally accessible from every side (see Figure 2.24).

A close examination of the processes involved in the design of the altar at Ronchamp reveal the extent of Le Corbusier's efforts to achieve a satisfactory solution. By his own admission Le Corbusier found its organization very difficult. It was here that he seems to have most problems with balancing the demands of the Church with his own thinking, a process which filled him with 'turmoil':

> 'the stone for saying Mass, consecrated and which is brought, which is fitted into 1 cavity (otherwise filled with a dead stone) although marked with 1 or with 5 crosses and which will receive the Host and ?[sic] two materializations of the highest sacrifice. The stone will be carried out by the officiant at the end of Mass . . . The altar which is the most maximum block of solid stone with proportions cubit and Modulor'.[6]

The problem was to balance this with the rest of the 'elements . . . of the interior choir . . . that testify to the Christian drama', the Virgin and the cross. Two years after the dedication ceremony – the chapel was not consecrated until 2006 – he wrote that he was beginning to feel an 'increasing uneasiness' about the position of the wooden cross 'the latter occupying a position on the axis of the high altar, produces a mutual lessening in importance of these two opposing elements'.[7] This is an intriguing passage. Why do the cross and the altar oppose each other? He made sketches of a new arrangement which would bring 'order, hierarchy and dignity' between the 'protagonists', the altar, the Tree (cross) and the Virgin (Figure 6.1).

> The consecration cf the host is performed on the altar under the sign of the cross placed on the tabernacle dominating the axis which commands the architectural arrangement of the building. But close by and obliquely sited, upright and full sized is the witness, the tree, upright standing alone and embedded in the ground.

In the new version the tree is set apart, in some way special, centred between the altar and Virgin. 'The protagonists are apparent, clearly visible, they are not confused on an opposing axis'.[8]

Perhaps the ultimate symbol of Le Corbusier's cosmos, the tree, simultaneously refers back to nature, the tree of life, the tree of the alchemical process and the tree of the iconostasis in his *Poem*. Just why they are considered to be protagonists is unclear, but the 'drama' that unfolds at

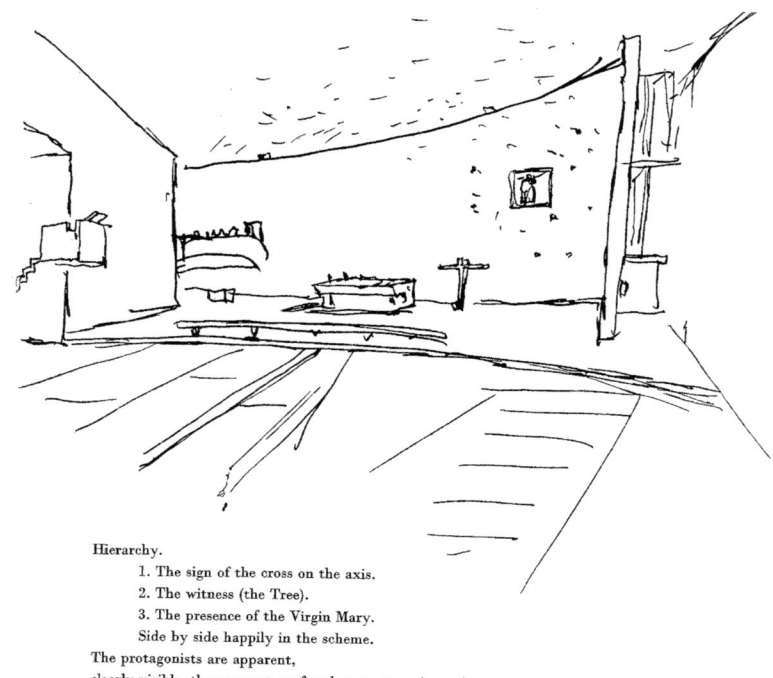

Hierarchy.
  1. The sign of the cross on the axis.
  2. The witness (the Tree).
  3. The presence of the Virgin Mary.
  Side by side happily in the scheme.
The protagonists are apparent,
clearly visible, they are not confused on an opposing axis.

Figure 6.1 Le Corbusier's sketch of the altar at Notre-Dame du Haut, Ronchamp (1955)

the altar may well be a representation of conflicting strands of spiritual thought at work in the chapel. It is highly reminiscent of the images in alchemical texts where the tree is flanked on one side by the sun (symbolized by Christ) and on the other by the moon (symbol of Mary), in which case we have here an example of the *coniunctio*, the union of opposites, both spiritual and sexual, a favoured point of reference for Le Corbusier.[9]

In his *Sketchbooks* is a note dated 4 June 1955. It reads: 'I discover in Catholicism the continuation of the most ancient, the most human rites, (human scale, and pertinent)'.[10] The preparation of bread and wine has clear ritual significance at the altar of a church. The act of cooking within the home would, for Le Corbusier, be a similarly charged event. The family meal was a 'solemn occasion', which he believed was 'too often neglected', an 'ancient family tradition' that 'must live again'.[11] Le Corbusier clearly enjoyed the pleasures of dining and cooking alfresco. This may be why some of his most celebratory tables are provided for eating outside. Of particular note are those that form part of a window frame, the best known being that in the hanging garden of the Villa Savoye (Figure 6.2). A similar arrangement appears on the terrace of the house that Le Corbusier designed for his mother on the lake at Vevey.[12] Both are connected to unglazed windows framing spectacular views beyond. They share in the altar-like quality that I believe characterizes much of

Figure 6.2 Table in roof garden of Villa Savoye (1930)

Le Corbusier's table design and fits in with his ideas of the sacredness of domestic space.

One of the most altar-like surfaces of Le Corbusier's oeuvre is the marble table that appeared in front of the photomural of microscopic organisms in the Pavillon Suisse (Figure 6.3).[13] Here the grain of the marble echoed the forms in the mural – blown up images of water, stone, and indeed the structure of the building.[14] One of the photomurals (Figure 6.4) was replaced with a long mural painted by Le Corbusier, including such key figures from his painted work as Icône. A sketch shows the relationship between the painting and the table below (Figure 6.5).[15] The rich stone surface gives value to the goddess figure beyond, rendering her a figure of veneration.

Like the chairs discussed in Chapter 2, Le Corbusier's tables are often made of succulent shiny materials, pleasurable to touch, adding extra cachet to the event for which they provide the backdrop. The *table en tubes d'avion* (see Figures 2.21 and 3.12), for example, was developed for dining. It was made of 'hollow steel-sheet supports, ovoid in cross section resembling the struts that connect the parallel wings of a biplane) and painted azure, topped by a seven-foot long gold-flecked slab of Saint Gobain glass'.[16] As in much of Le Corbusier's furniture design, there is, as McLeod points out, a clear delineation between that which supports and that which is supported 'although their relationship is inverted: here

La fresque photographique considérée comme «détournement de mineurs»

Figure 6.3 Photomural in Pavillon Suisse (1933). Photo from Le Corbusier's *Oeuvre Complète*

Figure 6.4 Original photomural Pavillon Suisse (1933)

Figure 6.5 Mural in Pavillon Suisse (1933), FLC 15653

a rather massive frame holds up a relatively thin cantilevered plane'.[17] At each corner a small rod allows the height of the table top to be adjusted, it also contributes to the feeling that the glass is floating, creating a notional line, between the two elements. McLeod makes the significant point that: 'The table's strong aesthetic – its objectlike presence – somewhat belied its role as a table-type. As was so often the case with Le Corbusier and

Perriand, an interest in the effect of forms and materials on the senses coexisted with an adherence to the ideas of type and standardization'.[18] Perhaps paradoxically, Le Corbusier's altars are special – yet, ostensibly, standardized.

6.2   Fire – the hearth

Just as the altar at Ronchamp was composed of three elements, each in dialogue with one another, Le Corbusier's domestic altars need to be read in their compositional entirety. The dining-table altars of Le Corbusier's houses appear in close conjunction with the kitchen or 'ancient fire, the hearth of tradition',[19] another sacred site within the context of the home. When Le Corbusier refers to foyer or hearth, it is never clear whether he is referring to the kitchen or to the fireplace itself, or, as is most likely in French usage, to the home and to the woman who presides over it. Certainly the fireplace receives a similar, if not greater, degree of celebration to that of the kitchen within the Corbusian home, in spite of an increasing reliance on mechanical heating systems.

Le Corbusier spoke of the kitchen of the Unité apartment as 'the fire, the hearth, that is to say something ancestral, that eternal thing which is the very key to everything'.[20] The kitchen space is here separated from the dining space by a counter top. When the folding windows of the brise soleil are pushed back out of sight whoever is cooking benefits from an uninterrupted view of mountains or of sea, almost as though cooking in a cave. Le Corbusier also brought the kitchen within easy reach of the living space in order to make the experience of cooking more sociable. Gaelle Rio, the current owner of Jaoul Maison B, speaks enthusiastically of the convenience of this organization in her own home where a movable shutter subdivides the two spaces (Figure 6.6).[21] Here the dining table is flanked by kitchen and fire place, reinforcing its special role within the house. The fireplace actually faces in the opposite direction, but a painted panel on its rear side, an illusionistic fire screen, makes the link clear (Figure 6.7).

In early buildings such as the Villa Savoye, the fireplace – built of brick – stood out alone in the middle of the room (Figure 6.8), or was housed in one of the casiers – as in the Maison Cook and Maison Guiette 1926.[22] However, when Le Corbusier returned to more traditional forms of construction, the chimney gravitated back into its load-bearing position, occupying a brick flue within the stone wall (Figure 6.9),[23] before escaping from the wall altogether, as it eventually did at the Maison de Petite Weekend (Figure 6.10).[24] At Jaoul Maison B the freestanding chimney has sprouted various limbs that separate space without limiting visibility across it (Figure 6.7). At roof level, like many Corbusian flues, it appears like a lone Greek column left standing in the wilderness (Figure 6.11).

Figure 6.6
Hatch from dining space
to kitchen, Maison Jaoul B
(1955)

Figure 6.7
Fireplace seen from dining
space, Maison Jaoul B
(1955)

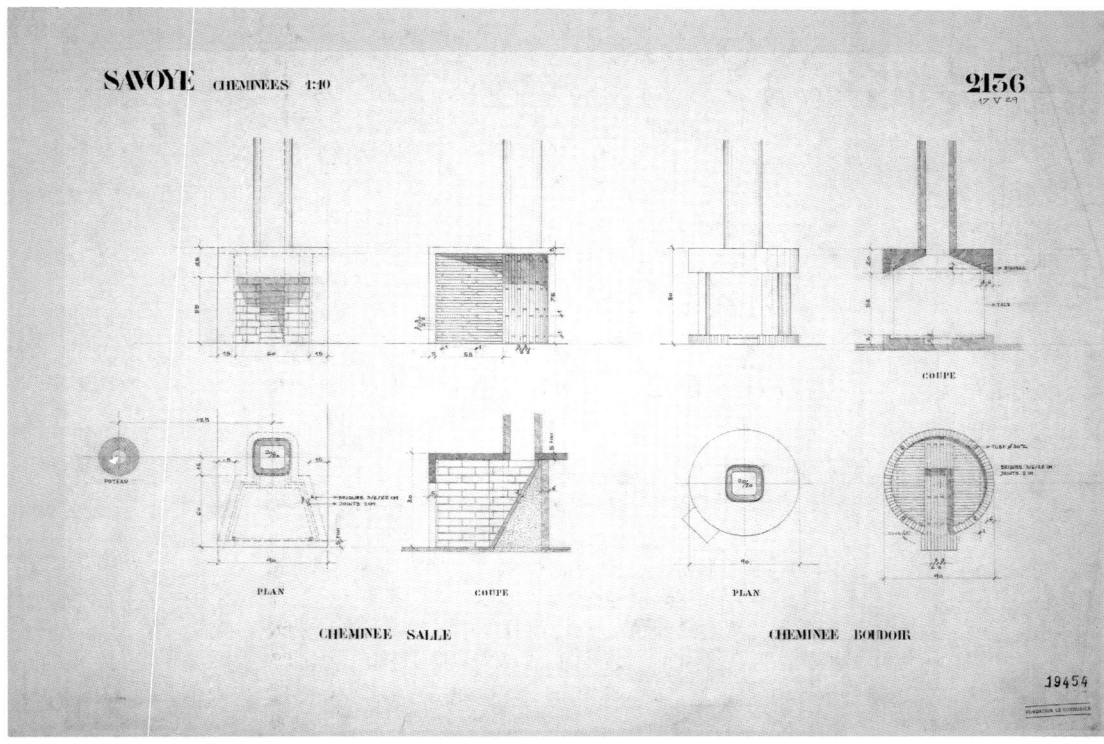

Figure 6.8   Drawing for fireplaces in Villa Savoye (1930), FLC 19454

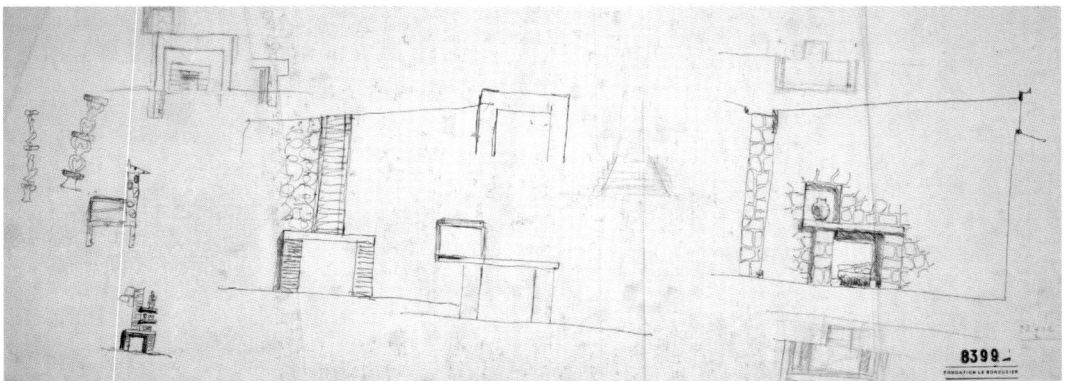

Figure 6.9   Sketches for fireplace Villa aux Mathes (1935), FLC 8399

In the solarium of the Bestegui apartment the ornate fire surround, surmounted by a distant Arc de Triomphe, provides a playful poke at the niceties of the bourgeois hearth, recalling Le Corbusier's own hatred of etiquette (See Figure 2.22). It is an indoor space in the open air. Down below is a very different fire place experience. Here in the library, the fire consists of a simple white cube set between two floor-to-ceiling

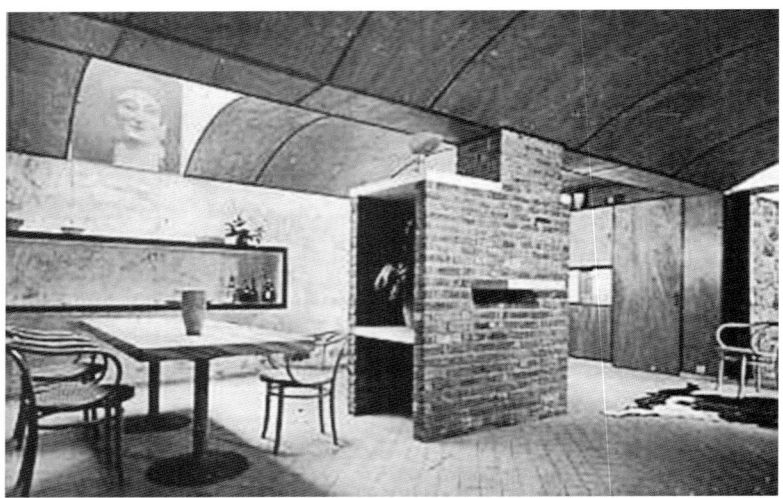

Figure 6.10
Fireplace, Petite Maison
de Weekend (1935)

Figure 6.11
Chimney, Maison Jaoul B
(1955)

Figure 6.12   Fireplace, de Bestegui apartment (1930). Photo from Le Corbusier's *Oeuvre Complète*

windows with a hearth of shiny black stone (Figure 6.12). It is as though Le Corbusier was hoping to evoke the experience of sitting before a fire in the open air yet within the interior of the apartment – an outdoor space within.[25]

The exterior fireplace, whether for cooking or contemplating, is one that appears repeatedly in Le Corbusier's work.[26] In his plan for the houses of the Permanent City at La Sainte Baume the simple word 'fire' appears in the garden just beyond the cave-like space beneath the house. That the architect was trying to evoke a more archaic and simple form of lifestyle is obvious from sketches of this space in use. The 'perspective of the fire', the title of one sketch, was drawn from the point of view of a person deep within the cavernous zone beneath one of the houses (Figure 6.13). By extending the rocks and vegetation of the landscape beneath the undercroft of the building, the distinction between the two is blurred. It is late into the evening and the shadows are long. A group of people are sitting, relaxed, around a fire in the garden, enjoying the tranquillity of the evening. A woman is attending to the cooking. For Le Corbusier she would be 'the soul of the dwelling, the home, the fire'.[27] This image succinctly captures the peaceful and contemplative lifestyle which Trouin and Le Corbusier envisaged for La Sainte Baume, what Trouin called 'a certain state of collective soul' the 'the natural goal of communal life'.[28] Parallels can be drawn between this scene and an illustration in *Le Livre de Ronchamp*, where the congregation can be seen sitting clustered in a circle around a fire by the exterior altar. with the figure of the Virgin Mary looking on from above (Figure 6.14).

Figure 6.13 'Perspective of Fire', La Sainte Baume, FLC 17730

Figure 6.14
Exterior altar at Ronchamp
from Le Corbusier's
Le Livre de Ronchamp

6.3   Water

Associated with woman, the womb, the tides, rhythm and the balance of the inner ear, water always exists in counterpoint with the sun, or indeed with fire, in the work of Le Corbusier. Rainwater gulleys feature repeatedly in the rather limited selection of construction drawings present in the *Oeuvre Complète*.[29] It is always possible that they weighed on Le Corbusier's mind because of the practical problems of draining water from the flat roofs of his buildings, but it seems to me that he was, even in his early career, aware of their potential to carry meaning. Later in his career Le Corbusier rarely missed an opportunity to celebrate the passage of rainwater from roof to ground. To visit the cloister of La Tourette in the rain is to see innumerable gulleys and spouts (Figure 6.15) come alive, giving the building yet another rhythm (Figure 6.16).

The symbolism of water receives perhaps its most extreme expression at the chapel at Ronchamp. Here the roof was designed to collect water sending it running through a tapering breast-like gargoyle (Figure 6.17), past the pregnant bulge of the confessionals into a uterine pool containing a trinity of Platonic forms, one of the most cryptic unities to be found in Le Corbusier's work (Figure 6.18). Water is the milk of Terre Mere and is to be cherished. The topos is not dissimilar to that of the Villa Shodhan where 'a rain spout sticks rigid from the slab, poking towards the soft, female shape of the pool in its grassy hummock' fulfilling, as Curtis suggests 'some private erotic agenda of the building's meaning'.[30]

At the Church of Saint Pierre Firminy, recently completed under the guidance of José Oubrerie, formally of Le Corbusier's atelier, a remarkably playful gutter traverses the entire square cone of the church itself

Figure 6.15   Gargoyle detail, La Tourette (1959)

Figure 6.16
Gargoyles La Tourette
(1959)

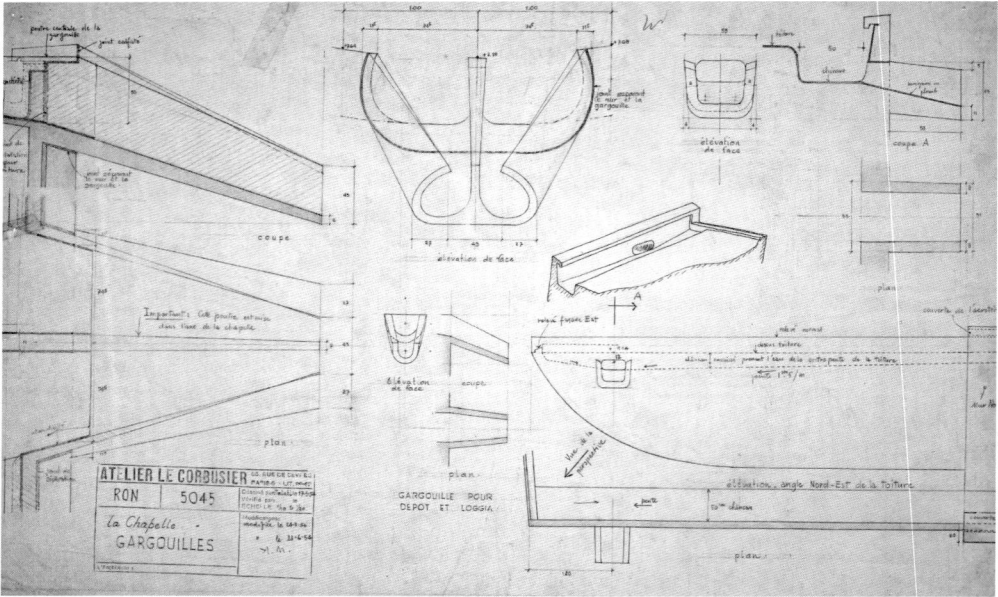

Figure 6.17 Drawing of gargoyle, Notre-Dame du Haut, Ronchamp (1955), FLC 7201

Figure 6.18
Gargoyle, west façade of
Notre-Dame du Haut,
Ronchamp (1955)

gathering the water slipping down every one of its faces and collects it at the base (Figure 6.19). Lights are hidden behind glass on the under-side of the gutter so that at night it reads as a spiral of light. According to Oubrerie, Le Corbusier, who always looked to the roots of religion, wanted to create within the church a pool for baptism by total immersion, an idea that proved unacceptable to the church.[31] It seems instead that he designed the entire building as a form of immersion, immersion in its wonderful watery blue light, circumnavigated by the spiralling rainwater without (Figure 6.20).

Water is evoked at the entrance to the Director's apartment at the Maison du Brésel where it is very much the theme, as will be seen in the next chapter. Here, set into the wall, is an often photographed panel of the deepest blue glass. What is less frequently photographed, and indeed seems, irritatingly, to obstruct a well composed shot of the aforementioned glass, is a small metal spout that drains the window

Figure 6.19
Detail of gutter, St- Pierre,
Firminy-Vert (started 1960,
completed 2006)

 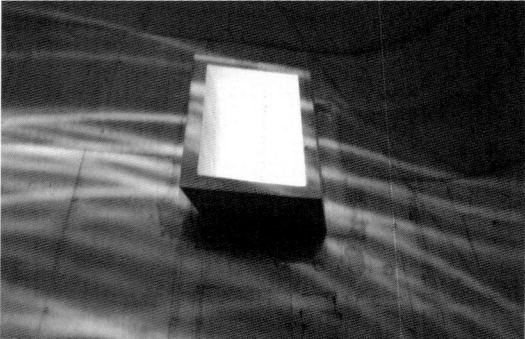

Figure 6.20   St-Pierre, Firminy-Vert (construction started 1960, completed 2006)

Figure 6.21   Entrance to director's apartment at the Maison du Brésel (1957)

ledge above (Figure 6.21). Highly unorthodox form of drainage it must have been designed this way in order to avoid the fussy clutter of a protruding sill and to increase the clean white planarity of the wall in the days before rain screen cladding. It would have been very easy to position the spout further along the wall – perhaps somewhere out of sight – but Le Corbusier chose to position it there on the wall left of the glass in a watery dialogue reminiscent of those grander dialogues present at Ronchamp and elsewhere.

A sketch, drawn during Le Corbusier's *Journey to the East* of a 'water temple' built into the side wall of a house indicates an early interest in how sacred water might be brought into a domestic setting.[32] Colin Rowe has written of the entrance of the Villa Savoye (Figure 6.22):

> As we further enter the vestibule of this temple and house, just how are we intended to interpret the so prominently displayed lavabo or sink? Scarcely as a functional accessory. For any details which one might associate with the act of washing (towels and soap) are conspicuously absent and would surely damage the pristine impact of this very obsessive little statement. Is it then a place of ritual purification, the equivalent of a holy water stoop? Personally, I think that it is; and, though we have scarcely arrived within the house, an item so poetically obtrusive as this one could usefully prompt a little digression.[33]

The sink is displayed prominently at the entrance to several of Le Corbusier's early dwelling designs.[34] The act of cleansing, for example at baptism, is a universal symbol of new beginnings. At the start of this book I made reference to Le Corbusier's Law of Ripolin (whitewash), to his desire to cleanse and purify the home. His enthusiasm for whitewash

Figure 6.22   Sink at entrance to Villa Savoye. Photo from Le Corbusier's *Oeuvre Complète*

was fuelled by his *Journey to the East* where he noted the way that people painted their cottages each year as a sign of renewal. It is my suggestion that the act of washing held for Le Corbusier connotations of rebirth and initiation, themes that were central to Rabelais' description of Panurge's visit to oracle of the holy bottle in the pages of *Gargantua and Pantagruel* mentioned in the last chapter.[35]

At a more prosaic level, bathing was increasingly celebrated for its health benefits, for preventing disease and for purposes of exercise. Sea bathing, something which Le Corbusier himself loved doing, became very fashionable at the start of the twentieth century. Similarly, sunbathing would be celebrated for its health-giving properties.[36] The 'Solarium' or sun bath appears in several of Le Corbusier's schemes, for example the Villa Savoye, the Pavillon Suisse and the Unité[37] where it forms the culmination of the route. Curtis writes that the 'roof garden became a dominant theme related to Le Corbusier's celebration of natural forces – the rain, the vegetation, the sun, and even the moon, since he hoped that the roofs would be used by night'.[38]

The connection between health and bathing was one that Le Corbusier obviously treated with great seriousness. In a survey of housing conditions in Rouen taken in 1949, more than half the flats had no running water. There were no bathrooms or inside lavatories and women frequently had to fetch water from the local fountain and wash in the river, a situation that persisted well into the 1950s.[39] The provision of bathing facilities within the home was a novel and luxurious development, well

Weewee and Co.

Cloakroom

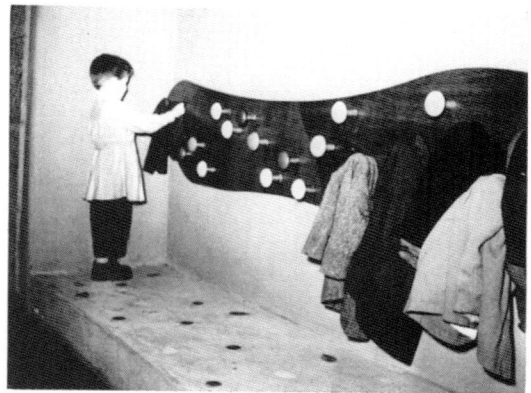

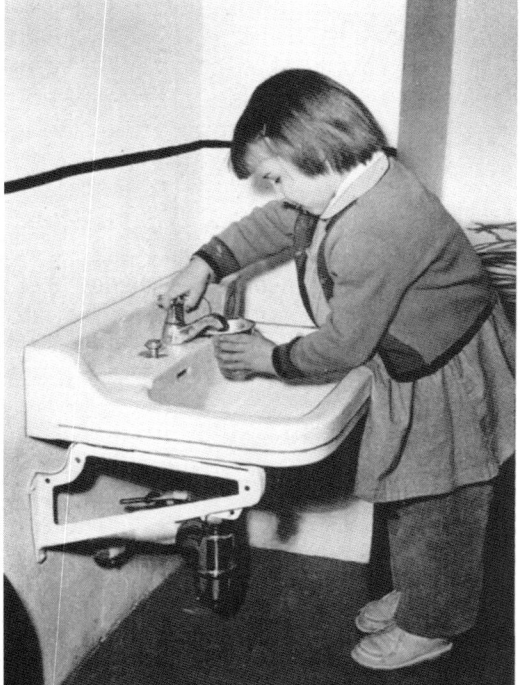

The miraculous fountain of water

Figure 6.23   'Weewee and Co.' from Le Corbusier's *The Nursery Schools*

worth celebrating. In *The Decorative Art of Today* Le Corbusier commented on the way that internal bathrooms were now entering everyday language. It was a subject that Le Corbusier felt very strongly about, one that caused lengthy fights with his clients for the Pavillon Suisse who argued against his plans to provide showers in each individual student room.[40]

A page from Le Corbusier's book *The Nursery Schools* illustrates 'The miraculous fountain of water' starting with a photo of a little boy (Figure 6.23) at a urinal – 'Weewee and Co.' – the arc of water that projects from a little bulbous nozzle in the ceiling above the paddling pool on the Unité Marseilles, seemingly a memory of this act, a humorous abstraction of a cherub in a pompous municipal fountain (Figure 6.24). Le Corbusier then moves on to the pleasures of a little girl washing her hands in a large basin at child height.[41] Rowe writes that for Le Corbusier 'there was always the greatest anxiety (amounting sometimes to fetishism) positively to celebrate the triumph of running water'.[42] For this reason it would never do to use standard baths or sinks from catalogues. Indeed, much of the effort of the Corbusier atelier seems to have gone into the design of bathrooms. During the lean period that accompanied the War a study was made analysing the functions of the 'blocs d'eau'.[43] A similar study, this time for the Unité Marseilles, entitled 'Se Laver' – to wash oneself – is devoted to the multiple possibilities of washing; both allude to Le Corbusier's desire to avoid any preconceived ideas of what this might be about (Figure 6.25).[44]

Like the staircases discussed in the previous chapter, it seems that Le Corbusier thought of the bathroom as another of the houses 'organs', one that needed its own form of tectonic and formal expression. Rüegg writes of the sink in Le Corbusier's apartment that appears silhouetted against a panel of glass block (Figure 6.26):

> Popular opinion would hardly have found the sink's surface-mounted tangle of pipes either attractive or practical. Here again, one need not assume that Le Corbusier simply tolerated this crude construction, but rather one suspects a sort of conspiracy with French craftsmanship. Artfully backlit, the network of pipes, seen in proximity to the oval shell of the sink, looks like an anatomical specimen in which the blood vessels supply a beautifully formed organ. The system's form seems to be a metaphor for its function.[45]

Although they are fully functional, Le Corbusier's bathrooms are, as Rowe put it, 'poems about hydraulics'.[46] He continued to write of the 'polemical and ritual status' of the bidet which is achieves notoriety in *The Decorative Art of Today*.[47] Apparently when Le Corbusier installed just such an object next to their bed, in full view of the dining table (with the bedroom door open) his wife Yvonne – not known for her prurience – covered it up in disgust.[48] The prominent presence of the bidet in his bedroom at 24 Rue Nungesser et Coli brings to mind Le Corbusier's vociferous pronouncements on the hypocrisy of the Catholic Church in denying the importance of sex. Taya Zinkin, once the object of Le Corbusier's amorous advances,

Figure 6.24   Paddling pool on roof of Unité, Marseilles Michelet (1952)

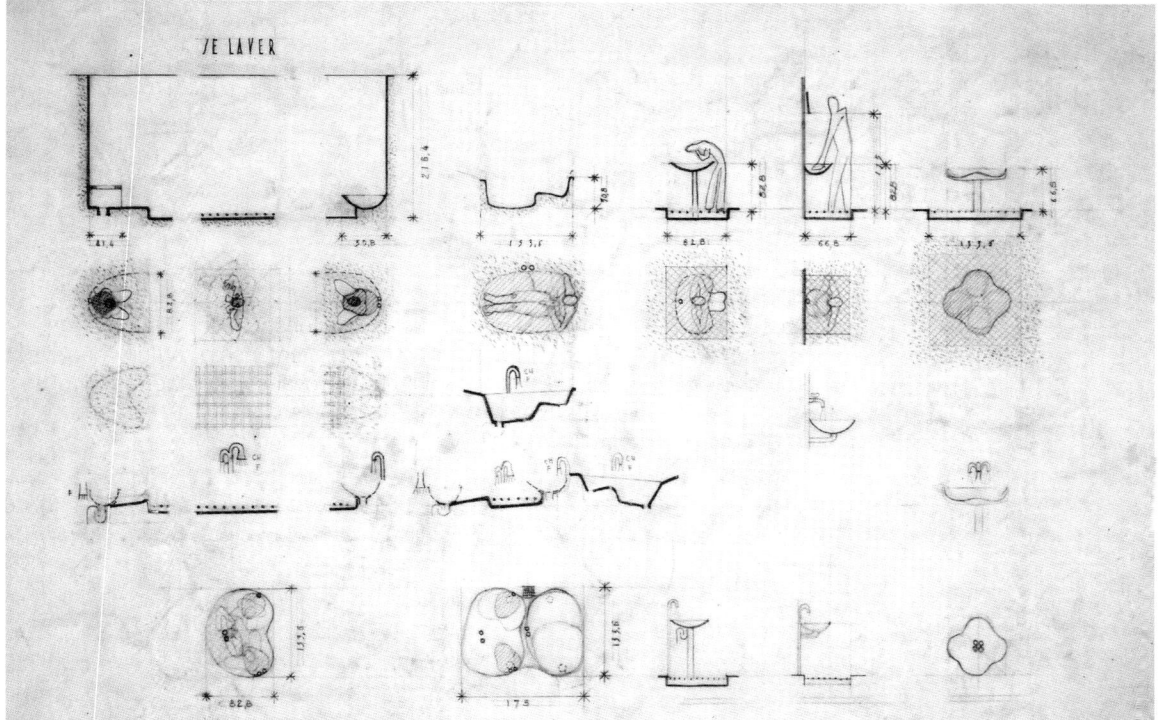

Figure 6.25   'Se Laver', FLC 27064

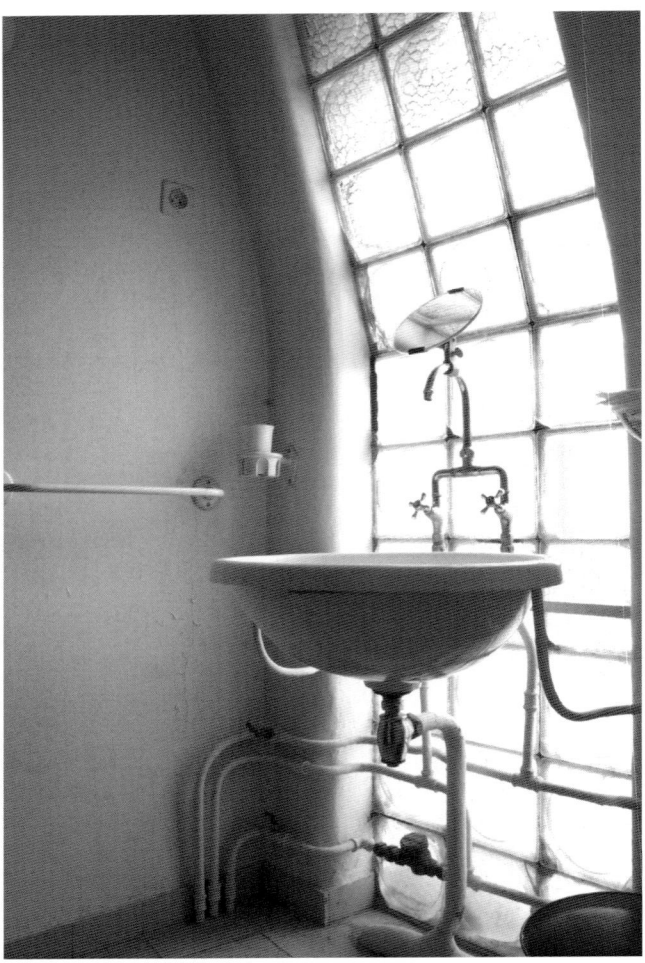

Figure 6.26
Sink in Le Corbusier's
bedroom penthouse, 24
Rue Nungesser et Coli
(1934)

recalled that if she had not studied medicine she would have 'found his anatomical precision embarrassing'.[49] Clearly he had certain exhibitionist tendencies in this regard. In my opinion, what he believed to be a new era of sexual and bodily frankness was celebrated in Le Corbusier's bathrooms.[50]

For Le Corbusier such spaces were often housed within a framework of curves which seem to echo the bodies which they contain. In the opinion of Rowe the 'spatial complexity' of the bathrooms on the Villa at Garches gives them the character of an 'event'.[51] The shower of Le Corbusier's own bathroom at 24 Rue Nungesser et Coli[52] is highly uterine (Figure 6.27),[53] but the bathroom pod receives perhaps its most extreme expression in the scheme for the Maisons Loucheur of 1929 where it appears freestanding at the very centre of the room. That same year Le Corbusier designed a cylindrical shower enclosure visible both from the living and dining spaces of an exhibition stand entitled 'Equipment for the dwelling'.[54] Similarly the apartments of the first, 1945, Unité

Figure 6.27   Shower pod, penthouse, 24 Rue Nungesser et Coli (1934)

scheme were each to have almost stand-alone lavatory and bathing pods.[55] The master bedroom of Jaoul Maison B has a beautiful sculptural bathroom pod which, through its form, serves simultaneously to protect the threshold of the door, yet facilitate the transition within.

A further foray into the standardized design of bathrooms was made by Le Corbusier around 1957, with a commission for bathroom fixtures from the Italian firm Ceramica Pozzi . 'At this stage in life', writes Rüegg, 'Le Corbusier was only interested in radical, elemental solutions, which is undoubtedly why the project was never realised'.[56] The intention of the project was clearly to in some way mimic the bathing conditions of 'primitive man' (Figure 6.28).[57]

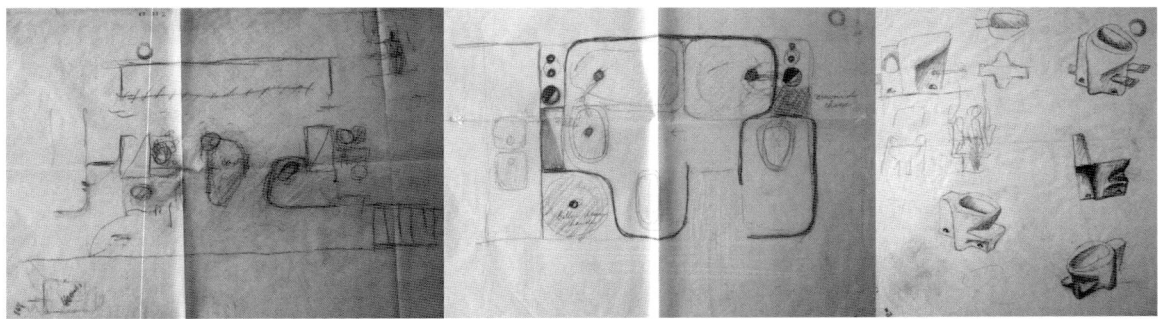

Figure 6.28   Sketch of shower unit for Ceramic Pozzi

Two of his sketches show a cavelike plastic element combining the shower, sitz bath, and toilet in one component. This unit, with evokes anthropomorphic comparisons, would have been augmented by an *arbre sanitaire*, a post on which a sink, cabinet, mirror, and towel bar were all mounted. A working drawing exists for the device. It shows two sinks attached to the common stem of the drain pipe. Warm and cold water were to have been supplied by pipes that were mounted on the ceiling and also supported an open cabinet element and a pivoting, framed mirror.[58]

In the opinion of Rüegg what was at stake here was 'the juxtaposition of male and female forms that is characteristic of Le Corbusier's concept of dialectic oppositions'.[59] If so, even the art of plumbing could be used to convey aspects of Le Corbusier's wider philosophy to the initiated.

6.4   Conclusion

Much has been written on the tryptich of enigmatic objects, the fish, fan and the coffee pot that are dispersed around the kitchen counter top of the Villa Savoye in one well-known photograph (Figure 6.29). David Leatherbarrow asks: 'can one not ease the opposition between settings such as the altar in the temple and the table in the domestic dining room, as Le Corbusier seems to have imagined when composing his provocative view?'[60] It is this slippage between the domestic and the

Figure 6.29   Kitchen, Villa Sayoye (1930) from Le Corbusier's *Oeuvre Compléte*

sacred that is one of the most significant aspects of Le Corbusier's architecture and it is often achieved through small but significant tectonic gestures that can revivify the role of fire, water and food in daily life.

Notes

[1] Le Corbusier discussed what he calls 'the cult of the home' which has stayed the same for centuries, primarily represented by '*the roof!*' and then 'the other household gods' in Le Corbusier., *The Final Testament of Père Corbu: a Translation and Interpretation of Mise au Point by Ivan Zaknic* (New Haven, CT: Yale University Press, 1991), pp. 18–19.

[2] Ibid., p. 91

[3] A. Wogenscky, *Les Mains de Le Corbusier* (Paris: Grenelle, n.d.), p. 32. Charles Correa is more critical . C. Correa, 'Chandigarh: the view from Benares' in H. Allen Brooks (ed.), *The Le Corbusier Archive, Volume XX* (New York: Garland, 1983), p. x. Hereafter referred to as Allen Brooks, *Archive*.

[4] Le Corbusier, *When the Cathedrals were White* (New York: Reyner and Hitchcock, 1947), p. 89.

[5] I. Xenakis, 'The monastery of La Tourette' in Allen Brooks, *Archive, Volume XXVIII*, pp. xii.

[6] F. Samuel, 'A profane annunciation; the representation of sexuality in the architecture of Ronchamp', *Journal of Architectural Education*, 53:2 (1999), pp. 74–90.

[7] D. Leatherbarrow, *The Roots of Architectural Invention* (Cambridge: Cambridge University Press, 1993), p. 224.

[8] Le Corbusier, *The Chapel at Ronchamp* (London: Architectural Press, 1957), pp. 131–3.

[9] See M. Krustrup, *Porte Email* (Copenhagen: Arkitektens Forlag, 1991), p. 128

[10] Le Corbusier, *Sketchbooks, Volume 3* (Cambridge, MA: MIT, 1982), sketch 549.

[11] Le Corbusier, *The Marseilles Block*, (London: Harvill, 1953), p. 20. Originally published as *L'Unité d'habitation de Marseille* (Mulhouse: Editions Le Point, 1950).

[12] Le Corbusier, *Une Petite Maison* (Zurich: Editions d'Architecture, 1993), p. 24. Originally published 1954.

[13] See photo in Allen Brooks, *Archive, Volumes VIII*, p. 152.

[14] Le Corbusier and P. Jeanneret, *Oeuvre Complète Volume 2, 1929–34* (Zurich: Les Editions d'Architecture, 1995), p. 77. Originally published in 1935.

[15] FLC 15653 in Allen Brooks, *Archive, Volumes VIII*, p. 324.

[16] M. McLeod (ed.), *Charlotte Perriand: An Art of Living* (New York: Harry N. Abrams 2003), p. 54.

[17] Ibid.

[18] Ibid.

[19] F. Pottecher, 'Que le Fauve soit libre dans sa cage', *L'Architecture d'Aujourd'Hui*, 252 (1987), p. 62.

[20] Ibid.

[21] Conversation with author in April 2006. An early version of this shutter appears in the project for the Immeuble Feuardent, 1934, in Allen Brooks, *Archive, Volume XII*, p. 189.

[22] Le Corbusier and P. Jeanneret *Oeuvre Complète Volume 1, 1910–1929* (Zurich: Les Editions d'Architecture, 1995), p. 135 Originally published in 1937.

[23] FLC 8409 in Allen Brooks, *Archive, Volume XII*, p. 516.

[24] Ibid., p. 537.

[25] Le Corbusier and Jeanneret, *Oeuvre Complète Volume 2*, p. 57.

[26] See, for example, the fire niche in the hanging garden on Garches. Le Corbusier and Jeanneret *Oeuvre Complète Volume 1*, p. 149. Colin St John Wilson was highly critical of the planning of the fireplace Villa de Mandrot where it was flanked by doors that would presumably make it both draughty and uncomfortable. C.St. John Wilson, *The Other Tradition of Modern Architecture* (London: Academy, 1995), p. 105.

[27] Le Corbusier, *Sketchbooks 2* (London: Thames and Hudson, 1981), sketch 497. See also 'le cœur du logis/feu foyer// Marseille'. Ibid., sketch 508.

[28] Trouin called it 'un certain état d'âme collectif' the 'aboutissement naturel de la vie commune'. E. Trouin, 'Appel au Monde en faveur du Plan d'Aups', n.d., FLC 13 01 370.

[29] S.P.A. Lannezman house type for an engineer. Construction sections through house and details showing roof make-up, balustrade, showing how rainwater gully on terrace works at large scale. Le Corbusier, *Oeuvre Complète Volume* 4, p. 37.

[30] W. Curtis, *Le Corbusier: Ideas and Forms* (Oxford: Phaidon, 1986), p. 210.

[31] Email, José Oubrerie to author April 2006.

[32] Le Corbusier, *Journey to the East*, (Cambridge MA: MIT, 1987), p. 240. Originally published in 1966.

[33] C. Rowe, *The Architecture of Good Intentions* (London: Academy Editions, 1994), p. 60.

[34] The Maison Lipchitz, the Maison Guiette at Anvers, 1926, the Villa at Carthage (1929) where the sink is directly opposite the door, Projets Wanner in Geneva of 1928/9, the Immeuble pour artistes 1928/9, the apartments of Maison Locative at Alger, 1933.

[35] F. Samuel, 'Le Corbusier Rabelais and Oracle of the Holy Bottle,' *Word and Image: a Journal of verbal/visual enquiry*, 16, (2000), pp. 1–13.

[36] Le Corbusier, *Precisions on the Present State of Architecture and City Planning* (Cambridge, MA: MIT, 1991), p. 44.

[37] Le Corbusier, *Oeuvre Complète Volume 5, 1946–1952* (Zurich: Les Editions d'Architecture, 1995), p. 214. Originally published in 1953.

[38] Curtis, *Le Corbusier: Ideas and Forms*, p. 212.

[39] C. Laubier, *The Condition of Women in France: 1945 to the Present* (London: Routledge, 1990), p. 2.

[40] I. Zacnic, *Le Corbusier: Pavillon Suisse: The Biography of a Building* (Basel: Birkäuser, 2004), p. 137.

[41] Le Corbusier, *The Nursery Schools* (New York: Orion, 1968), p. 70.

[42] Rowe, *The Architecture of Good Intentions*, p. 60.

[43] FLC 19370 Allen Brooks, *Archive, Volume XV*, p. 143.

[44] FLC 27064 in Allen Brooks, *Archive, Volume XVII*, p. 345.

[45] Arthur Rüegg, 'Transforming the bathroom: Perriand and Le Corbusier, 1927–57' in McLeod, *Charlotte Perriand*, p. 116.

[46] C. Rowe, *The Architecture of Good Intentions*, p. 60.

[47] Ibid.

[48] C. Jencks, *Le Corbusier and the Continual Revolution in Architecture* (New York: Monacelli Press, 2000), p. 191.

[49] Ibid., p. 104.

[50] See F. Samuel, *Le Corbusier: Architect and Feminist* (London: Wiley, 2004) for a development of this discussion.

[51] Rowe, *The Architecture of Good Intentions*, p. 60.

[52] For a lengthy series of developmental drawings see, for example, FLC 13444, FLC 13547 FLC 28235 in Allen Brooks, *Archive, Volume XI*, pp. 67, 115 and 303.

[53] Le Corbusier and Jeanneret, *Oeuvre Complète Volume 2*, p. 148.

[54] McLeod, *Charlotte Perriand*, p. 53.

[55] Le Corbusier, *Oeuvre Complète Volume 4, 1938–1946* (Zurich: Les Editions d'Architecture, 1995), p. 172. Originally published in 1946.

[56] Rüegg, 'Transforming the bathroom', p. 129.

[57] Lotissement 1933 Barcelona. Le Corbusier and Jeanneret, *Oeuvre Complète Volume 2*, p. 199.

[58] Rüegg, 'Transforming the bathroom', p. 129.

[59] D. Leatherbarrow, *The Roots of Invention*, p. 224.

[60] Rüegg, 'Transforming the bathroom', p. 129.

Clouds 1959 7

'Trinity, I love that word', wrote Le Corbusier.[1] Like the trinity of platonic forms that inhabit the cistern at Ronchamp (see Figure 6.3), and the trinity of coloured rooflights that beam down upon the crypt of La Tourette (see Figure 3.11), a trinity of elements float across the entry to Le Corbusier's Maison du Brésel (1957–59).[2] These form the focus of this chapter, a reflection on detail and its meaning in context – a lesson in geography, perspective and interior urbanization, for in Le Corbusier's work 'the outside is always an inside'.[3]

In an early photograph the trinity consisted of two clouds and a sun (Figure 7.1), but now the trinity is rather different, although its purpose, I would suggest, is very similar. The first element, in natural wood, encompasses the door handle, its brown form evocative of a land mass when seen from above, or possibly a cloud. The other two, flanking the two side walls of the draught lobby, are emphatically clouds but they are painted in a satin red (Figure 7.2). Restrained by their metal fixings they do not touch the glass itself, but are held proud of it as befits their floating state (Figure 7.3). The first red cloud is fastened to the glass with four fixings, the second with three – which when added make seven, each a loaded number in Le Corbusier's Pythagorean cosmos. Together the three elements join together to form a clue to the possible meaning of the space which they introduce – a fictive landscape of water and rock, bathed in the sun, drawn from Le Corbusier's distinct memories of his travels around and above South America.[4]

A similar arrangement to that of the lobby of the Maison du Brésel, though rather more literal, can be found in Le Corbusier's scheme for a stand at the Ideal Home Exhibition in London (1938–39), under the banner 'The radiant city: Sun, Space, Greenery'. Here sun and cloud are vast three-dimensional objects formed of papier mâché that hover

Figure 7.1 Lobby, Maison du Brésel. Photo from *Oeuvre Complète*

Figure 7.2
Red cloud, lobby, Maison
du Brésel (1957)

Figure 7.3
Lobby, Maison du Brésel
(1957)

above a model depicting Le Corbusier's radiant city proposal for London
(Figure 7.4). Below them float a vast eye and an ear. All three are connected to the model by the rays of the sun, literally 'radiant'. While the
suggestion seems to be that the eye and the ear focus on the city via
the rays below, they actually focus outwards towards the horizon. It is
as though they are responding both to the particular and the universal
at the same time. This makes sense as this was one of the main tenets
of Le Corbusier's work. The model was designed to, in Le Corbusier's
words 'call and intrigue the visitor and leave him with a reminder of the
essential and decisive principals capable of driving the new urbanism
and the new architecture'.[5]

The sun, the cloud, the eye and the ear are all framed within a block
of gridded steel, intentionally evocative of the Unité.[6] The visitor was
to be brought into the picture, literally, up a ramp and into a pavilion
(also enveloping a tree) that cantilevered out into the frame and over the
model city. He or she would occupy the space just below the eye/ear and
would be associated with them by proximity. The Ideal Home Exhibition

Figure 7.4 Le Corbusier's scheme for a stand at the Ideal Home Exhibition in London (1938–39)

and the lobby of the Maison du Brésel appear to share three elements, cloud, frame and map/model (both aerial views). The sun is present at the Maison du Brésel in its original form of light, pouring through the ondulatoires from all sides. It is my suggestion that the eye/ear seemingly missing from its lobby is actually present in the form of you or I, the visitor who completes the composition. This is not the first time that Le Corbusier does such a thing. I have described a similar arrangement in Chapter 2 where the presence of the visitor is required to make the composition whole. In this way the building acts as a highly personal initiatory experience to those 'with eyes to see'.

7.1 Brazil

As if lifted from the pages of his book *The Poem of the Right Angle* (1990), the clouds and the land are familiar elements of Le Corbusier's symbolic language but the sheer redness of the lobby clouds is startling. Red,[7] in terms of *The Poem of the Right Angle* is the colour of fusion, of carnality, of sex. It was about the body, the unconscious and basic instinct, qualities that he sweepingly ascribed to the Brazilian people, qualities that he revelled on his debauched visits to the favellas accompanied by the painter Emiliano Di Cavalcanti.[8] Le Corbusier was impressed by the

Brazilians, by their music, by their ability to enjoy life to the full (as he saw it) and their seemingly innate ability to create vibrant space.[9]

An enthusiastic swimmer, he delighted in the omnipresence of the sea in Rio. 'I swim in front of my hotel; I go back to my room by elevator in a bathrobe, at 30 metres above the sea; I stroll about on foot at night; I have friends at every minute of the day, almost till sunrise; at seven in the morning, I am in the water.'[10] This experience caused him to posit a vast town planning scheme where cars were to travel at roof level maximizing contact with sea in what he called a 'seascraper', which would give vast bodies of people vital access to the beach.[11]

'Brazil is one of those hospitable and generous places which one loves to be able to call a friend', wrote Le Corbusier. These words are prefaced by a description of the country's topography which he described as one of the great 'privileged areas on the planisphere, between the mountains, on the plateaus and the plains where flow the great rivers which go to the sea'.[12] For Le Corbusier, Brazil meant Rio 'blue bays, sky and water . . . edged by white quays or pink beaches'.[13] Further, 'everything rises; islands piercing the water, peaks falling into it, high hills and great mountains'.[14]

7.2   Geography lesson

Always an admirer of Venice for its watery foundations, Le Corbusier viewed cities in terms of their elemental geography.[15] 'The site is the base of the architectural composition', he wrote, a lesson that he learned when he first visited the Parthenon in 1911.[16] Further, 'What is Manhattan? It is a peninsular bounded by water and space'.[17] This tendency to see the world from an aerial perspective was reinforced by his enthusiasm for aeroplanes and the views therefrom, given such emphasis in *Precisions*, the book that records his thinking as he travelled across Latin America.

> When one has gone up in a plane for observation and glided like a bird over all the bays, has turned around all the peaks, when one has entered the intimacy of the city, when one has torn away in a single glance of the gliding bird all the secrets that it hid so easily from the poor terrestrial on his two feet, one has seen everything, understood everything . . .
>
> . . . When, by plane, everything has become clear, and you have learned this topography, this body so hilly and so complicated; when, having conquered difficulties, you have been seized with enthusiasm, you have felt ideas being born, you have entered into the body and the heart of the city, you have understood part of its destiny . . .
>
> . . . But when everything is on holiday in Rio, when everything is so sublime and so magnificent, when one has taken a long flight over the city like a bird gliding, ideas attack you.[18]

Such an experience would be available to the inhabitant of Le Corbusier's seascraper apartment whose home would be 'almost the nest of a gliding bird'.[19]

Le Corbusier's preoccupation with topography was expressed in two 1936 schemes for Rio. The first for the City University, where great emphasis was placed on framing the mountain at the head of the complex.[20] A further project, the Palais du Ministère de L'Éducation Nationale et de la Santé Publique, provides yet more evidence of Le Corbusier's preoccupation with the forms of the islands and rocky outcrops around the city which are continually present through vast plate-glass windows – 'this sea, seen from the room of a palace, is a geography map of the time of the Conquest, with its gulfs, its mountains, its boats'.[21]

A variety of means were to be used to bring the landscape into his architecture. In one sketch of the Palais du Ministère De l'Éducation Nationale (1936) – a view of the antechamber of the minister – a statue of a reclining woman is placed on axis with the room (Figure 7.5). It echoes in its form that of the islands in the bay beyond. The same statue appears again in a sketch of 'Minister Capanema's office', again mirroring the distant rocks (Figure 7.6). In a further drawing of an office space, a vast seated statue, 'Brasilian Man'[22] again echoes the form of the rocks in the bay.[23] This statue appears to reflect the mountains – one of which

L' antichambre du ministre

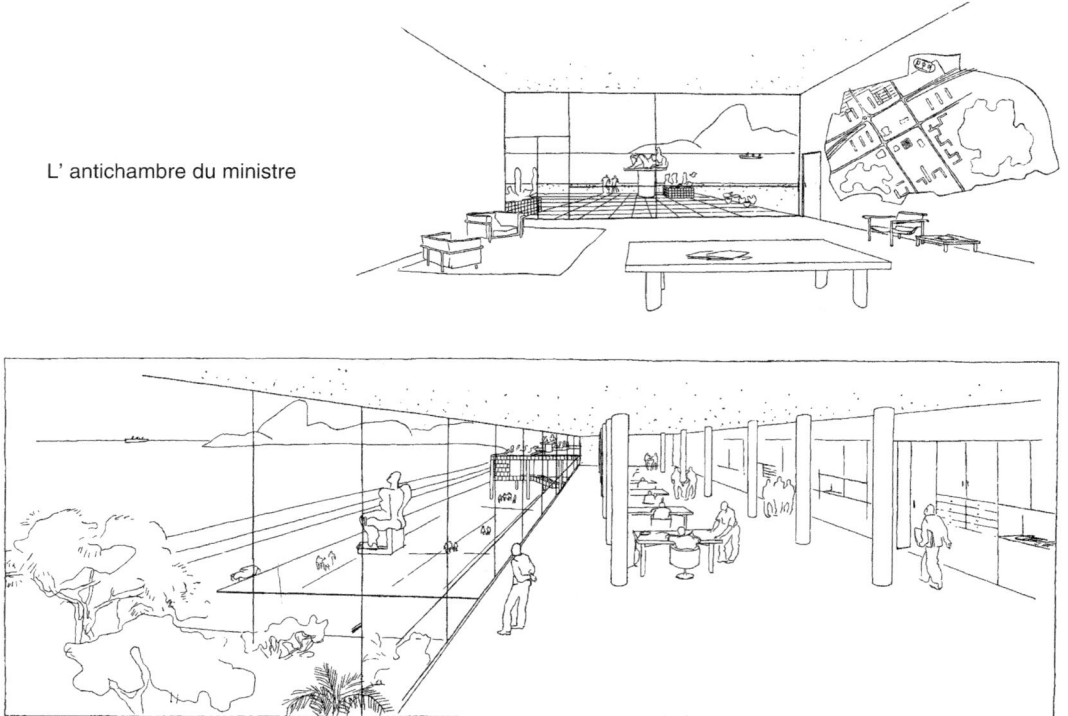

Figure 7.5 Sketch of the Palais du Ministère de l'Éducation Nationale (1936)

Le cabinet du
Ministre Capanema

Figure 7.6 'Minister Capanema's office'. Sketch of the Palais du Ministère de l'Éducation Nationale (1936)

is known as 'the stone man' – in a kind of dialogue (Figure 7.5).[24] Their names reflect the synergy between them. Similar perspective games would be played by Le Corbusier on the uppermost level of the Unité, where he borrowed the rocky crags beyond Marseilles, drawing them visually into the fictive terrain of his roof where they appear as one with what he called his 'artificial mountains' (Figure 7.7).[25]

Le Corbusier's response to the Rio landscape was celebrated in an intriguing series of sketches in the *Oeuvre Complète* in which he pulled the exterior environment into the confines of a box-like room through the framing of views (Figure 7.8). This intention is clearly expressed in a series of sketches in the *Oeuvre Complète*, the first of which is of the 'celebrated' rock at the centre of the bay of Rio de Janeiro. The second sketch shows the rock framed by sea. The view has panned out further in the third sketch to encompass a man sitting in an armchair enjoying the view 'the palm trees, the banana trees; the tropical splendour animates the site. We stop, we put an armchair there'.[26] In the fourth and final sketch 'a frame surrounds it all! The four planes of a perspective! The room is positioned in front of the site. Within the room one is entirely within the landscape'.[27] The lobby of the Brazil pavilion would fulfil a parallel function to the room in the sketches. In this case it would cause a strange inversion of space giving an impression of the landscape from an aerial perspective.

Figure 7.7 'Artificial mountains' on roof of Unité, Marseilles Michelet (1952)

Ce roc à Rio de Janeiro est célèbre

Autour de lui se dressent des montagnes échevelées; la mar les baigne

Des palmiers, des bananiers; la splendeur tropicale anime le site. On s'arrête, on y installe son fauteuil

Un cadre tout autour! Les quatre obliques d'une perspective! La chambre est installée face au site. Le paysage entre tout entier dans la chambre

Figure 7.8   Framing of a view. Series of sketches from Le Corbusier, *Oeuvre Complète Volume 4*

7.3   Perspective

Le Corbusier took great delight in playing spatial games. 'Try to look at the picture upside down or sideways. You will discover the game', he wrote.[28] Vertical and horizontal – the right angle at the very heart of his personal philosophy – are blurred. Colin Rowe devoted much energy attempting to chart the 'perceptual intricacies' of Le Corbusier's work.[29] Indeed, he wrote of La Tourette: 'For, if floors are horizontal walls, then, presumably, walls are vertical floors; and, while elevations become plans and the building a form of dice, then the complete aplomb with which Le Corbusier manages his church may, in some faint degree be explained'.[30] The same could be said of the lobby of the Maison du Brésel. If, as Le Corbusier wrote, 'The floor . . . is really a horizontal wall'[31] then in this case too the wall is really a floor giving a vertical view through space. In Le Corbusier's words 'Bird flight, bird sight, extraordinary conquest. Harmonized destiny'.[32]

Le Corbusier was fully conversant with the way in which the perspectival space of Renaissance and Baroque churches was designed intentionally around a viewer standing in a particular position. Indeed, he wrote with vehement disgust of the way the Beaux Arts School continued to encourage this form of design. In his opinion 'an architecture must be walked through and traversed . . . our man walks about . . . in the midst of a succession of architectural realities'.[33]

At the Maison du Brésel this 'rule of movement' has been 'brilliantly exploited' in Le Corbusier's terms. It is built around the viewer while utilizing, and indeed flouting, the rules of perspective. The visitor's horizontal, human viewpoint is temporarily held in suspense, replaced for an extraordinary and fleeting moment with a bird's eye view of clouds, land and sea – an entirely different 'architectural reality' – as he or she moves through the lobby, where it is restored – upon opening the door into the hall itself – once more to the horizontal. 'Architecture', wrote Le Corbusier, 'particularly for emotional reasons' offers 'up the anticipation or surprise of doors which reveal unexpected space'.[34]

Jerzy Soltan recalled that for Le Corbusier the ground floor of a building 'represented the poetic and purely visual longing to express the "new space", the "continuum of space", a relatively recent notion introduced by science and visually tackled already by Cubism'.[35] Certainly the rotating viewpoint created in the lobby of the Maison du Brésel shares something of Le Corbusier's Purist paintings and, indeed, his early forays into Cubism which he described as a 'serious revolutionary shock . . . driving towards an architectural synthesis . . . a plastic epic'.[36] In his painting *Deux bouteilles* of 1926 (Figure 7.9)[37] the bottles in question are experienced from above and below, from within and without simultaneously. Le Corbusier wrote in *Talks with Students* of the way in which ethnography offered 'us the opportunity to readjust our points of view'.[38] It may be that he was implying that ethnography allows us to see a multitude of other viewpoints, or he may have been alluding to an entirely different experience of space rendered visible by a study of 'so called

Figure 7.9   Le Corbusier, *Deux bouteilles (1926)*

primitive art'.[39] The latter point seems to be more likely as this statement it followed by a discussion of the way in which the 'major arts' were 'vigorously refurbished' through the discovery of this 'modern science' and, further, that 'Here we confront all the implications of that strange term Cubism. Since the post war years, architecture has been touched by its fruitful stirrings'.[40] This curious juxtaposition of ethnography and perspective experiment leads us back to the Maison du Brésel where, as well as giving us the experience of the Brazilian landscape, Le Corbusier may be giving us what he felt to be a more 'primitive' experience of space, the drug-induced interior flight of the shaman, the mythopoetic world where all things, including viewpoints, are one. Certainly the thresholds of reality are called into question, a rupture occurs that brings to mind Le Corbusier's own description of 'the miracle of inexpressible space'.[41]

Curtis writes of the hallway of the Carpenter Centre that 'its many glazed surfaces, projections, and boundaries' create a kind of visual confusion about the very limits of the space itself 'thus exterior features are experienced as interior ones, and it even requires slight effort to

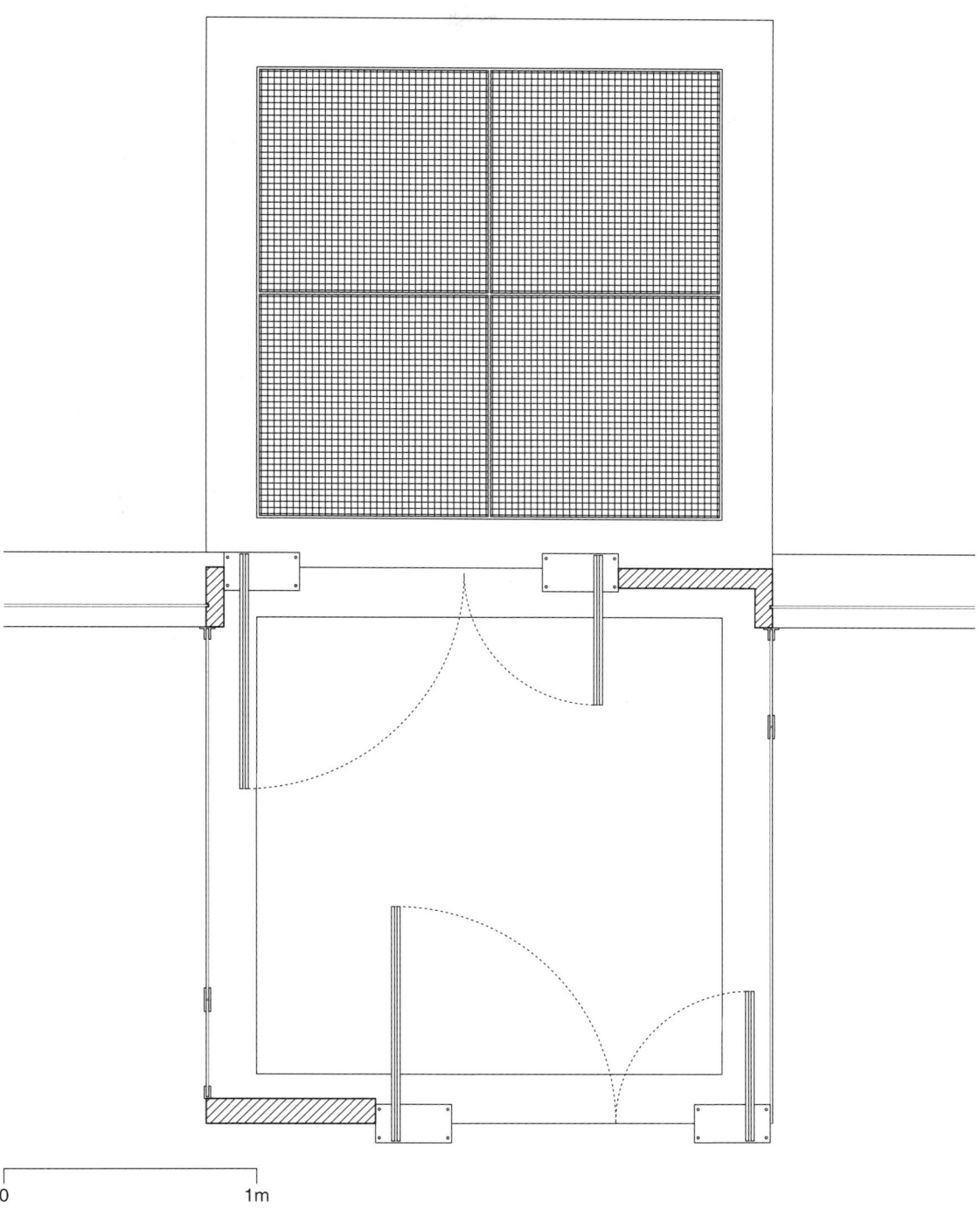

Figure 7.10 Plan of Lobby Maison du Brésel (1957)

0   1m

concentrate on the room itself'.[42] A similar experience occurs in the shifting space of the hallway of the Maison du Brésel where, at times, the walls of the lobby completely disappear leaving only the trace of clouds behind.

On the exterior elevation the glass of the box sits just slightly proud of the glazing on either side, giving it a special presence within the wall (Figure 7.10). That this was the intention is evident from a number of design sketches.[43] Formed out of sheets of glass fixed by means of metal plates to walls and floor, the draft lobby is at the same time an expanded version of the glass display cases, *casiers*, which he sometimes chose to build into windows, discussed in Chapter 4. They invite the viewer to see past the objects to the world beyond. The Carpenter Centre at Harvard is a still larger version of the same thing, a 'built cube',[44] a vast cabinet, this time physically traversed by the visitor on elevated ramps, a place where 'the students of the university could, while crossing this main path, look-in from the outside, eventually enter and register to work'.[45]

The glass box of the cube in the Maison du Brésel was built to Le Corbusier's favourite dimensions: 226 × 226 cm, the 'application revelatrice', applied both to his Cabanon and his own 'working cell' in the Rue de Sèvres.[46] Like many spaces in Le Corbusier's oeuvre, it would provide a place of initiation into the Orphic power of number, which would be perceived at a gut level as sensation, before moving on to the brain as thought.

7.4 Interior urbanism

As if floating upon water, or standing in a lagoon, the Maison du Brésel sits on a plane of rippling black slate, laid in waves to Modulor proportions, moving almost seamlessly from exterior to interior. The built-in furniture of the hall is in strong contrast with this hard shiny floor, particularly the soft white matt leather covering the cushions on the concrete banquettes, perhaps an island, perhaps a cloud – it strongly evokes the image of buildings seen from water by night, on the cover of *Precisions* (Figure 7.11). There is something almost indecent about the leather in its expense, in its impracticality, in its approximation to skin (Figure 7.12). On the first page of *The Poem of the Right Angle* Le Corbusier wrote of the influence of the sun in the life of 'our' earth. In the illustration above, his body appears as a rocky landscape extending out into the sea (Figure 7.13). The image, based on an experience Le Corbusier had in a bath in a hotel room in London in 1953, serves to blur the difference between the earth and the body, a central theme of *The Poem*, and one that may well have found its way into the hall of this Paris block of student accommodation. Sekler writes of one of Le Corbusier's paintings from 1945 which carries the 'telltale title *The islands are bodies of women half immersed who hold boats in their arms*' (Figure 7.14). In Sekler's opinion 'it was entirely in keeping with his way of looking at the world that he compared the forms of man and his inhabitation to trees and stones, rivers and clouds'.[47] This same painting, this time translated into

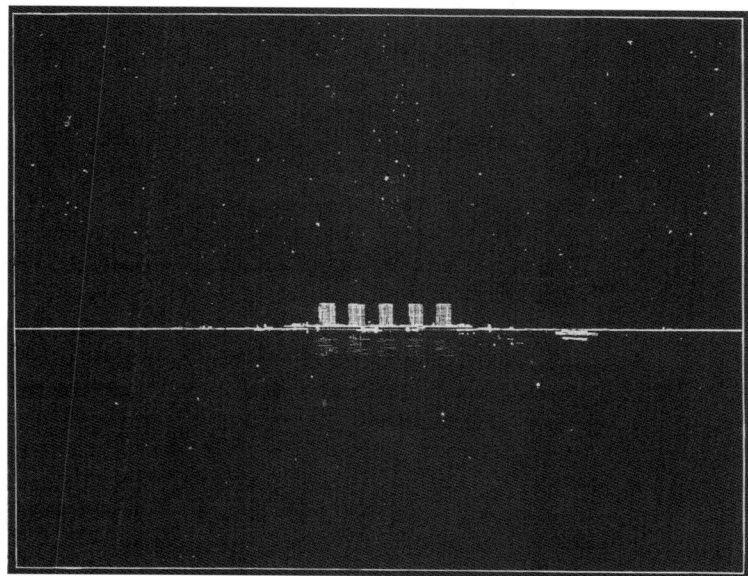

Figure 7.11
Cover of Le Corbusier's
Precisions, based on his
journey round South
America

Figure 7.12
White leather banquettes.
Maison du Brésel (1957)

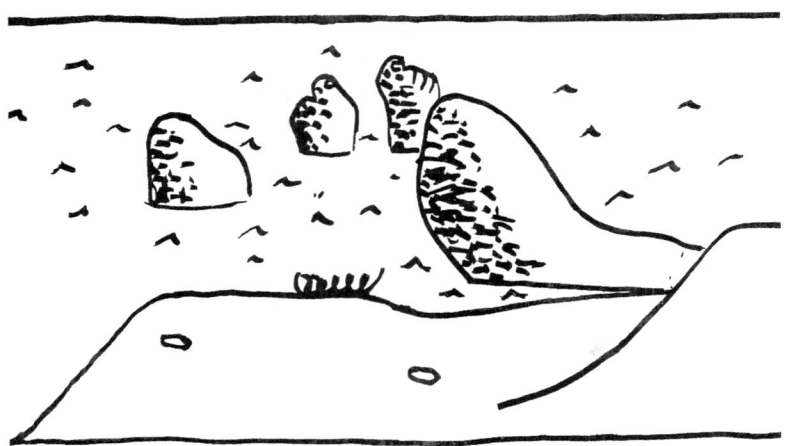

Figure 7.13 Detail, Section A1, *The Poem of the Right Angle* (1955)

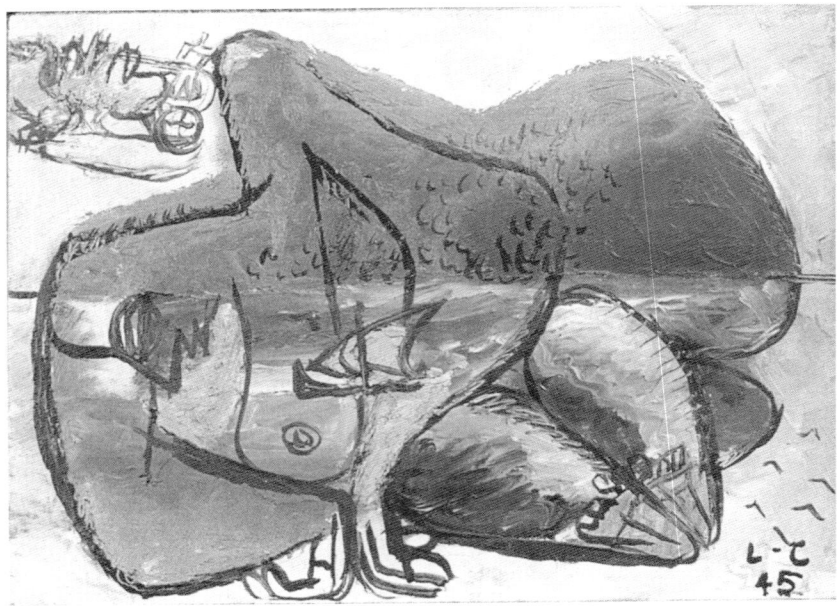

Figure 7.14 'Les îles sont des corps de femmes', FLC 4231 (1945)

tapestry, appeared on exhibition at the Museum of Modern Art in Rio de Janeiro in 1952, perhaps because of its connection with that city.[48] As Le Corbusier himself wrote: 'I have never ceased to draw and to paint, searching for the secrets of form where I could find them. One must not search elsewhere for the key to my labours and my research.'[49]

A further type would enter Le Corbusier's furniture repertoire in the 1950s – the banquette. Such free-standing elements – 'a natural urbanization of space contemplated'[50] – the urbanization of the

Figure 7.15   Banquette. Pavillon Suisse (1957–59)

interior and the urbanization of the city being much the same thing in Le Corbusier's eyes. In his examination of Le Corbusier's 1957–59 refurbishment of the Pavillon Suisse, Ivan Zacnic, discusses their development in some detail (Figure 7.15):

> From the start Le Corbusier described the Banquettes as something already designed, down to the last detail. They were to be made out of ordinary brick and cement, 40 cm high, faced with enamel panels similar to those of the Ronchamp chapel door. Le Corbusier would paint them himself, free of charge: 'I cannot give them to a third person to be painted', he admitted. The dimensions provided were also quite specific: 226 cm by 70 cm each, equipped with two dunlopillo cushions measuring 113 by 70 by 10 and upholstered with a washable fabric of his own choice both in quality and colour. Modulor was not mentioned as proportioning system, but the specifications make it obvious that it was applied.[51]

Apparently the steel and cement framework of each banquette weighs some 400 kilos – each had casters, but they soon wore out.[52] Clearly such a structure was inappropriate for movable furniture so Le Corbusier must have had some other reason for making them so heavy. It is my suggestion that he wanted them to feel like something that would more appropriately be placed outdoors, like stone. Indeed, at the Maison du Brésel, banquettes, this time without wheels, appear both on the interior and the exterior (without cushions), contributing to the blurring of indoor and outdoor space which is so very central to the scheme.

At low altitude we cruise past the block of pigeonholes, a miniature Unité, cast, not of concrete, but of glass (Figure 7.16). A block – a casier

Figure 7.16   Pigeonhole block, Maison du Brésel (1957)

indeed – not of apartments but of pigeonholes. It is formed of three bands – first a concrete foundation, the patterns of its timber formwork exactly that of the exterior of the Maison du Brésel. Onto this founda-tion are mounted translucent pilotis sheltering the polished grey com-munal ground plane occupied now by a variety of potted plants and

Figure 7.17
Detail, pigeonhole block,
Maison du Brésel

newspapers. The numbered glass cells above provide individual homes
for assorted letters and junk mail for people. They are bolted together with
metal plates like those of the lobby beyond with which the pigeonhole
block is in conversation (Figure 7.17). The 'jewel'[53] of the building, natural
focus of the space, it is lit from beneath, like an altar, like the Unité itself,
throwing a ripple of light onto the bulging concrete of the ceiling above.
From my seascraper nest I look back to clouds, red clouds, hot clouds,
sun and water both.

Notes

[1] Le Corbusier, *Journey to the East* (Cambridge, MA: MIT, 1987), p. 83.
[2] The initial design was prepared by Lucio Costa, but documentary evidence suggests
that Le Corbusier was decisive in his influence. Charlotte Perriand was also involved in
the interiors. See C. Rodrigues dos Santos, M. Campos da Silva Pereira, R. Veriano da

Silva Pereira, V. Caldeira da Silva, *Le Corbusier e o Brasil* (São Paulo: Projecto Editora, 1987), pp. 244–301 for an account of the genesis of the building as well as selected correspondence relating to its progress.

[3] Le Corbusier, *Precisions on the Present State of Architecture and City Planning* (Cambridge, MA: MIT, 1991), p. 78. Originally published as Précisions sur un état présent de l'architecture et de l'urbanisme (Paris: Crès, 1930).

[4] Nationalistic concerns were of course an issue in the building. Costa was concerned that the building should be in some way Brazilian, but Le Corbusier made the point that students coming to Paris should engage with the country that they were staying in. Exchange of letters, Costa Le Corbusier 1956 in ibid, pp. 273–4. The grey, blue, red and white of the façade were the 'predominant colours of France'. They were there in response to the boulevard which the façade addresses. Ibid., p. 267.

[5] Le Corbusier, *Oeuvre Complète Volume 4, 1938–1946* (Zurich: Les Editions d'Architecture, 1995), p. 14. Originally published in 1946.

[6] Ibid.

[7] Although the colours in the bedrooms vary slightly, a band of bright red consistently floats across the zone occupied by the bed, apparently causing complaints from the students sleeping beneath who insist that it is detrimental to their sleep. Conversation with Denise Leitao Curator at the Maison du Brésel, 24 April 2006.

[8] R. Segre, 'Un moment brésilien', Le Corbusier Moments biographiques, Paris, Fondation Le Corbusier, 8 December 2006.

[9] See J. Odgers, F. Samuel and A. Sharr (eds), *Primitive* (London: Routledge, 2006) for a discussion of the complexities of Le Corbusier stance vis-à-vis colonialization.

[10] Le Corbusier, *Precisions*, p. 234.

[11] Ibid., p. 239.

[12] Le Corbusier, *Oeuvre Complète Volume 7, 1957–1965* (Zurich: Les Editions d'Architecture, 1995), p. 8. Originally published in 1965.

[13] Le Corbusier, *Precisions*, p. 233.

[14] Ibid., p. 2.

[15] 'These are the three chief bases of city planning and architecture: The sea and the immense harbour. The magnificent vegetation of the Park of Palermo, the sky of Argentina. . .' Le Corbusier, *Precisions*, p. 24.

[16] Le Corbusier, *Talks with Students* (New York, Princeton: 2003), p. 41.

[17] Ibid., p. 67.

[18] Le Corbusier, *Precisions*, pp. 235–6. See also 'From a plane, one understands still many other things'. Ibid., p. 5.

[19] Ibid., p. 244.

[20] Ibid., p. 42.

[21] Ibid., p. 234. It should be noted that Le Corbusier was heated in his disgust at the damage done by the colonizers.

[22] 'L'homme Brésilien'. This was the result of collaboration between Le Corbusier and the sculptor Celo Antonio, FLC Carnet B4-258.

[23] Le Corbusier and P. Jeanneret, *Oeuvre Complète Volume 3, 1934–38* (Zurich: Les Editions d'Architecture, 1995), p. 79. Originally published in 1938.

[24] H. Usill (ed.), *The Story of the World in Pictures* (London: Oldhams Press, 1934), p. 227.

[25] Le Corbusier, *Oeuvre Complète Volume 5, 1946–1952* (Zurich: Les Editions d'Architecture, 1995), p. 214. Originally published in 1953.

[26] Le Corbusier, *Oeuvre Complète Volume 4*, p. 80.

[27] Ibid., p. 81.

[28] Le Corbusier, *The Chapel at Ronchamp* (London: Architectural Press, 1957), p. 47. Curtis writes of 'Architecture Pure Creation of the Mind' in Le Corbusier's *Towards a New Architecture* where the Parthenon is portrayed in a 'stunning montage of near and far views. The effect of these images and their captions is almost like a film – an analogue to the dynamic experience of a building from various points of view, and to the flux of thought and feeling as the artists recalls one of his most profound architectural experiences'. W. Curtis, *Le Corbusier: Ideas and Forms* (Oxford: Phaidon, 1986), p. 54.

[29] C. Rowe, *The Mathematics of the Ideal Villa and Other Essays* (Cambridge, MA: MIT, 1976), p. 192.

[30] Ibid., p. 197.

[31] Le Corbusier, *Towards a New Architecture* (London: Architectural Press, 1982), p. 172. Originally published as *Vers une Architecture* (Paris: Crès, 1923). See the Mill Owners' Building in Ahmedabad where there is a spine wall clad in stone that looks very much like a wall.

[32] Le Corbusier, *Oeuvre Complète Volume 4*, p. 71.

[33] Le Corbusier, *Talks with Students*, p. 45.

[34] Ibid., p. 46.

[35] Soltan, 'Working with Le Corbusier', in H. Allen Brooks (ed.), *The Le Corbusier Archive, Volume XVII* (New York: Garland, 1983), p. xvi. Hereafter referred to as Allen Brooks, *Archive*.

[36] Le Corbusier, *Oeuvre Complète Volume 4*, p. 155.

[37] M. Krustrup, *Le Corbusier, Painter and Architect* (Arkitekturtidsskrift: Nordjyllands, 1995), p. 167.

[38] Le Corbusier, *Talks with Students*, p. 66.

[39] 'L'Art dit primitif'. This was the name of an exhibition that was held in Le Corbusier's penthouse at 24 Rue Nungesser et Coli.

[40] Le Corbusier, *Talks with Students*, p. 66.

[41] Le Corbusier, *Modulor 2* (London: Faber, 1955), p. 71. Originally published as *Le Modulor II* (Paris: Editions d'Architecture d'Aujourd'hui, 1955).

[42] E. Sekler, and W. Curtis, *Le Corbusier at Work: The Genesis of the Carpenter Centre for the Visual Arts* (Cambridge, MA: MIT, 1978), p.26.

[43] FLC 12724 and 12725 in Allen Brooks, *Archive, Volume XXVIII*, p. 229.

[44] Le Corbusier quoted in Sekler and Curtis, *Le Corbusier at work*, p. 81.

[45] Le Corbusier, *Oeuvre Complète Volume 7*, p. 54.

[46] Le Corbusier, *Oeuvre Complète Volume 5*, p. 185.

[47] Sekler and Curtis, *Le Corbusier at Work*, p. 230.

[48] Rodrigues dos Santos et al., *Le Corbusier e o Brasil*, p. 223.

[49] Le Corbusier, *Creation is a Patient Search* (New York: Praeger, 1960), p. 197.

[50] Letter to Pierre Baudoin, 10 May 1958. J. Jenger, *Le Corbusier Choix de Lettres* (Basel: Birkhauser, 2002) p. 419. I. Zacnic, *Le Corbusier: Pavillon Suisse: The Biography of a Building* (Basel: Birkäuser, 2004), p. 354.

[51] Ibid., p. 332.

[52] Ibid.

[53] I owe this word to Denise Leitao who described it as 'our jewel' when showing us around the space.

Conclusion

Tectonic decisions, even at the level of structure, convey a great deal about the architect's view of the world – whether they are jaded and cynical or full of idealism. There is something very moralistic about Le Corbusier's architecture. In accordance with his own doctrine of hard work and asceticism, his buildings are about self-denial, knowledge, courage and reward and are detailed in accordance with these precepts.

Le Corbusier thought continually in terms of the way the body would respond to his architecture. Nowhere is that relationship so intense as in the sphere of detail, yet, as Banham has observed:

> The new body was to be, it seems, the 'masterly, correct and magnificent play of muscles brought together in light'. This rehabilitated image of the Greek athlete, and the rehabilitated classical architecture to house it, are clearly aspects of the same vision, yet they seem to have no organic relationship. Standing upon a *terrain ideal*, not our common earth, each is a free-standing conception, absolute and unconditioned by the other, bathed by the same sun, but that sun does not shine through the windows of the ideal building into the eyes of the ideal body, nor does the breath of the ideal nose condense upon ideal glass.[1]

In my book *Le Corbusier: Architect and Feminist* (2004) I illustrated a number of inconsistencies between Le Corbusier's ideal vision of women and his treatment of women that he knew. What Banham describes is something similar; Le Corbusier's inability to resolve fully the differences between art and life, a problem that dogged the construction of his buildings, a problem of which he was fully aware – representing himself as Don Quixote tilting at the windmills of his ideals. Banham, too, was aware of this, tempering the acidity of his statement by adding that

'Le Corbusier was neither totally unaware of environmental problems, nor indifferent to the human need to solve those that he recognised.'[2] Further 'he was probably no worse than the rest of his generation' in this regard.[3]

Banham highlights the vexed issue of functionalism in the work of Le Corbusier by quoting from an article by Yves Labasque from *L'Esprit Nouveau* (the journal edited by Le Corbusier and Amédée Ozenfant) in which the author stated that 'Useful objects must not dissimulate their functions'.[4] Then, creating a slippage of meaning between the terms 'natural law' and 'functionalism', he points out that 'if it is an offence against natural law to disguise an electric lamp, what constitutes an undissimulated one?'[5] It is tempting to draw parallels between Le Corbusier hatred of the false – 'The reform to be undertaken is profound; hypocrisy reigns over love, marriage, society, death; we are entirely and totally falsified, we are false!'[6] – and his architecture. Yet for Le Corbusier, functionalism and natural law were not synonymous – although Banham could well be forgiven for equating the two (especially if we remember Le Corbusier's early statements about the house being a 'tool' and 'a machine for living'). However (at the same time that he made these dictats) Le Corbusier also made the point that:

> One commonplace among Architects (the younger ones): *the construction must be shown.*

> Another commonplace amongst them: *when a thing responds to a need, it is beautiful.*

> But... To show the construction is all very well for an Arts and Crafts student who is anxious to prove his ability. The almighty has clearly shown our wrists and our ankles, but there remains all the rest! ...

> Architecture has another meaning and other ends to pursue than showing construction and responding to needs (and by 'needs' I mean utility, comfort and practical arrangement).

> ARCHITECTURE is the art above all others which achieves a state of platonic grandeur, mathematical order, speculation, the perception of the harmony which lies in emotional relationships. This is the AIM of architecture.[7]

In the foreword of his *Oeuvre Complète Volume 5*, Le Corbusier was at pains to emphasize his interest in poetry rather than functionalism, his stated aim being 'harnessing technics to the aims of culture'.[8] Functionalism may have played a role in Le Corbusier's early work but it was a word for which he was to express a marked abhorrence as it denied the 'magical' qualities of architecture.[9]

> it is the proportion that counts – another architectural concept, and a very demanding one. Architecture, architectural doctrine? Yes, indeed, and it is imperative.

> People insist in making me exclusively into a man of the 'machine for living'. I have never ceased to affirm that beauty, harmony, purity, the smile,

proportion are, in a word, the definitive motive of architectural creation. And this harmony does not come about from external appearances (arrangement of the façade etc) but from within the very essence of creation.

Having satisfied the absolute imperatives of the programme (biology, function, price) I demand therefore the right to crown the work with harmony.[10]

Geometry, harmony and beauty were key to Le Corbusier's vision of natural law, issues that were not addressed by the bald term 'functionalism', or rather 'Functionalism' the movement, especially when used by some of his more extreme colleagues. In spite of his early rhetoric it does not seem to have taken him long to realize that the question of functionalism was as difficult to define and resolve as that other Modernist chestnut 'truth to materials', especially when applied to the sphere of architectural detail. Instead, he seems largely to have contented himself with what he called 'from the constructional point of view, a clear definition of elements: stonework, woodwork, loadbearing and open areas'.[11]

Le Corbusier's approach to handrails, doors, windows, stairs, skirtings, and so on, described herein, is remarkably consistent with his approach to architecture as a whole, both governed by his Orphic theories. Emphasis is placed on asceticism, bodily experience, number, space and proportion, as well as knowledge gained through initiation. 'The architectural idea is strictly an individual phenomenon, inalienable. It is good to push an idea to a state of purity', wrote Le Corbusier as a young man.[12] Pushing the 'idea to a state of purity' meant working, working and reworking a design until all its parts fitted together in an inalienable whole, the Modernist dream to which many of us still aspire – the making of order in a terrifyingly chaotic world – 'associations of incongruous ideas conjure up contrasts, analogies and then deductions!'[13]

This has been a journey through Le Corbusier's work seen close up. I have swept away dust and felt my way into the ridges and cracks of his buildings. Like most things subject to intense scrutiny, they appear riddled with flaws, mostly in terms of technology which has only recently begun to rise to the challenges that Le Corbusier set almost a century ago. However it seems to me that there is a remarkable degree of unity between his stated aims, his work as a whole and Le Corbusier in detail, all the more surprising given his tendency to neglect the project once on site.[14]

Recognizing the degree that Le Corbusier's own inner world impacted upon his work, it is, as Summerson states, 'impossible, alas, to design like Le Corbusier unless one happens to be Le Corbusier',[15] and – given new forms of building contract, ever stricter regulation and the advance of a new breed of professionals who are taking over the architects traditional constructional role – it is nowadays more and more difficult to push an 'idea to a state of purity'. But if that is not the primary role of the architect then what is?

You employ stone, wood and concrete, and with these materials you build houses and palaces; that is construction. Ingenuity is at work.

But suddenly you touch my heart, you do me good, I am happy and I say: "This is beautiful". That is Architecture. Art enters in.

My house is practical. I thank you, as I might thank Railway engineers or the Telephone service. You have not touched my heart.

But suppose that walls rise towards heaven in such a way that I am moved. I perceive your intentions. Your mood has been gentle, brutal, charming or noble. The stones you have erected tell me so. You fix me to the place and my eye regard it. They behold something which expresses a thought. A thought which reveals itself without word or sound, but solely by means of shapes which stand in a certain relationship to one another.[16] . . . By the use of inert materials and *starting from* conditions more or less utilitarian, you have established certain relationships which have aroused my emotions. This is Architecture.[17]

Notes

[1] R. Banham, *The Architecture of the Well-Tempered Environment* (London: Architectural Press, 1969), p. 146.

[2] Ibid., p. 147. See for example cross ventilation diagram for the Secretariat at Chandigarh, FLC 2827 in H. Allen Brooks (ed.), *The Le Corbusier Archive, Volume XXIII* (New York: Garland, 1983), p. 79 (hereafter referred to as Allen Brooks, *Archive*) or the 'grille climatique', FLC5602 in Allen Brooks, *Archive, Volume XXV*, p. 64.

[3] Banham, *The Architecture of the Well-Tempered Environment*, p. 143.

[4] Ibid., p. 150.

[5] Ibid.

[6] Le Corbusier, *Precisions on the Present State of Architecture and City Planning* (Cambridge, MA: MIT, 1991), p. 10

[7] Le Corbusier, *Towards a New Architecture* (London: Architectural Press, 1982), p. 102. Originally published as *Vers une Architecture* (Paris: Crès, 1923).

[8] Le Corbusier, *Oeuvre Complète Volume 5, 1946–1952* (Zurich: Les Editions d'Architecture, 1995), p. 7. Originally published in 1953.

[9] A. Wogenscky, *Les Mains de Le Corbusier* (Paris: Éditions de Grenelle, n.d.), p. 41. See also C.St. John Wilson, *The Other Tradition of Modern Architecture* (London: Academy, 1994), p. 55 for a further critique of Le Corbusier.

[10] Letter Le Corbusier to Honnorat, President of the Cité Universitaire, 15 October 1932, quoted in I. Zacnic, *Le Corbusier: Pavillon Suisse: The Biography of a Building* (Basel: Birkäuser, 2004), p. 194.

[11] Le Corbusier, *Sketchbooks Volume 4, 1957–1964* (Cambridge, MA: MIT, 1982), p. 30.

[12] Le Corbusier, *Precisions*, pp. 133–4.

[13] Le Corbusier, *Journey to the East* (Cambridge MA: MIT, 1987), p. 128. Originally published in 1966.

[14] Commentators have repeatedly noted that the details within ape, both in form and intention, the buildings within which they are housed. See for example. C. Rowe, *The Mathematics of the Ideal Villa and Other Essays* (Cambridge, MA: MIT, 1976), p. 195.

[15] J. Summerson, *Heavenly Mansions* (New York: Norton, 1963), pp.190–1.

[16] Le Corbusier. *Towards a New Architecture*, p. 187.

[17] Ibid.

Select bibliography

Allendy, R., *Capitalisme et Sexualité: le conflits des instincts et les problèmes actuels*, Paris: Denoel, 1931, in FLC.

Arnheim, R., 'Notes on creative invention' in E. Sekler and W. Curtis, *Le Corbusier at Work: The Genesis of the Carpenter Centre for the Visual Arts*, Cambridge, MA: MIT, 1978.

Bacon, M., *Le Corbusier in America*, Cambridge MA: MIT, 2001.

Bahga, S. and Bahga, S., *Le Corbusier and Pierre Jeanneret: Footprints on the sands of Indian Architecture*, New Delhi: Galgotia, 2000.

Baker, G. and Gubler, J., *Le Corbusier: Early Works by Charles-Edouard Jeanneret Gris*, London: Academy, 1987.

Banham, R., *The New Brutalism, Ethic or Aesthetic*, London: Architectural Press, 1966.

Banham, R., *The Architecture of the Well-Tempered Environment*, London: Architectural Press, 1969.

Banham, R., 'La Maison des homes and La Misère des villes; Le Corbusier and the architecture of mass housing' in H. Allen Brooks (ed.), *The Le Corbusier Archive, Volume XXI*, New York: Garland, 1983, pp. ix–xix.

Benton, T., 'Villa Savoye and the architects' practice' in H. Allen Brooks (ed.), *The Le Corbusier Archive, Volume VII*, New York: Garland, 1983.

Benton, T., *The Villas of Le Corbusier 1920–1930*, London: Yale, 1987.

Benton, T. (ed.), *Le Corbusier Architect of the Century*, London: Arts Council, 1987.

Benton, T., 'The petite maison de weekend and the Parisian suburbs', in Mohsen Mostafavi (ed.), *Le Corbusier and the Architecture of Reinvention*, London, AA Publishing, 2003, pp. 118–39.

Benton, T., 'From Jeanneret to Le Corbusier: rusting iron, bricks and coal and the modern Utopia', *Massilia*, 2 (2003), pp. 28–39.

Benton, T., 'Pessac and Liège revisited: standards dimensions and failures', *Massilia*, 3 (2004), pp. 64–99.

Billeter, E., *Le Corbusier Secret*, Laussanne: Musée Cantonal des Beaux Arts, 1987.

Birksted, J.K., "'Beyond the clichés of the hand-books": Le Corbusier's architectural promenade', *Journal of Architecture*, 11, 1 (2006), pp. 55–132.

Bozdoğan, S., 'Journey to the East: ways of looking at the orient and the question of representation', *Journal of Architectural Education*, 41, 4 (1989), pp. 38–45.

Breton, A., *Arcane 17*, Paris: Jean-Jacques Pauvert, 1971, p. 66. Originally published 1947.

Brooks H. Allen (ed.), *The Le Corbusier Archive*, New York: Garland, 1983.

Brooks, H.A., *Le Corbusier's Formative Years*, London: University of Chicago Press, 1997.

Buchanan, S. (ed.), *The Portable Plato*, Harmondsworth: Penguin, 1997.

Cali, F., *The Architecture of Truth: The Cistercian Abbey of la Thoronet in Provence*, London: Thames and Hudson, 1957.

Carl, P., 'Le Corbusier's penthouse in Paris: 24 Rue Nungesser et Coli', *Daidalos*, 28 (1988), pp. 65–75.

Carl, P., 'Architecture and time: a prolegomena', *AA Files*, 22 (1991), pp. 48–65.

Carl, P., 'Ornament and time: a prolegomena', *AA Files*, 23 (1992), pp. 49–64.

Carl, P., 'The godless temple, "organon of the infinite"', *Journal of Architecture*, 10, 1 (2005), pp. 63–90.

Celik, Z., 'Le Corbusier, orientalism, colonialism', *Assemblage*, 17 (1992), pp. 61–77.

Christ-Janer, A. and Mix Foley, M., *Modern Church Architecture*, London: McGraw Hill, 1962.

Cohen, J.L. and Martin Mueller, G. (eds), *Liquid Stone: New Architecture in Concrete*, Basel : Birkhäuser, 2006.

Coll, J., 'Le Corbusier. Taureaux: an analysis of the thinking process in the last series of Le Corbusier's plastic work', *Art History*, 18, 4 (1995), pp. 537–68.

Coll, J., 'Structure and play in Le Corbusier's art works' *AA Files*, 31 (1996), pp. 4–14.

Colli, L.M., 'Le Corbusier e il colore; I Claviers Salubra', *Storia dell'arte*, 43 (1981), pp. 271–91.

Colli, L.M., 'La Couleur qui cache, la couleur qui signale: l'ordonnance et la crainte dans la poètique corbuséenne des couleurs' in *Le Corbusier et La Couleur*, Paris: Fondation Le Corbusier (1992), pp. 21–34.

Colomina, B., 'Mies Not', in D. Mertens (ed.), *The Presence of Mies*, New York: Princeton Architectural Press, 1994, pp. 193–221.

Colquhoun, A., 'The significance of Le Corbusier' in H. Allen Brooks (ed.), *The Le Corbusier Archive, Volume 1*, New York: Garland, 1983, pp. xxxv–xliii.

Constant, C., *Eileen Gray*, London: Phaidon, 2000.

Coombs, R., 'Le Corbusier and vernacular architecture: a newly discovered drawing for the bergerie at Sainte Baume', *Minutes of the 83rd ACSA Meeting*, 1995, p. 149.

Corner, J. (ed.), *Recovering Landscape*, New York: Princeton University Press, 1999.

Correa, C. 'Chandigarh: the view from Benares' in H. Allen Brooks (ed.), *The Le Corbusier Archive, Volume XXII*, New York: Garland, 1983, pp. ix–xiv.

Curtis, W., *Le Corbusier: Ideas and Forms*, Oxford: Phaidon, 1986.

De Smet, Catherine, *Le Corbusier Architect of Books*, Baden: Lars Müller, 2005.

Denèfle, S., Bresson S., Dussuet, A. and Roux, N., *Habiter Le Corbusier: Pratiques sociales et théorie architecturale*, Rennes: Universitaire de Renne, 2006.

Deplazes, A. (ed.), Constructing Architecture: Materials Processes Structures, A Handbook (Basel: Birkhauser, 2005).

Devoucoux du Buysson, P., *Le Guide du Pèlerin à la grotte de sainte Marie Madeleine*, La Sainte Baume: La Fraternité Sainte Marie Madeleine, 1998.

Dodds, G., *Building Desire: On the Barcelona Pavilion*, London: Routledge, 2005.

Dodds, G. and Tavernor, R. (eds), *Body and Building: Essays on the Changing Relation of Body and Architecture*, Cambridge, MA: MIT, 2002.

Dupont, R., 'Près de Marseille Dans les forêts millenaires de la Sainte-Baume la 'cathédrale engloutie' surgira pour devenir la basilique de la Paix', *L'Aube* (2 June 1948), front page.

Duport, L., *Le Corbusier: Les Maisons Jaoul*, Paris: Les Lieux Editions, 2004.

Evans, A.B., *Jean Cocteau and His Films of Orphic Identity*, London: Associated University Press, 1977.

Evenson, N. 'Yesterday's city of tomorrow today' in H. Allen Brooks (ed.), *The Le Corbusier Archive, Volume XV*, New York: Garland, 1983, pp. ix–xvii.

Fagan-King, J., 'United on the threshold of the twentieth century mystical ideal', *Art History*, 11, 1 (1988), pp. 89–113.

Faure, É., 'La ville radieuse', *L'Architecture d'aujourd'hui* , 11 (1935), pp. 1–2.

Faure, É., *Fonction du Cinéma: de la cinéplastique à son destin social*, Paris: Éditions Gonthier (1995), p. 12. Originally published 1953.

Forty, A., *Words and Buildings*, London: Thames and Hudson, 2000.

Forty, A., 'Cement and multiculturalism' in F. Hernandez, M. Millington and I. Borden (eds), *Transculturation: Cities, Spaces and Architectures in Latin America*, Amsterdam and Atlanta: Rodopi, 2005, pp. 144–54.

Frampton, K., *Studies in Tectonic Culture: The Poetics of Construction in Nineteenth and Twentieth Century Architecture*, Cambridge, MA: MIT, 1996.

Fraser, I. and Henmi, R., *Envisioning Architecture: An Analysis of Drawing*, New York: Van Nostrand Reinhold, 1994, pp. 1–24.

Friedman, A.T., *Women and the Making of the Modern House*, New York: Harry N. Abrams, 1998.

Garrier, C. and Arnaud, Y., 'Eglise Sainte Pierre Le Corbusier Firminy', www.st-etienne.archi fr/corbu/corbu.html, accessed 16 March 2006.

Ghyka, M., *Esthetique des proportions dans le nature et dans les arts*, Paris: Gallimard, 1927.

Ghyka, M., *Nombre d'or: rites et rhythmes Pythagoriciens dans le development de la civilisation Occidental*, Paris: Gallimard, 1931.

Gimpel, J., *Les Bâtisseurs de Cathédrales*, Paris: Éditions Seuil, 1959.

Glancey, J., *Swimming toward the Sun: A Look at the Architect Le Corbusier and the Cathars*, BBC Radio 3, 29 September 2002.

Golan, R., *Modernity and Nostalgia: Art and Politics in France between the Wars*, London: Yale, 1995.

Gresleri, G., 'Prima da Ronchamp La Sainte Baume: Terra e cielo, ombra e luce', *Parametro*. 207, (1995), pp. 34–43.

Griffin, F. and Millet, M., 'Shadey aesthetics', *Journal of Architectural Education*, 37/3:4 (1984), pp. 43–60.

Gronberg, T., *Design on Modernity: Exhibiting the City in 1920s Paris*, Manchester: Manchester University Press, 1998.

Guillén, M.F., *The Taylorized Beauty of the Mechanical. Scientific Management and the Rise of Modernist Architecture*, Princeton, NJ: Princeton University Press, 2006.

Guthrie, W.K.C., *Orpheus and Greek Religion*, London: Methuen, 1935.

Hagan, S., *Taking Shape: A New Contract between Architecture and Nature*, London: Architectural Press, 2001.

Hartoonian, G., *Ontology of Construction*, Cambridge: Cambridge University, 1994.

Haskins, S., *Mary Magdalene*, London: HarperCollins, 1993.

Hawkes, D., *Environmental Imagination*, London: Routledge, 2006.

Hicken, A., *Apollinaire, Cubism and Orphism*, Aldershot: Ashgate, 2002.

Hill, J., *Immaterial Architecture*, London: Routledge, 2006.

Ingersoll, R., *A Marriage of Contours*, Princeton, NJ: Princeton Architectural Press, 1990.

Jencks, C., *Le Corbusier and the Tragic View of Architecture*, London: Allen Lane, 1973.

Jencks, C., *Le Corbusier and the Continual Revolution in Architecture*, New York: Monacelli Press, 2000.

Jenger, J., *Le Corbusier Choix de Lettres*, Basel: Birkhäuser, 2002.

Jung, C.G., *Alchemical Studies, Collected Works 13*, London: Routledge and Kegan Paul, 1951.

Kagal, C., 'Le Corbusier: the acrobat of architecture. Interview with Balkrishna Doshi, 1986', *Architecture and Urbanism*, 322 (1997), pp. 168–83.

Krustrup. M., *l'Illiade Dessins*, Copenhagen: Borgen, 1986.

Krustrup, M., 'Poème de l'Angle Droit,' *Arkitekten*, 92 (1990), pp. 422–32.

Krustrup, M., *Porte Email*, Copenhagen: Arkitektens Forlag, 1991.

Krustrup, M., 'The women of Algiers', *Skala*, 24/25 (1991), pp. 36–41.

Krustrup, M. 'Persona' in *Le Corbusier, Painter and Architect*, Arkitekturtidsskrift: Nordjyllands, Denmark, 1995.

Lahiji, N., 'The gift of the open hand: Le Corbusier's reading Georges Bataille's La Part Maudite,' *Journal of Architectural Education*, 50, 1 (1996), pp. 50–67.

Lapunzina, A., 'The pyramid and the wall: an unknown project of Le Corbusier in Venezuela', *arq*, 5, 3 (2001), pp. 255–67.

Laubier, C., *The Condition of Women in France: 1945 to the Present*, London: Routledge, 1990.

Le Corbusier, *Towards a New Architecture*, London: Architectural Press, 1982. Originally published as *Vers une Architecture*, Paris: Crès, 1923.

Le Corbusier, *The Decorative Art of Today*, London: Architectural Press, 1987. Originally published as Le Corbusier, *L'Art décoratif d'aujourd'hui*, Paris: Editions Crès, 1925.

Le Corbusier, *The City of Tomorrow*, London: Architectural Press, 1946, p. 75.

Le Corbusier *Urbanisme*, Paris: Éditions Arthaud, 1980. Originally published in 1925.

Le Corbusier, *Une Maison – un palais, A la recherche d'une unité architecturale*, Paris: Crès, 1928.

Le Corbusier, *Precisions on the Present State of Architecture and City Planning*, Cambridge, MA: MIT, 1991. Originally published as Précisions sur un état présent de l'architecture et de l'urbanisme, Paris: Crès, 1930.

Le Corbusier, *The Radiant City*, London: Faber, 1967, p. i. Originally published as Le Corbusier, *La Ville Radieuse*, Paris: Éditions de l'Architecture d'Aujourd'hui, 1935.

Le Corbusier, *When the Cathedrals were White: A Journey to the Country of the Timid People*, New York: Reynal and Hitchcock, 1947. Originally published as *Quand les cathédrales étaient blanches*, Paris: Plon, 1937.

Le Corbusier and Jeanneret, P., *Oeuvre Complète Volume 1, 1910–1929*, Zurich: Les Editions d'Architecture, 1995. Originally published in 1937.

Le Corbusier and Jeanneret, P., *Oeuvre Complète Volume 2, 1929–34*, Zurich: Les Editions d'Architecture, 1995. Originally published in 1935.

Le Corbusier and Jeanneret, P., *Oeuvre Complète Volume 3, 1934–38*, Zurich: Les Editions d'Architecture, 1995. Originally published in 1938.

Le Corbusier, *Oeuvre Complète Volume 4, 1938–1946*, Zurich: Les Editions d'Architecture, 1995. Originally published in 1946.

Le Corbusier, *Oeuvre Complète Volume 5, 1946–1952*, Zurich: Les Editions d'Architecture, 1995. Originally published in 1953.

Le Corbusier, *Oeuvre Complète Volume 6, 1952–1957*, Zurich: Les Editions d'Architecture, 1995. Originally published in 1957.

Le Corbusier, *Oeuvre Complète Volume 7, 1957–1965*, Zurich: Les Editions d'Architecture, 1995. Originally published in 1965.

Le Corbusier, *Le Corbusier Talks with Students*, New York: Orion, 1961, p. 34. Originally published as *Entretien avec les étudiants des écoles d'architecture*, Paris: Denoel 1943.

Le Corbusier, *A New World of Space*, New York: Reynal Hitchcock, 1948.

Le Corbusier, *Poésie sur Alger*, Paris: Editions Connivances, 1989. Originally published in 1950.

Le Corbusier, *The Marseilles Block*, London: Harvill, 1953. Originally published as *L'Unité d'habitation de Marseille*, Mulhouse: Editions Le Point, 1950.

Le Corbusier, *Modulor*, London: Faber, 1954. Originally published as *Le Modulor*, Paris: Editions d'Architecture d'Aujourd hui, 1950.

Le Corbusier, 'Le Théatre Spontané' in A. Villiers (ed.), *Architecture et Dramaturgie*, Paris: Editions d'Aujourd'hui, 1980. Originally published in 1950.

Le Corbusier, *Une Petite Maison*, Zurich: Editions d'Architecture, 1993. Originally published 1954.

Le Corbusier, *Modulor 2*, London: Faber, 1955. Originally published as *Le Modulor II*, Paris: Editions d'Architecture d'Aujourd'hui, 1955.

Le Corbusier, *The Poem of the Right Angle* (1990), princeton architectural press *Le Poème de l'angle droit*, Paris: Editions Connivance, 1989. Originally published in 1955.

Le Corbusier, *The Chapel at Ronchamp*, London: Architectural Press, 1957.

Le Corbusier, *Le Poème Electronique*, Paris: Les Cahiers Forces Vives aux Éditions de Minuit, 1958.

Le Corbusier, *Journey to the East*, Cambridge: MIT, 1987. Originally published in 1966.

Le Corbusier, *The Final Testament of Père Corbu: a Translation and Interpretation of Mise au Point by Ivan Zaknic*, New Haven, CT: Yale University Press, 1997, p. 91. Originally published as *Mise au Point*, Paris: Editions Forces-Vives, 1966.

Le Corbusier, *The Nursery Schools*, New York: Orion, 1968. Trans. Eleanor Levieux. Les Carnets de la Recherche Patiente 3.

Le Corbusier, *Sketchbooks Volume 1*, London: Thames and Hudson, 1981.

Le Corbusier, *Sketchbooks Volume 2*, London: Thames and Hudson, 1981.

Le Corbusier, *Sketchbooks Volume 3, 1954–1957*, Cambridge, MA: MIT, 1982.

Le Corbusier, *Sketchbooks Volume 4, 1957–1964*, Cambridge, MA: MIT, 1982.

Leatherbarrow, D., *The Roots of Architectural Invention*, Cambridge: Cambridge University Press, 1993.

Léger, F., *Functions of Painting*, New York: Viking, 1965.

Loach, J., 'Studio as laboratory', *Architectural Review*, Special Issue, 181, 1079 (1987), pp. 73–7.

Loach, J., 'Le Corbusier and the creative use of mathematics,' *British Journal of the History of Science*, 31 (1998), pp. 185–215.

Lowman, J., 'Le Corbusier 1900–1925: the years of transition', doctoral dissertation, University of London, 1979.

Mâle, E., *The Gothic Image*, London: Fontana, 1961. Originally published as *L'Art Religieux du XIII° en France*, Paris: Armand Colin, 1910.

Mâle, E., *Religious Art in France: the Twelfth Century*, Princeton, NJ: Bollingen, 1973. Originally published as *L'Art religieux du XIIe siècle en France. Etude sur l'origine de l'iconographie du Moyen Age*, Paris: Armand Colin, 1922.

Maniaque, C., *Le Corbusier et les maisons Jaoul*, Paris: Picard, 2005.

Marcus. G.H., *Le Corbusier: Inside the Machine for Living*, New York: Monacelli, 2000, p. 85.

McLeod, M., 'Urbanism and utopia: Le Corbusier from regional syndicalism to Vichy', DPhil thesis, Princeton, 1985.

McLeod, M., 'Charlotte Perriand, her first decade as a designer, *AA Files*, 15 (1987), pp. 3–13.

McLeod, M. (ed.), *Charlotte Perriand: An Art of Living*, New York: Harry N. Abrams 2003.

Menin, S. and Samuel, F., *Nature and Space: Aalto and Le Corbusier*, London: Routledge, 2003.

Moles, A., *Histoire des Charpentiers*, Paris: Librairie Gründ, 1949.

Montalte, L. (E. Trouin pseud.), *Fallait-il Batir Le Mont-Saint-Michel?* St Zachaire: Montalte, 1979.

Moore, R.A., 'Le Corbusier and the *mecanique spirituelle*: an investigation into Le Corbusier's architectural symbolism and its background in Beaux Arts design', DPhil thesis, University of Maryland, 1979.

Moore, R.A., 'Alchemical and mythical themes in the Poem of the Right Angle 1947–65', *Oppositions* 19/20 (winter/spring 1980), pp. 110–39.

Odgers, J., Samuel, F. and Sharr, A., *Primitive: Original Matters in Architecture*, London: Routledge, 2007.

Ozenfant, A. and Jeanneret, C.E., 'After cubism' in C.S. Eliel (ed.), *L'Esprit Nouveau: Purism in Paris*, New York: Harry N. Abrams, 2001.

Pauly, D., 'The chapel at Ronchamp' *AD Profile 60*, 55, 7/8 (1985), pp. 30–7.

Pearson, C.E.M., 'Integrations of art and architecture in the work of Le Corbusier: theory and practice from ornamentalism to the "Synthesis of the Major Arts"', PhD thesis, Stanford University, 1995.

Peter, J., *The Oral History of Modern Architecture*, New York: Harry N. Abrams, 1994.

Petit, J., *Un Couvent de Le Corbusier*, Paris: Les Éditions de Minuit, 1961.

Petit, J., *Le Corbusier Lui-même*, Paris: Forces Vives, 1970.

Pevsner, N., *Pioneers of Modern Design*, Harmondsworth: Pelican, 1975.

Pico della Mirandola, G., *On the Dignity of Man*, Indianapolis, IN: Hackett, 1998. Originally written in 1486.

Pincus Witten, R., *Occult Symbolism in France: Joséphin Péladan and the Salons de la Rose-Croix*, New York: Garland, 1976, p. 55.

Plummer, H., 'Masters of light, first volume: twentieth century pioneers', *Architecture and Urbanism Extra Edition*, November 2003.

Pottecher, F., 'Que le Fauve soit libre dans sa cage', *L'Architecture d'Aujourd'Hui*, 252 (1987), pp. 58–66.

Provensal, H., *L'Art de Demain*, Paris: Perrin, 1904.

Pye, D., *The Nature and Art of Workmanship*, Cambridge: Cambridge University Press, 1968.

Rabelais, F., *Oeuvres Complètes*, Paris: Gallimard, 1951.

Réau, L., *Iconographie de l'art Chrétien Volume 1*, Paris: Presses Universitaires de France, 1955.

Réau, L., *Iconographie de l'art Chrétien Volume 2*, Paris: Presses Universitaires de France, 1957.

Renan, E., La *Vie de Jesus*, Paris: Calmann-Levy, 1906.

Rodrigues dos Santos, C., Campos da Silva Pereira, M., Veriano da Silva Pereira, R. and Caldeira da Silva, V., *Le Corbusier e o Brasil*, São Paulo: Projecto Editora, 1987.

Roller, T., *Les Catacombes de Rome. Histoire de l'art et des croyances religieuses pendant le premiers siècles du Christianisme, Volume II*, Paris: Morel, 1881.

Rowe, C., *The Mathematics of the Ideal Villa and Other Essays*, Cambridge, MA: MIT, 1976.

Rowe, C., *The Architecture of Good Intentions*, London: Academy Editions, 1994.

Rüegg, A. (ed.), *Polychromie Architecturale*, Basel: Birkhäuser, 1997.

Rüegg, A. (ed.), *Le Corbusier Photographs by René Burri: Moments in the Life of a Great Architect* Basel: Birkhäuser, 1999.

Samuel, F., 'Le Corbusier, women, nature and culture', *Issues in Art and* Architecture, 5, 2 (1998), pp. 4–20.

Samuel, F., 'A profane annunciation; the representation of sexuality in the architecture of Ronchamp' *Journal of Architectural Education*, 53, 2 (1999), pp. 74–90.

Samuel, F., 'Le Corbusier, Teilhard de Chardin and the planetisation of mankind' *Journal of Architecture*, 4 (1999), pp. 149–65.

Samuel, F., 'The philosophical city of Rabelais and St Teresa; Le Corbusier and Edouard Trouin's scheme for St Baume, *Literature and Theology*, 13, 2 (1999), pp. 111–26.

Samuel, F., 'The representation of Mary in Le Corbusier's Chapel at Ronchamp' *Church History*, 68, 2 (1999), pp. 398–417.

Samuel, F., 'Le Corbusier, Teilhard de Chardin and *La Planétisation humaine*: spiritual ideas at the heart of modernism', *French Cultural Studies*, 11, 2 (2000), pp. 181–200.

Samuel, F., 'Le Corbusier Rabelais and Oracle of the Holy Bottle,' *Word and Image: A Journal of Verbal/Visual Enquiry*, 16 (2000), pp. 325–338.

Samuel, F., 'Animus, anima and the architecture of Le Corbusier, *Harvest*, 48, 2 (2003), pp. 42–60.

Samuel, F., *Le Corbusier: Architect and Feminist*, London: Wiley/Academy, 2004.

Samuel, F., 'La Cité Orphique de La Sainte Baume in *Le Corbusier et le Sacré*, Paris: FLC/Editions La Villete, 2005.

Schumacher, T., 'Deep space shallow space', *Architectural Review*, 181, 1079 (1987), p. 41.

Schuré, E., *Les Grands Initiés: Esquisse secrete des religions*, Paris: Perrin, 1908, in FLC.

Sekler, E. and Curtis W., *Le Corbusier at Work: The Genesis of the Carpenter Centre for the Visual Arts*, Cambridge, MA: MIT, 1978.

Serenyi, P., 'Le Corbusier, Fourier and the monastery of Ema', *Art Bulletin*, 49 (1967), p. 297.

Silver. K., *Esprit de Corps: The Art of the Parisian Avant-Garde and the First World War, 1914–1925*, Princeton, NJ: Princeton University Press, 1989.

Soltan, J., 'Working with Le Corbusier' in H. Allen Brooks (ed.), *The Le Corbusier Archive, Volumes XVII*, New York: Garland, 1983, pp. ix–xxiv.

Spate, V., *Orphism: the Evolution of Non-figurative Painting in Paris in 1910–14*, Oxford: Clarendon, 1979.

Stirling, J., 'Ronchamp: Le Corbusier's chapel and the crisis of rationalism', *Architectural Review*, 119, 711 (March 1956), pp. 155–61.

Stirling, J., 'Garches to Jaoul: Le Corbusier as domestic architect in 1927 and 1953' in H. Allen Brooks (ed.), *The Le Corbusier Archive, Volume 20*, New York: Garland, 1983, pp. ix–xxi.

Summerson, J., *Heavenly Mansions*, New York: Norton, 1963.

Tafuri, M., "'Machine et mémoire": the city in the work of Le Corbusier', H. Allen Brooks (ed.), *The Le Corbusier Archive, Volume 10*, New York: Garland, 1983, pp. xxxi–xlvi. Trans. S. Sartarelli.

Treib, M., *Space Calculated in Seconds*, Princeton, NJ: Princeton University Press, 1996.

Turner, P., *The Education of an Architect*, New York: Garland, 1977.

Von Moos, S. and Rüegg, A. (eds), *Le Corbusier Before Le Corbusier*, New Haven, CT: Yale, 2002.

Walden, R. (ed.), *The Open Hand*, Cambridge, MA: MIT, 1982.

Weber, H. (ed.), *Le Corbusier the Artist*, Zurich: Editions Heidi Weber, 1988.

Willmert, T., The ancient fire, the hearth of tradition, combustion and creation in Le Corbusier's studio residences', ara. 10, 1 (2006), pp. 57–78.

Wogenscky, A., *Les Mains de Le Corbusier*, Paris: Éditions de Grenelle, n.d.

Wogenscky, A., 'The Unité d'Habitation at Marseille' in H. Allen Brooks (ed.), *The Le Corbusier Archive, Volumes 16*, New York: Garland, 1983, pp. ix–xvii.

Xenakis, I., 'The Monastery of La Tourette' in H. Allen Brookes (ed.), *The Le Corbusier Archive, Volume 28*, New York: Garland, 1983, pp. ix–xiii.

Audio interview with Le Corbusier, 15 March 1959, www.bbc.co.uk/bbcfour/audiointerviews/profilepages/lecorbusierc1.shtml.

Fondation Le Corbusier DVD, *Le Corbusier Plans, Echelle 1*, 2006.

Index

(Page numbers in italics represent figures)

Aalto, A., 28
Abstraction, 23, 42, 43
After Cubism, 41
Ahmedabad, 7, 10, 19, 134, *137*
   Museum, 57
Aimonetti, 7
Air conditioning, 78
Albigensianism, 74
Altars, 170–175
Alchemy, 3, 41, 56, 171, 172
   Metals, 54
Aluminium, 18, 83, 89, 109
Anatomy, 66
Anthropomorphism, 41–43, 66, 192
Apartment for a Young Man, 109
Apollinaire, G., 3, 74
Arches, 19, 28, 30
Architect, role of, 17, 23, 33, 217
Architecture, 217, 218
   classical, 215
   domestic, 169
   female, 41
   Japanese, 149
   male, 41
   modern, 80
   nautical, 132
   new, 21, 234, 26, 42, 76, 197
   poetic, 34
   public, 20
   religious, 169

Arts and Crafts, 17, 216
Asceticism, 4, 32, 75, 215, 217
ATBAT, 7
Aztec ritual, 170

Bacchus, 2
Baizeau, Villa, 64
Banham, R., 4, 79, 91, 95, 127,
   215, 216
Banquette, 42, 206, *207*, 208, 209
Barcelona, Plan Macia, 78
Bat'a Boutique, *6*, 48, 49, 110
Bauchant, A., *3*
Beaux Arts, 203
Benton, T., 4, 7, 8, 11, 19, 33, 34, 61,
   76, 102, 128, 153, 161, 162
   The Villas of Le Corbusier, 11, 160
Beton brut, 18, 19, 45
Biology, 16, 83, 217
Birksted, J., 148
Body, 4, 39–71, 73, 75, 96, 127, 129,
   152, 157, 198, 206, 215
Books, 108, 116, 172
Brasilia, French Embassy, 163
Brasilian Man, 200
Brick, 19, 20, 26, 31–32
Bridge, 137, 156, 157
Brise soleil, 24, 76, 78, 79–81, 82,
   110, 111, 112, 175
Brussels Exposition, 109

Brutalism, 19
Builders, 7, *8*, 19
Building site, 17

Cabanon, *33*, 94, 103, 133, *148, 150*
Calendar, 80, 88
Carl, P., 142
Caravaggio, 73
Carpaccio, 102
Carpenter Centre, 4, 11, 19, 20, 23, 24,
    28, 45, 66, 78, 81, 82–85, 92, 127,
    160, 161, 138, 204, 206, 208
Casier, 109–116, 123, 141, 175, 209,
    212, 206
Centrosoyus, 152, 162
Ceramica Pozzi, 191
Cervantes, 3
Chancellerie, French Embassy,
    Brazil, 81
Chandigarh, 10, 19
    Assembly, 75, 83, 88, 90, 148
    Parliament Building, 23
Chareau, P., 18
Cherchell, 31
Church, Villa, *89*
Cité de Refuge, 110, *128*, 127
Cleaning, 40, 75, 83, 185, 187
Clothes, 59
Coll, J., 42
Colour, 41, 42, 60, 64, 66, 117, 118,
    120, 129, 132, 148, 195, 198,
    200, 209
    Coding, 42, 85
Concrete, 4, 18–21, 24, 26, 30, 31, 34,
    45, 49, 51, 62, 64, 83, 88, 105,
    106, 118, 127, 138, 142, 149,
    152, 206, 210, 211
    See also beton brut
    Precast, 28
Condensation, 5, 76
Construction
    Ancient, 49, 51
    Honesty, 216
    Industry, 34
    New methods, 7
    Originality, 6
    Problems, 6
    Principles, 11
    Process, 19
    Prowess 4–6, 8
    Simple, 15, 32, 77
Contrast, 45, 60, 106, 132, 139,
    148, 159, 206
Cook, Villa, 76, 175
Correa, C., 79
Couturier, M.A., 74
Craftsmanship, 6, 17, 84, 188

Cubism, 203, 204
Curtis, W., 4, 7, 21, 23, 24, 45, 78, 83,
    85, 86, 118, 127, 161, 204
    Le Corbusier at Work, 11

Dark, 4, 73–100, 106, 129, 163
Death, 33, 56, 74, 94, 169
De Bestegui, C., 90
    Apartment, 61, 84, 85, 101, 132,
        157, 159, 177, *179*
Decorative Art of Today, The, 39,
    111, 188
De Mandrot, Villa, 7
Design 101
    Process, 7, 16, 64
    techniques, 30, 45, 104, 217, 203
Detail
    Hierarchy, 165
    Meaning of, 7
Deux Bouteilles, 203, *204*
Di Cavalcanti, E., 198
Dionysus, 3, 170
Domino, 21, *22*
Door, 4, *5*, 47–49, 130–149
Doshi, B., 7
Drawings, 10, 11
Dry construction *see* factory
    fabrication
Duport, L., 31

Economy, 15, 40
Egyptian architecture, 91
Ema, monastery at, 15
Emancipation, 21
Emotion, 39, 43, 64, 111, 218
Engineers, 7, 17, 23, 24
Environment,
    Local, 19
    Problems, 216
Eroticism, 41, 60, 61, 87, 101
Errazuriz, Maison, 19
Ethnography, 2053, 205
Eurythmy, 63

Factory fabrication, 17
Fallet, Villa, 17
Faure, E., 64
Femme à la fenêtre de Georges,
    118, 119
Film, 127
Five points for a new architecture, 21, 76
Floors, 61–63, 90, 92, 105, 163, 203
Fondation Le Corbusier, 11
Ford, E., 1, 4, 6, 77
    Details of Modern Architecture, 6
Framing, 101–125, 162, 172, 201, *202*
Frampton, K., 4, 20, 23, 26, 30

Free plan, 4, 21
Fruges, M., 20
Functionalism, 216, 217
Furniture, 10, 59–61, 107, 109, 110, 173, 208, 209

Gargoyles, 181–184
Garland Series, 11, 83, 92
Gate, 4
Garches, *see* Stein de Monzie
Garnier, T., 20
Gender, 56, 59
Geometry, 3, 4, 11, 16, 65, 66, 76–78, 117
George Washington Bridge, 24
Gide, A., 74
Green, C., 39
Glass
    paving stones, 84
    doors, 48, 138
    block, 18, 20
    plate, 20, 26, 76, 109, 200
Gnosticism, 3, 73, 74
God, 32, 73, 74, 79. 87
gods, 2, 24, 156, 149
Greek philosophy, 3
Guiette, Maison, 175

Hadrian's Villa, 86
Handles, 6, 34, 47–58, 93, 132, *133*, 141, 156
Health, 186
Hearth, 177–182
Heidi Weber Haus, 28, 29, 42, 50, *52*, 57, 106, 132, *133*, 134, 139, 150, 152
Hennibique, 21
Hervé, L., 42, 45, 73
Hervol, E., 23
Housework *see* cleaning
Housing
    Low cost, 32
    Mass produced, 16

Ideal Home Exhibition, London, 195–197
Icône, 42, *44*, 66, 93, 170
Iconostasis, 164, 165, 170, 171
Initiation, 3, 4, 129, 161, 186, 194, 206, 217

Jacob's Ladder, 129
Jaoul Houses, 30, 31, *32*, *40*, 49, 51, *52*, 53, 61, 64, 85, 105, 152, 157, *158*, *159*, *160*, 175, *176*, *178*, *191*
Jeanneret, A., 61
Jeanneret, C.E., 2
Jeanneret, Maison, 48, 61

Jesus, 32, 51, 170, 172
Jonas, H., 73
Journey to the East, 186

Kabbala, 3
Krustrup, M., 56

Labasque, Y., 216
Labour saving *see* cleaning
Lamps, 4, 91, *93*, *94*
L'Art Sacré, 74, 170
La Cité permanente, 33
L'Esprit Nouveau, 112, 114, 218
La Roche, Maison, 48, 61, 76, 89, 94, *95*, *108*, 134, 138, 150, 161
La Sainte Baume, 19, 30–33, 66, 74, *75*, 86, 90, 179
La Tourette, 19, 32, 63, 45, 51, *53*, 62, 65, 74, 81–83, *84*, 86, 87, 88, 90, 121, 129, 130, 134, 139, *140*, *141*, *156*, *182*, 203
Laugier, 16, 21
League of Nations, 65, 89, 103, 152
Leatherbarrow, D., 19, 192
Le Corbusier
    Books
        Decorative Art of Today, The, 39, 111, 188
        Journey to the East, 185
        Le Livre de Ronchamp, 179, *180*
        Mise au Point, 169
        Nursery Schools, The, 65, 163, *189*
        Poem of the Right Angle, 10, 44, 51, 75, 80, 117, *130, 131*, 145, *147*, 165, 170, 193, 198, 208
        Precisions, 39, 131, 199, 206, *207*
        Radiant City, The, 39, 54
        Talks with Students, 19, 203
        Towards a New Architecture, 9, 16, 18, 21, 24, *26*, 76, 116
        When the Cathedrals were White, 15, 42
    Paintings
        Femme à la fenêtre de Georges, 118, *119*
        Icône, 42, *44*, 66, 93, 170, 173
        Les îles sont des corps des femmes, 208
        Nature morte géométrique, 150, *151*
        Yvonne, 56, 78, 142, 144, 188
Le Corbusier: Architect and Feminist, 215
Léger, F., 112, *114*
Light and dark, 4, 11, 63, 73–100, 107, 120
    See also lamps
Locksmith, 4

Logos, 6
Loucheur, Maison, 105, 190
Louis XVI, 16
Love, 15, 75

Magdalene, Mary, 33, 50, 54–57, 120
Manhattan, 199
Mary, Virgin, 57, 74, 87, 120, *121*, 139,
    173, 179, 181
Maison du Brésil, 11, 20, 45, *51*, 81, 83,
    85, 90, 110, 144, 145, *146*, 147,
    183, 195–211
Maison des Jeunes, 45, 47, 83, *150*
Maniaque, C., 11
    *Le Corbusier et les maisons
        Jaoul*, 11
Manichaen, 73–75
Masonry, 3, 19, 20, 31, 110, 148
Masons, 7, 73
Mass Production
    Houses, 16, 20
Materials
    Experience of, 18
    Fixed, 18
    Natural, 18, 19
    Safety, 19
McLeod, M., 59, 60, 173
Meyer, Mme, 102
Mill Owners Association Building, 4, 7,
    19, 57, *58*, 105, 134, *137*
Minotaure, 57
Mirror, 89
Mise au Point, 169
Modular architecture, 34
Modulor, 16–18, 57, 62, 63, 65, 83, 101,
    104, 110, *113*, *114*, 160–161, 170
Moellon blocks, 20
Monol houses, 30
Monasticism, 15
Moore, R., 65
Murondins, 31
Museum of Unlimited Growth, 150
Music, 3, 44, 65, 66, 73, 83, 87,
    127, 161, 199

Naegele, D., 117
Nationalism, 19
Natural Law, 216
Nature, 1, 2, 15–17, 19, 59, 64, 79,
    101, 116, 150, 171
    See also Biology
Nature morte géométrique, 150, *151*
Nautical architecture, 4, 132
Neo-Platonism, 3
Nivola, C., 28
Nomadism, 26
Nursery Schools, The, 65, 163, 181

Objects, 10, 101, 107–116
Oeuvre Complète, 11, 16, 17, 24, 33, 78,
    80, 85, 86, 101, *107*, 112, *115*, 119,
    120, *173*, *179*, 181, *186*, *192*, *196*,
    202, 201
Oppositions, 4
Opus optimum, 62, 63
Order, 1, *17*, 23, 34, 61, 110, 123,
    171, 217
Orphism, 1, 4, 11, 15, 206, 217
Orpheus, 3, 74, 75
Oubrerie, J., 181, 183
Ozenfant, A., 41, 76, 172, 218
    Atelier, 128, 150, *151*, 153, 216

Painting, 4, 17, 41, 42, 44, 49, 57, 64, 66,
    89, 93, 102, 112, 117, 118, 138, 139,
    150, 152, 173, 203
    See also Le Corbusier paintings
Palladio, 21
Paris, 16
Parthenon, 16, 24, 116, 199
Partition, 76, 105, 110
Pavillon
    des Temps Nouveaux, 26, *27*, *91*
    Esprit Nouveau, 59, 85, 112, *114*
    Suisse, 9, 20, 24, 25, 48, 85, 92, 105,
        110, 162, 173, 174, 186, 188, 209
Pearson, C., 42
Perriand, C., 59
Pessac, 20, 33, 118
Perret, A., 20
Petite Maison de Weekend, 20, 30,
    31, *178*
Petite Villa au bord du Lac Leman, 105
Phidias, 24
Philips Pavilion, 27, 66
Philosophy, 3, 47, 101, 192, 203
Piero della Francesca, 138, 139
    Flagellation, *139*
Pilotis, 21–24, 25, 28, 45–47, 89, 90, *92*,
    128, 161, 210, 212
Pisé, rammed earth, 31–33
Planarity, 78, 185
Planeix, Maison, 152
Planets, 54
Plato, 3, 39
Plummer, H., 97
Poem of the Right Angle, 10, 44, 51, 75,
    80, 117, *130*, *131*, 145, *147*, 164, 165,
    170, 198, 206
Precisions, 39, 131, 199, 206, *208*
Primitive, 21, *26*, 31, 32, 33, *191*, 204
Primitive hut, 21, 31
Prakash, V., 148
Promenade architecturale, 11, 127–165

Proportion *see* geometry
PFSF Bank, 24
Purism, 4, 6, 21, 64, 89, 152, 203,
    216, 217
Pythagoras, 3, 73

Rabelais, 3, 161, 186
Radiant City, The, 16, 30, 39, 40, 41, 54,
    109, 111, 195, 197
Rebutato, R., 51, *133*
Reflection, 73, 89–91, 102
Regionalism, 19
Regulations, building, 11
Relationship, men and women, 40
Religion, 16, 42, 75, 74, 120, 172–174, 183
Renan, E.,
    La Vie de Jesus, 32
Right angle, 9, 26, 94
Rio de Janeiro, 201, 202
    City University, 200
    Museum of Modern Art, 208
    Palais du Ministère de L'Éducation
        Nationale, *200*
Ritual, 4, 11, 169–194
Roman architecture, 30
    Pompeii, 116
Ronchamp, 7, *8, 9,* 19, 42, *43,* 45, 46, 56,
    57, *62,* 64, 66, *87,* 92, 107, 117–120,
    145, 146, *147,* 148, *153, 154,* 156,
    157, 163, *171,* 172, 175, 179, *180,*
    181, 182, 183, 185, 195, 209
Roof, 2, 4, 54, 81
    Bestegui, 61, 157, 159
    curved, 28
    garden, 21, 32, 61, 85, 102, 127, 128,
        149, 159, *172,* 186
    open, 4
    parasol, 28, 85
    play area, 47, 65
    solarium, 162
    tent, 26
    terraced, 88
    Unité Marseilles, *2, 106,* 153, *154, 155,*
        189, 201
    vaulted, 28
    Villa Savoye, *172*
    Villa Stein, 153, 159
Rooflights, 84–88
    Mitraillette, *86*
Rowe, C., 21, 23, 31, 42, 77, 78, 87, 101,
    110, 121, 129, 132, 165, 185, 188,
    190, 201, 203
Rue de Sèvres, 3, 104, 206
Rüegg, Arthur, 109, 115, 188, 191, 192
Rue Nungesser et Coli, 78, 94, *96, 104,*
    115, 132, *133,* 139, 141, *142,* 143,
    144, 188, *190, 191*

Saint Gobain, 76, 173
Saint Pierre, Firminy, 88, 181
Salon d'Automne, 61, 109, 110
Salubra, 64
Saporta, 65
Savoir habiter, 15, 129
Savoye, Villa, 7, 21, *77,* 91, 92, 102, 107,
    110, 152, 153, 159, 162, 172, 175,
    177, 185, *186,* 192
Schumacher, T., 139–140
Sekler, E., 5, 7, 11, 204
    Le Corbusier at Work, 11
Senses, 41, 49, 141, 175
Sexual responses *see* eroticism
Schuré, E., 74
Schwob, Villa, 121, *122*
Science, 16, 203, 204
Senses, 41, 49, 65
Services, 42, 61, 150
Shadow gap, 105–7
Shodhan house, 30, 85, 181
Skin, 42, *43*
Sign of the 24 hour day, 28, *29,* 74, 80,
    94, 132
Silver, K., 41
Site visits, *8*
    Frequency, 7, 217
Skylight, 4, 6, 85
Society, 15, 216
Solarium, *61, 102,* 132, 162, 177, 186
Solomite, 18
Soltan, J., 3, 4, 17, 18, 23, 122, 203
Sound, 65–66
Space, 66, 68, 77, 78, 101, 108, 110,
    116–122, 127, 131, 132, 142, *144,*
    176, 195, 203, 204, 206, 211
    see also geometry
Standardization, 15–37, 59, 60, 171, 191
Stairs and Ramps, 149, 145–164
Stein de Monzie, Villa, 21, 110, 127,
    159, *160*
Stirling, J., 1, 33, 48, 119, 129
Structure
    Concrete, 20, 31, 34, 156, 210
    Parasol, 28, 81
Steel, 18–20, 24
    Sections, 26
Stirling, J., 7, 33, 48, 119, 129
Stone, 18, 19, 26, 45, 62, 74, 84, 132, 148,
    153, 170, 173, 206, 217
Summerson, J., 78
Sun, 4, 15, 40, 42, 74, 80, 86, 132,
    172, 195

Table en tubes d'avion, 60, 173
Taureau, 49, *51,* 57

Taylorism, 17
Techne, 6
Technology, 6
Temporary structures, 26
Temple
   Primitive, 21, *26*
Tent, 26
Timber, 17, 18, 19, 32, 49, 51, 62, 77, 132,
   133, 141, 148, 156, 157, 210
Time, 33
Touch, 44–47
Towards a New Architecture, 9, 16, 18, 21,
   24, *26*, 76, *116*
Treib, M., 26
Troubadours, 3
Trouin, E., 74, 86, 91, 179

Ubu, 42
Unité, 211, 212
   Firminy, 45, *47*, 80, 83, *150*, 163
   Marseilles, 2, *5*, 7, *8*, 18, 39, 41, 45, 47,
     51, 64, 67, 78, *79*, 80, *92*, 105, *106*,
     110, *111*, *112*, *113*, *114*, 118, *135*,
     136, *137*, *150*, *153*, 140, 156, 163,
     188, *189*, 201, 203
   Meaux, 45, *46*
   Rezé les Nantes, 51
Unity, 1, 4, 15–37, 74, 122, 128
   Structural, 21
Urbanism, 197, 206–211

Varese, E., 66
Vaucresson, Villa, 138
Vaults, 28–33, 86, 92, 95
Venice, 201
Venice Hospital, 34, 199
Ventilation, 76, 83
   Aerateur, 83
Villas and houses, 8
   au bord du Lac Leman, 105
   Aux Mathes, 117, *177*

Cherchell, 31
Church, *89*
Cook, 76, 175
De Mandrot, 8
Errazuriz, 19
Fallet, 17
Jaoul, 30, 31, *32*, *40*, 49, 51, *52*, 53, 61,
   64, 85, 105, 152, 157, *158*, *159*,
   160, 175, *176*, *178*, *191*
Loucheur, 105, 190
Planeix, 152
Schwob, 121, *122*
Savoye, 7, 21, 77, 91, 92, 102, 107,
   110, 152, 153, 159, 162, 172, 175,
   177, 185, *186*, 192
Shodhan house, 30, 85, 181
Stein de Monzie, 21, 110, 127, 153,
   159, 160
Vaucresson, 138

Watch making, 17
Water, 4, 42, 62, 76, 89–90,
   181–192
Wall, 4, 23, 26, 31, 45
Weber, H., 28, 57, 152, 157
Weston, R., 77
When the Cathedrals were White, 15, 42
Windows, 6, 26, 34, 49, 75–78, *117*, *118*,
   128, 129, 172, 175, 200, 206, 215
   Pan de verre, 76, 78
   Brise soleil, 24, 76, 78, 79–81
   Horizontal, 21, 76, 78, 102
   Ondulatoire, 76, 82–84
Wogenscky, A., 7, 9, 17, 65, 169

Xenakis, I., 83, 88, 170

Zacnic, I., 209
Zinkin, T., 188
Zurich Pavilion, *see* Heidi Weber Haus